Greatest Moments in
Pittsburgh
Steelers History

Edited by
Francis J. Fitzgerald

From the Sports Pages of the
Pittsburgh Post-Gazette

Published by

Louisville, Ky.

ACKNOWLEDGEMENTS

Research assistance: Tim Rozgonyi and the *Pittsburgh Post-Gazette* library; Joe Gordon, Mike Fabus and the Pittsburgh Steelers; Fritz Huysman, Ed Bouchette, Ron Cook and Gary Dulac of the *Pittsburgh Post-Gazette* sports department; AllSport U.S.A.; AP/Wide World Photo; Bettmann Archives, the National Football League, NFL Properties and *The Detroit News*.

ISBN 1-887761-07-1

ISBN 1-887761-12-8 (Leatherbound edition)

Book Design by Chris Kozlowski and David Kordalski.
Cover Design by David Kordalski.
Typefaces: Kis-Janson, Herald Gothic

Published by:
AdCraft Sports Marketing
Kaden Tower, 10th Floor
6100 Dutchmans Lane
Louisville, KY 40205
(502) 473-1124

Royalties to the Pittsburgh Post-Gazette from the sale of this book will be donated to the Dapper Dan Charities Youth Sports Leagues operated by the Boys and Girls Clubs of Western Pennsylvania.

Contents

LABEL OF 'GREATEST' GOES TO THE STEELERS

By Fritz Huysman, *Assistant Managing Editor/Sports*
Pittsburgh Post-Gazette
June 19, 1996

I DON'T NORMALLY LIKE TO PIN THE LABEL OF "ALL-TIME great" on an athlete or sports team.

There have been so many greats through the years – the Bulls and Celtics, Ken Griffey Jr. and Barry Bonds – that it's almost impossible to pick the best of the best.

However, identifying the greatest is much easier for a native Pittsburgher like myself when the subject is professional football.

San Francisco and Dallas have won more Super Bowls, but no team ever dominated professional football like the Pittsburgh Steelers of the 1970's. Consider:
■ Four Super Bowl victories in four tries and the only team to win two straight Super Bowls twice.
■ Six players – Joe Greene, Jack Ham, Mel Blount, Terry Bradshaw, Franco Harris and Jack Lambert – and the head coach, Chuck Noll, are members of the Professional Football Hall of Fame. Members of the news media, who do the Hall of Fame voting, acknowledge that this glut of players from the same era has hurt the Hall of Fame chances of several deserving teammates, including Mike Webster, L.C. Greenwood, John Stallworth and Lynn Swann.

■ NFL Films a few years ago declared the 1978 Steelers the greatest team in National Football League history following its series of computerized games involving all of the Super Bowl champions.
■ Steelers officials and former players from the 1970's consider the 1976 squad – not 1978 – as the greatest Steelers team. With a rookie quarterback, Mike Kruczek, starting most of the way due to an injury to Bradshaw, Pittsburgh recorded five shutouts and yielded only 28 points in winning the last nine regular-season games. The Steelers lost to Oakland, the eventual Super Bowl winner, when injuries kept both starting running backs, Harris and Rocky Bleier, from playing in the AFC championship game.

The 1970's were truly heady times for Pittsburgh sports fans. With the Pirates and University of Pittsburgh football team also winning championships, Pittsburgh immodestly referred to itself as The City of Champions. But, make no mistake about it, the Steelers, win or lose, have always been No. 1 in Pittsburgh.

It seems that each player from the era had his own fan club. Franco's Italian Army, Lambert's Lunatics, Kolb's Kowboys, Gerela's Gorillas and Dobre Shunka (that's Polish for Great Ham) were a few.

And, everybody was selling something. Remember Franco Harris and the talking car? The Super Steelers were so hot that a reserve defensive tackle, Steve Furness, had his own television commercial for a convenience store.

Even today, Steelers fans remain fiercely proud of the 1970's teams' blue-collar style of play. Tough-earned victories won the Pittsburgh way – with hard work, determination and guts.

Greatest is also a very appropriate description of the late Arthur J. Rooney, the Steelers' founder/owner.

Affectionately know to his friends as "The Chief," Rooney had a remarkable ability to relate to people at all levels. He was a gentleman and the only person I've known who may not have had an enemy.

At the league level, Rooney had the attention and respect of all factions of

NFL ownership. That was no easy feat for a group better known more for its litigious – rather than clubby – nature.

When he passed away in 1988 at age 87, Ronney's funeral was attended by most of the big names in professional football. They included league Commissioner Pete Rozelle, the Maras of New York, Art Modell of Cleveland and Al Davis of Oakland.

Ironically, Rooney was inducted into the Pro Football Hall of Fame in 1964 when the Steelers were perennial losers, often the laughingstock of the league.

Little went right for Rooney's club before the 1970's. Bad teams, bad coaching and bad trades led to 40 years of losing.

It was a Steelers coach, for example, who cut Hall of Fame quarterback John Unitas as a rookie, labeling him dumb.

The same coach featured an offense in the mid-1950's that started each game with an off-tackle plunge by a plodding fullback named Fran Rogel. The play was so predictable that fans at Forbes Field would chant "hi-diddle-diddle, Rogel up the middle" as the Steelers' offense approached the line of scrimmage for the first time.

It all started in 1933 when Rooney paid $2,500 for the Pittsburgh franchise in the fledgling National Football League. The club was named the Pirates, and remained so until it was renamed the Steelers in 1941.

During the early years the crowds were slim. The Pirates' uniforms were the familiar black and gold but the color of the team's business ledgers was all red ink.

Rooney had considerable talent for picking horses but the luck of his football team was all bad. There was little fan and media interest in the Pirates and making the payroll each week was often a challenge.

Sharing Forbes Field with the major league baseball Pirates, Rooney's club managed to break even on the field only once during the 1930's and fared only slightly better over the next three decades.

It was a paradox that it took Pittsburgh four decades to win a title since few professional football owners knew the game as well as Rooney. A boxer and all-around athlete as a young man, he had played and coached football.

Rooney always left his football team, however, in the hands of others to manage and coach. The Chief viewed the club as a fun enterprise, something he and his friends could enjoy. This philosophy continued until his son, Dan, took over the day-to-day operations in the mid-1960's.

The truth is, Art Rooney's vision of pro football as a sport rather than a business and his penchant for hiring and rehiring his cronies as coach were part of the problem during the losing years.

Forrest (Jap) Douds was the first coach, followed in quick order in the 1930's by Luby DiMelio, Joe Bach, player-coach Johnny (Blood) McNally and Walt Kiesling, who had three stints as head coach and four more as an assistant.

Eight different men coached in the 1940's and there were four coaching changes in each of the next two decades.

The Steelers did come close to winning their division in 1947 and 1963, falling one game short each year. The first championship of any kind did not come until they won a division title in 1972.

During the first four decades, however, the franchise was best known for the players who got away. The club's bad trades and errors in judging talent are legendary.

Bill Dudley, the NFL's Most Valuable Player in 1946, was traded to Detroit the next season because of differences with Coach Jock Sutherland.

It was the inflexible Kiesling who dismissed Unitas as a third-string quarterback in 1955 because he had difficulty remembering the plays in his first professional training camp. Unitas was the NFL's MVP in 1957, leading the Baltimore Colts to the first of two consecutive world championships.

Kiesling's successor, Texan Buddy Parker, had four winning seasons in eight years. But, his disdain for young players and his penchant for cutting veterans following losses was so well known around the league that one general manager would regularly call Parker at his suburban Upper St. Clair home after Steelers losses to talk trade.

It was Parker who got rid of young quarterbacks Jack Kemp and Len Dawson and who made the infamous "Dial for Nothing" trade in which the Steelers gave up star receiver Buddy Dial to the Dallas Cowboys for the right to negotiate with college defensive tackle Scott Appleton. A consensus all-America at Texas, Appleton signed with the Houston Oilers of the rival American Football league and never amounted to anything as a pro.

Bill Austin's hiring in 1966 marked the first time the club went outside Art Rooney's circle of cronies for a head coach. Austin was just as tough as Vince Lombardi, his mentor, but not nearly as good. His winning percentage of .298 (11-28-3) is the worst of any Steelers coach who lasted more than two seasons.

It was during Austin's last presea-

Art Rooney, right, accepts the Vince Lombardi Trophy from NFL Commissioner Pete Rozelle after the 1975 Super Bowl.

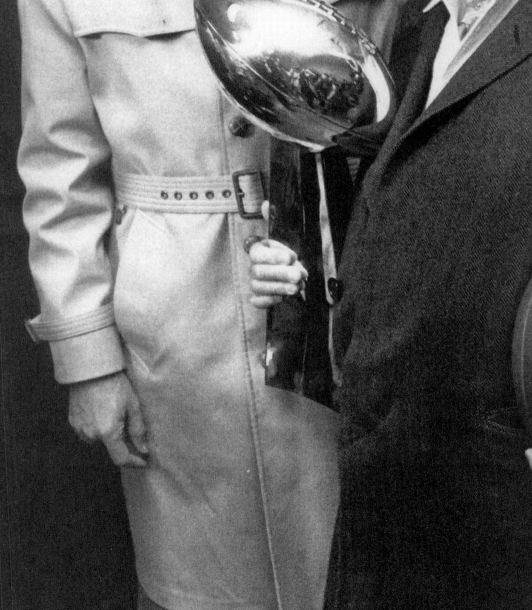

son in 1968 that the expansion Cincinnati Bengals won their first game ever against the Steelers, 19-3, in Morgantown, W. Va. A headline in a Pittsburgh newspaper the next day read, "Same Old Steelers, 19-3."

Through the years of losing SOS (Same Old Steelers) had become an acerbity for every faux pas, every mistake, every misjudgment committed by the Steelers. The originator of the phrase was Art Rooney.

Although it wouldn't be apparent for another four years, Dan Rooney in 1969 made the most important decision in Steelers history when he replaced Austin with Chuck Noll, a Baltimore Colts assistant who learned the game as an offensive guard under Paul Brown at Cleveland.

The Rooney's hired Noll after Penn State coach Joe Paterno turned the job down.

Despite a 1-13 record his first year, Noll never lost his poise. His approach to rebuilding differed from his predecessors. He chose to hold onto his draft choices rather than mortgage the future of the franchise with quick-fix trades for veterans nearing the end of their careers.

Decades of losing, however, had left the Pittsburgh media and fans skeptical.

When Noll's first act in 1969 was to draft future Hall of Fame defensive tackle Joe Greene No. 1 out of tiny North Texas State, a local newspaper heralded the move with the headline, "Steelers Draft Joe Who?"

Jon Kolb and Greenwood joined the Steelers in the same draft. Bradshaw and Blount were selected in 1970. Ham and Harris arrived the next year from Penn State.

With the arrival of Lambert, Swann, Stallworth and Webster in 1974, the rebuilding was complete. The Steelers were ready to settle some longstanding scores around the league.

Pittsburgh won the first of six consecutive AFC Central titles in 1974 and, paced by its Steel Curtain defense, defeated Minnesota, 16-6, in Super Bowl IX at New Orleans.

Using the same formula of dominating defense and conservative offense, the 1975 Steelers repeated in Super Bowl X, defeating the Cowboys, 21-17, in Miami.

By 1978, the offense under Bradshaw had matured to the point that the Steelers could win with big-play offense and defense. Pittsburgh finished the regular season with a league-leading 14-2 record and again defeated Dallas, 35-31, in Super Bowl XIII in Miami.

By 1979, the defense had begun to age, but Bradshaw was at the top of his game. Two long fourth-quarter Bradshaw-to-Stallworth passes allowed the Steelers to defeat the Los Angeles Rams, 31-19, in a come-from-behind victory in Super Bowl XIV.

History would reveal that the dynasty ended that day in Pasadena, Calif.

In the 1980's the Steelers' stars faded, the losses mounted and the Super Bowls became a distant memory. Dwight White, a dominating end with the Steel Curtain, knocked the defense of the mid-1980's as "soft and cheesy."

After making the playoffs only once in seven years, Noll retired after the 1991 season. His 209-159-1 with the Steelers ranked fifth in victories among coaches in NFL history. Noll was elected to the Hall of Fame 11 months after his retirement.

Dan Rooney then made perhaps the second most important decision in club history when he hired Bill Cowher as Noll's replacement. A 35-year-old Pittsburgh native, Cowher was a very successful defensive coordinator with the Kansas City Chiefs.

Cowher inherited a solid group of veterans that included Rod Woodson and Greg Lloyd, both perennial Pro Bowl performers. To that group Cowher and Tom Donahoe, the director of football operations, added several key players through the draft and shrewd use of a new system of free agency that Dan Rooney helped formulate.

In the process, the young coach energized a franchise and an entire city with what became known as "Cowher Power."

Although his style consists of more in-your-face emotion and discipline than Noll, Cowher found that the 1970's formula of strong defense was the quickest way back to the Super Bowl.

Featuring a gambling pass-rushing defense that became know as Blitzburgh, the Steelers returned to the Super Bowl last January in Cowher's fourth season.

The defense couldn't overcome mistakes by the offense, particularly two second half interceptions, and the Steelers lost to Dallas, 27-17, in Tempe, Ariz.

Greatest Moments in Steelers History is a record of all five Super Bowl teams, the Rooneys, Noll and Cowher.

It also chronicles performances by some of the teams from the losing era. Any book about the Pittsburgh Steelers would be incomplete without mention of Ernie Stautner, John Henry Johnson, Jack Butler, Jim Finks, Bobby Layne, Elbie Nickel, Dick Hoak, Lynn Chandnois, Ray Mathews, Pat Brady, Roy Jefferson and Bullet Bill Dudley.

Although a few still hold club records, the feats of these SOS stars are largely forgotten because they played before the Steelers were super.

Pittsburgh's Love Affair With The Steelers

By Gerry Dulac

IT HAD TAKEN 16 YEARS, ENVELOPED A GENERATION of diehard maniacs, and yet Bill Cowher, Pittsburgh-born, was there to finally bridge the gap. He was standing on a makeshift podium in the middle of Three Rivers Stadium, looking up at the adoring 60,000-plus throng that was celebrating his team's victory in the American Football Conference championship game, holding the trophy that proclaimed the Steelers as the best team in the AFC. Finally, with a trip to the Super Bowl in the making, he felt the emotion, understood the meaning, of something he had managed to witness as a teenager growing up in Pittsburgh.

Steeler-mania.

"It was great, the scene that took place in that stadium, the memories of the 1970's," Cowher said. "The generation, it was kind of carried over. The kids that were kids in the 70's are now proud parents who had their kids with them. When you can do that in a city, a city that's as special as Pittsburgh, it's very gratifying."

Cowher is one of them. He grew up in Crafton, five miles from Three Rivers, and graduated from Carlynton High School in 1975, the year the Steelers would win their second Super Bowl. Now he and his wife, Kaye, have three daughters, ages 5 through 10. When Cowher began to cross the field in the moments after the Steelers' 20-16 victory against the Indianapolis Colts in the AFC title game, tears welled in his eyes and he had a look as though he were watching his daughter get married.

Even Dan Rooney, stoic, often placid in public, was nearly overcome with emotion. The Steelers president said he could not look at the stadium scoreboard during the celebration because it flashed a picture of his father, team founder Art Rooney. He was afraid he would start crying.

"Coming out of that tunnel, seeing that Terrible Towel waving, it's a spectacle," Cowher said. "I'm just happy that the city can go through this. That's why it's great. It unites everybody."

On a brisk January afternoon, the city of Pittsburgh recaptured Camelot with its Steelers. The fans who once danced in Franco's Italian Army and waved Terrible Towels until their rotators ached had now come full cycle with the team that dominated the 1970's. The Steelers were going back to the Super Bowl for the first time since the 1979 season, and that could mean only one thing.

Euphoria.

Grown men wearing hard hats with beer cans on top.

Women knitting black-and-gold sweaters.

Polka music with Steeler lyrics.

Television sets with Terrible Towels draped across like a doilie, as though they were filtering some magical power through the screen.

Pittsburgh is a town of small neighborhoods with deep-rooted ethnicity, a city where the former mayor and the No. 1 broadcaster can be celebrated for having shrill, nasal voices that can wake cats. It is a city in metamorphis, a place whose infrastructure has changed from blue collar to almost white, from steel mills to corporate parks, from Grimy Gulch to glitzy skyline.

More important, they embrace their sports teams like a cousin. They rallied

Brothers Brian (left) and David Henderson of McKeesport wait to greet the Steelers upon their return from the Super Bowl win over the Los Angeles Rams in 1980.

Slippery Rock boosters (left to right) Dan O'Leary, Randy Patterson, Amy Porneluzi, Jim Thompson and beth Thompson share their Steelers Christmas card prior to the 1974 playoff game against Buffalo.

for the Terrible Towel and Gerela's Gorillas, to name a few. "High school football was so big around here. Football became even more important here when the steel industry went down the tubes and so many people were out of work. The Steelers gave them something to be happy about, something to cheer."

So did Cope. His distinguishable voice set him apart as the team's most colorful supporter and perhaps the most popular celebrity in town. He would do radio commentaries that actually were weekly guidelines for Gerela's Gorillas, a zany, band of characters whose hero was former kick Roy Gerela. At Christmas, he would adapt his own lyrics to "Deck the Halls" and sing it on television. You can't find anyone in Pittsburgh who hasn't heard the infamous verse, "Deck the Broncos, they're just Yonkos."

Pittsburgh loved Cope because they loved the Steelers.

"The games on Sunday helped you get started on Monday," Cope said. "It was a psychological shot in the arm. People in Pittsburgh had fallen on hard times and they needed to feel like a winner. We had great Steeler teams and we became known as the City of Champions and we were celebrated on national television. We had a lot of fun things like the Terrible Towel. We swarmed into other cities. Everybody knew it when Pittsburgh came to town. Everybody was wearing black and gold and waving their towels."

"I always thought that football in that town reflected life in that town, and that tradition has carried on," said former center Ray Mansfield, who played on two Super Bowl teams and still lives and works in Pittsburgh. "Pittsburgh has always represented a team that is proud of its hard-nosed past. I remember when I was with the Eagles, we were always

to keep the baseball Pirates in town when other cities wooed them with fervor. They passionately follow the Penguins and their magical superstar, Mario Lemieux. And, when it comes to the Steelers, why, not even Mister Rodgers can spellbind a city the way this team can. They followed the Steelers with the passion of college alumni, strutting into cities wearing their bold black-and-gold getups and waving yellow towels. Their success in the 70's, coupled with the Pirates' two World Series titles in 1971 and 1979, was the reason Pittsburgh was dubbed, "City of Champions."

"This has always been great football territory," said Myron Cope, the diminutive television and radio broadcaster whose theatrics were responsible

Prior to Super Bowl XIV, the city of Pittsburgh paid tribute to the Steelers by repainting one of its street trolleys.

A pair of Steeler fans, Ruthie (left) and Bonnie, celebrate their teams' 35-31 win over Dallas in Super Bowl XIII.

afraid to play Pittsburgh. You may win the game, but they beat the hell out of you and you felt it for three weeks.

"And, like the Steelers, the town always had a bad reputation. I remember when I was driving to Philadelphia as a rookiewith my wife and we were on the Pennsylvania Turnpike and we saw a sign for Pittsburgh. Our conception of Pittsburgh was this big, black cloud with stuff coming out of the steel mills. We thought that was Pittsburgh."

It was, but only to people who did not live there. Steelers fans became equally protective of their team. When you ridiculed one, you ridiculed the other. And you dare not affend them. Even country rocker Charlie Daniels scolded in one of his songs, "Don't ever place your hand on a Pittsburgh Steeler fan."

"Nothing brings everybody closer together than when the rest of the world is laughing at you," Mansfield said. "The hapless Steelers, up until 1972, were in

the same position as the town."

How did this mania evolve? What fueled the passion? For starters, consider the team's history. No playoff appearances in 40 years of existence. An owner, Art Rooney, known as The Chief, who was loved by everybody, even his opponents. The Steelers were a bumbling, stumbling organization that cut players such as John Unitas and traded Len Dawson, and only twice in their history did they win more than seven games (1947 and 1962) in a season.

So what happened?

The cornerstone of the team's Super Bowl success was laid in January 1969, when the Steelers signed a 37-year-old defensive backfield coach with the Baltimore Colts named Chuck Noll as their head coach. His first draft pick: Joe Greene, the lynchpin of the Steel Curtain defense and a future Hall of Famer. The Steelers embodied Greene's pride and nastiness, and he was the bandleader of a defense that carried them through the 1970's as the team of the decade.

But the Steelers' romance with the city and its fans didn't begin until 1972, their first playoff season, and it began with a running back with Italian and African-American descent. When Franco Harris burst onto the scene as a rookie out of Penn State, he almost immediately enraptured a city with his tough, brilliant running, not to mention that disarming smile and Greek-god good looks.

"That started everything," Mansfield said.

Harris became the catalyst of the offense, rushing for 1,055 yards and 10 touchdowns as a rookie and leading the Steelers to their first-ever playoff appearance. But he also became the player around whom the city — eventually, a nation — rallied.

Because of Pittsburgh's strong, ethnic communities, and being the son of an Italian mother, Harris became an instant hero, thanks to a local baker named Tony Stagno. It was Stagno and his friends who started "Franco's Italian Army," a motley collection of round-bellied supporters who waved Italian flags — and sometimes loaves of bread — on opposing defenses. As Harris rose the chart among the league's rushing leaders, so, too, did his band of supporters swell. The Army reached its

Pittsburgh's Mark Cordell was the first in line to buy a ticket for the 1975 Steelers-Oakland AFC Championship game at Three Rivers Stadium.

greatest moment the week preceding the final regular season game in San Diego. The Steelers were training in Palm Springs, Calif., getting ready to face the Chargers, and Harris had become a national star by now. So, with the help of Cope, the Army inducted the biggest piasano of them all right there in the desert. Frank Sinatra, Ol' Blue Eyes, showed up at practice and was sworn in as an honorary member. But even that could not properly set the stage for what was to follow in the next two weeks.

In their first-ever playoff appearance, after finishing with an 11-3 record, the Steelers defeated the Oakland Raiders, 13-7, in the game that has come to be known as the Immaculate Reception. It was only fitting that Harris would be the central character — catching the deflected pass that was ruled to have hit

off the shoulder pad of Raiders safety Jack Tatum as he was making a hit on Frenchy Fuqua. Harris scooped the ball off his shoetops, raced down the left and got past one final defender, safety Jimmy Warren, into football immortality. To this day, no single event, not even Bill Mazeroski's home run in the 1960 World Series, generates more goose bumps among the Pittsburgh sporting faithful than Franco's Immaculate Reception.

Harris was not alone in the city's embrace. Pitttsburgh took to the Steelers with such passion that, seemingly, each player had a wild following. Linebacker Jack Ham, Polish-born, had his "Dobre Shunka" section. Translated, that meant — what else? — good ham. Inside linebacker Jack Lambert, perhaps the most popular Steeler of them all, had his Lambert Lunatics.

Strangely, though, after Franco's Italian Army, the biggest following belonged to a hawk-nosed, pigeon-toed kicker named Roy Gerela. For what reason, nobody seems to know why. But Gerela's Gorillas became something of a cult following, perhaps because the ringleader showed up every Sunday, warm or cold, wearing the same outfit — an oversized, gorilla suit. His name was Bob Bubanic, "Tingle" to his friends, and you could find him at every game, sitting in the left corner of the end zone opposite the Steelers bench, looking quite Magilla-like.

The Gorillas became a popular bunch because they would hang a sign at each game, taunting or challenging the opposing team's kicker. The message changed for each home game, and it was delivered to the Gorillas in mid-week on the radio, by Cope, who devoted a whole morning commentary to that week's sign. You would have thought the president was delivering his state of the union message

CONGRAT'LATIONS
SUPER BOWL NO. "14"
YOUR COUNTY COMMISSIONERS
TOM FOERSTER

Downtown Pittsburgh was packed with Steeler fans celebrating the team's third Super Bowl win.

the way Pittsburghers tuned in to get that week's pscyhe job.

Cope got so caught up in the frenzy he once even suggested to former Coach Chuck Noll that he was part of the reason for the Steelers success. Noll looked at the diminutive sportscaster somewhat wryly and said, "Gee, I thought it was because we had a good football team."

The madness that enveloped the 1970's gave way to a complacency in the 1980's. The Steelers never got back to the Super Bowl after they won No. 4 in 1980. The closest they came was in 1984 when they made it to the AFC

Steelers lineman Sam Davis at the 1980 Super Bowl celebration at Point State Park.

Championship game, only to lose at Miami, 28-6. But that all changed in the 90's, when Cowher was brought in to replace Chuck Noll, who retired following the 1991 season.

It began to grow in 1994, when the Steelers got back to the AFC title game and came within 3 yards of advancing to the Super Bowl. Then, of course, it reached endemic proportion when the Steelers steamrolled the Buffalo Bills and rallied to beat the Colts last season to advance to Super Bowl XXX in Tempe, Ariz. Never mind that they lost to the Cowboys, a team it had defeated in Super Bowls X and XIII.

The passion was back.

"That was always something to me, the way the fans took to our team," said

former running back Rocky Bleier. "We would be on the road sometimes and I would swear there would be more Steeler fans in the stand than the other team."

"We might have been a dirty, hard-nosed city," Mansfield said, "but we had the greatest football team in the world."

When the Terrible Towel resurfaced last season, the mania had come full cycle. The towel-waving was so prevalent at Super Bowl XXX that most of Sun Devil Stadium appeared to be awash in a sea of yellow whenever the Steelers did something to incite their faithful.

"It's like one big happy family," Cowher said. "And I want to make them even happier."

STEELERS 63, GIANTS 7: HARD TO BELIEVE, ISN'T IT?

By Pat Livingston, *The Pittsburgh Press*

PITTSBURGH, NOV. 30, 1952 — STEELERS 63, GIANTS 7.

That was it!

Believe it or not, it was the story of the football game at Forbes Field yesterday.

Perhaps TV broadcaster Harry Wismer, a fellow who has watched the "defense-conscious" Giants all year and an inveterate New York fan, had the right answer.

"Now I know how those people in Hiroshima felt," he muttered as he walked out of the press box.

The 15,140 hoarse fans in the stands fully agreed with him. It was just as though an atomic bomb dropped at Forbes Field from the moment Lynn Chandnois returned the opening kick-off 91 yards for a touchdown.

NEVER IN DOUBT

The Giants were never in the ball game as the Steeler line outcharged, outfought and outsmarted the supposedly superior New York forward wall. And the Steeler backs, from All-League Ray Mathews down to Rookie Tom Calvin, who never had a chance to show what he could do until yesterday, were superb as they stormed over and through the high-flying Giants.

SCORE BY PERIODS

N.Y. Giants	0	0	7	0	7
Pittsburgh	14	14	7	28	63

Even Dick Hensley, a Giant castoff whom the Steelers picked up this year, had a field day. The unheard-of end caught seven passes for 154 yards and two touchdowns.

Quarterback Jim Finks, the kid who was on trial as Coach Joe Bach pondered whether to go for tackles or a quarterback in the draft, answered the question to Pittsburgh's delight. The 175-pounder from Tulsa University completed 12 of 24 passes for 254 yards and four touchdowns.

Bach would hardly dare draft a quarterback first, now that Finks passed his most severe test with flying colors.

VERY BIZARRE

The Giants' lone score, the only thing you haven't heard about yet, was strictly a freak. Tom Landry, a defensive halfback who was pressed into the quarterback spot after Charlie Conerly and Fred Benners were injured, passed to end Bill Stribling from his own 30.

Stribling made a beautiful catch even though he was closely guarded by Steeler linebacker Darrell Hogan. He cut toward the center of the field, and when he was stopped by a swarm of Steelers, he lateraled to Joe Scott. Scott was immediately trapped by the Steelers, but got the ball back to Stribling, who raced all the way from the Steeler 35 for a score.

That was the unbelievable extent of the Giants' scoring.

Meanwhile, the Steelers had piled up a 28-0 lead in the first half before either of the Giants' quarterbacks was injured.

They scored first on Chandnois' brilliant run with the opening kickoff after the losers disdainfully won the toss but elected to kick to the Steelers.

CHANDNOIS AND MATHEWS

It was midway through the period again before the Steelers scored their second touchdown as Chandnois and Mathews, running as though they never heard of the Giants' impregnable defense, drove 47 yards. Chandnois capped the drive with a 5-yard sprint around end behind magnificent blocking.

In the second quarter, Finks passed 21 yards to Elbie Nickel and 42 yards to Mathews for two more scores to make it 28-0.

Both teams scored in the third stanza, the Steelers first on a 25-yard pass to Hensley, and then the Giants on their double lateral play.

On the first play of the fourth quarter, Finks passed to Hensley for a 60-yard TD. Hensley was tackled by halfback Emlen Tunnell on the Giant 15, but got up and raced over the goal line for the touchdown.

Minutes later, guard Dale Dodrill blocked Landry's quick kick and opportunist George Hays picked up the ball on the 3 and stepped across.

Gary Kerkorian, who graciously permitted Mathews to convert after one of the Steelers' nine touchdowns, sparked the last two scores. The first came on a 20-yard pass to Jack Butler and the second on a 3-yard sweep by Ed Modzelewski after Kerkorian set it up with a 26-yard pass to Hensley.

Jim Finks completed 12 of 24 passes for 254 yards and four touchdowns.

LAYNE, ORR TEAM UP TO RIP CARDINALS, 38-21

By Pat Livingston, *The Pittsburgh Press*

PITTSBURGH, DEC. 13, 1958 — UNLEASHING ONE OF THE most awesome displays of offensive football ever seen in the National Football League, the Steelers walloped the Chicago Cardinals 38-21, at Pitt Stadium yesterday.

The Steelers, striking on the fantastic passing combination of quarterback Bobby Layne and rookie Johnny Orr, rolled up 683 yards on an icy, slippery, gridiron that would have been more appropriate for the Ice Capades.

Only one other pro team ever exceeded the Steelers' offensive output yesterday — the Los Angeles Rams, who in 1951 overwhelmed the New York Yanks with a total of 735 yards.

Orr, the Los Angeles castoff, was fantastic in the Steeler victory, a win that kept alive a streak that has now reached seven games without defeat.

The 185-pound end, a graduate of the University of Georgia, who is a candidate for Rookie of the Year honors, made a bold bid for the award with his performance yesterday.

Orr caught six passes for 205 yards. Three of them were for touchdowns as he moved the ball on scoring plays of 86, 17 and 72 yards. The productive afternoon made him the Steelers' all-time single-season receiving leader with a total of 910 yards on 32 receptions – an average of 29 yards a pass.

SCORE BY PERIODS

Chicago	0	7	14	0	21
Pittsburgh	0	17	7	14	38

The offensive display swept all the Steelers to new team records. Tom Tracy, who had to battle all afternoon on the slippery field, gained 35 yards to give him 714 yards for the season. It eclipsed Joe Geri's mark of 705, set eight years ago.

Tom Miner and Layne shattered old Steeler marks, too. Miner's eight points gave him 73 for the season and Layne's 409 yards passing put them into the record books with new Steeler highs.

A paid crowd of 16,660 and 6,330 youngsters (Steeler guests), sat in the frigid weather and watched the brilliant display of the home team.

START IN SECOND QUARTER

Actually, the Steelers didn't get started until the second quarter, when Orr took Layne's arching pass in the end zone for the first Steeler score. By halftime, they had a 17-7 lead as Layne, running instead of passing, went 17 yards for the second touchdown as he raced the clock in a last-minute drive.

Before that Miner kicked a 13-yard field goal.

Meanwhile, the Cardinals had been hard pressed to contain the Steelers, though Ollie Matson made it respectable with another of his specialties, the kickoff runback.

Matson, who ran 101 yards against the Steelers in Chicago, duplicated his touchdown route to tie the score, 7-7. Taking the kickoff, he raced 92 yards, evading the onswarming charge of Steelers at the 30-yard line and like a lonesome halfback, strolled unmolested over the goal line.

It was in the second half that the Steelers, who punted but twice all day, went into orbit.

Tank Younger, who contributed 106 yards in 13 carries for his best day as a Steeler, became the running threat while Layne picked away at the Cardinal defenses as he nailed Ray Mathews, Jack McClairen, Tracy and Orr with yard-consuming tosses.

McClairen alone caught nine for 139 yards, his best day, too, with the team.

CARDS KEEP PRESSURE ON

Despite the Steeler offense, the

The afternoon was cold but the Steelers' offense was hot, racking up 683 yards of offense against the Chicago Cardinals at Forbes Field. It was the second-highest offensive total in NFL history behind the L.A. Rams' 735 yards against the N.Y. Yanks in 1951.

Cardinals kept making it interesting right down to the wire. They pulled to within three points, 17-14, early in the third quarter on a 49-yard pass from rookie Mack Raynolds to Bobby Watkins.

They made it 24-21 later in the same period when Matson, stopped at the middle of the line, changed direction suddenly and swept across from the 1.

Meanwhile, Orr had eluded the Cardinal secondary in the end zone to take Layne's baseball pitch back of the goal line to keep the Steelers ahead of their pesky, unyielding foes.

But it was the first Steeler play of the final quarter that finally broke the Cardinals' back. Starting as an end run, this time Tracy saw Orr all by himself and led the hot-headed rookie perfectly. Orr took the ball on the Cardinal 28 – a 50-yard pass – and was all by himself as he raced over the goal line.

A final touchdown by Billy Reynolds, sweeping wide to his right

from 5 yards out with three minutes to play ended the scoring.

There were defensive heroes, too.

For the Cardinals, rookie Bobby Joe Conrad swiped three enemy aerials and, for the Steelers, Dean Derby, who drew the assignment of covering Matson deep, duplicated the feat.

The victory gave the Steelers a 7-4-1 mark, the second best in their history. Only the late Jock Sutherland's team, 8-4 for the season, did better than that.

Receiver Buddy Dial was one of the Steelers' few bright spots in this humbling contest.

GIFFORD SAVES GIANTS WITH FANTASTIC CATCH

By Pat Livingston, *The Pittsburgh Press*

NEW YORK, DEC. 15, 1963 — THE NEW YORK GIANTS ARE the Eastern Division champions and Y.A. Tittle, their aging quarterback, was the star of the show. But to the crushed Steelers, the real nemesis was 33-year-old Frank Gifford.

"Gifford was the guy who killed us," said disappointed Coach Buddy Parker after yesterday's head-on collision between the Giants and Steelers for the division title. "He made the play that sewed up the ball game."

Although Tittle threw for three touchdowns in the Giants' 33-17 victory, it was a real dog-fight until Gifford's diving, one-handed catch in the third quarter pulled the Giants out of a hole.

After trailing, 16-0, as the opportunistic Giants cashed in on a pair of early game breaks, the Steelers had rallied until they were behind by only six points, at 16-10. The Giants, with third and 7 on their own 23, appeared to be losing control of the ball game.

The Steelers had stopped the Giants on the first series of downs of the second half and, as far as the 63,240 pleading fans were concerned, they were stopping them again.

But suddenly Tittle, evading a powerful Steeler rush, fired a low liner just out of Gifford's reach. Somehow, the fabulous Giant flanker reached down for the ball, grabbed it in his right

SCORE BY PERIODS

Pittsburgh	0	3	14	0	17
N.Y. Giants	9	7	14	3	33

hand, and gathered it to his chest before it hit the ground for a 30-yard gain.

"That play did it," added Parker. "We were getting to them up until that time. That was the play that gave them the spark they needed."

Two plays later the exuberant Giants cashed in the impossible catch for another touchdown and the Steelers were out of it, 23-10.

The Giants had forged ahead with Tittle, who completed a fabulous 17 of 26 for his afternoon's work, throwing a 41-yard touchdown pass to Del Shofner and a pair of less spectacular throws — 4 yards and 22 yards — to halfback Joe Morrison.

Morrison, a lumbering 195-pound back who never before had been anything but a minor annoyance to the Steelers, scored his third touchdown of the game with a 1-yard dive after

another great Gifford catch had moved the ball in to that point.

Morrison almost had a fourth, too. But, Tittle overthrew him in the open. Tittle was so unhappy with his near-miss that he yanked off his helmet exposing his bald head to the frigid afternoon, and danced in a fit of despair in the middle of the field.

As effective as Tittle was for the Giants, his counterpart with the Steelers, Ed Brown, was as ineffective. Brown, playing his poorest game of the year, threw for two touchdowns — 21 yards to Gary Ballman and 40 yards to Buddy Dial — but he did nothing else right.

He was overthrowing wide-open receivers all afternoon as he completed only 13 of 33 throws, even though his protection was much better then Tittle's.

Al Sherman, the Giant coach, felt his team played a remarkable game.

"It was the best we played for five or six weeks," said Sherman. "If it had been anything else, the Steelers would be playing the Chicago Bears."

In the last analysis, however, justice triumphed.

With the whole season down on the line, with the playoff money at stake in the one big game that really counted, the Giants earned their trip to Chicago.

They had to beat an excellent team to get there.

THE STEELERS: PRO FOOTBALL'S GASHOUSE GANG

By Myron Cope
True, September 1964

CONTRARY TO GENERAL BELIEF IT WAS NOT Y.A. TITTLE'S passing arm that hoisted the New York Giants to the Eastern Division title of the National Football League in 1963. There is sound reason to believe that the Eastern race was, in fact, decided by a Pittsburgh quarterback's impetuous decision to go on the wagon.

That is precisely what Ed Brown did. On the final day of the 1963 season the Steelers played the Giants in New York, winner-take-the-money. The Giants led the standings by percentage points, but the Steelers, who earlier in the season had humiliated them, 31-0, needed only to win this game to become Eastern champions. To the utter dismay of those who know their Steelers best, quarterback Brown, a strapping former marine buck sergeant, took the big game too seriously. On the Wednesday preceding the showdown battle, he disappeared from his favorite saloon. He went into training.

Now Brownie is not the kind of guy who has to dry out before a game. On the contrary, he is rather a high-class drinker, favoring liquid ensembles — for example, Scotch whiskey on crushed ice with a thin layer of Drambuie added. He has black hair, a chiseled jaw, and broad shoulders and he is a bachelor who can name all the good songs from Armstrong to Kenton. So it is not in his nature to lock himself in a room.

Moreover, although his intentions were good when he decided to train for the big game, he contravened the very motto that had carried the Steelers to the brink of the title: "Stay loose." He vanished from the nocturnal stomping grounds of his teammates.

Brownie's defection went unnoticed amid the general hilarity with which other Steelers approached the crucial contest. Indeed, the New York press, covering the Steelers' and Giants' workouts in Yankee Stadium the day before the game, was startled by the contrasting attitudes of the two clubs. The Giants appeared grim, high-strung. The Steelers crackled with noisy confidence, tickled by the prospect of kicking the daylights out of all those New York players who pose for Madison Avenue's shirt ads — and then celebrating their victory up and down Broadway.

Sunday came up cold and wet. The field was a great pigpen of mud. But our Steelers — and I say "our" Steelers because I have been privileged over the past few years to spend many a robust evening with the boys — were undeterred. Our pass receivers galloped ebulliently through the slop, leaving New York's defensive backs flat on their muddied faces. Our boys held their hands aloft and yelled, "Here I am, Brownie! Put 'er here."

But Brownie did not put her there.

He threw long yards beyond his receivers. His body well rested, his insides dry as a temperance union president's, his head disgustingly clear, he totally lost his timing and sangfroid. Time and again he overthrew receivers who had no one between them and the goal line. In short, Brownie had trained himself into the most miserable performance of his career. Thus were the Giants able to win the Eastern title.

Now the 1964 football season is at hand. NFL title races being the dogfights they usually are, it is impossible to venture where the Steelers will finish. But red-blooded men must make Pittsburgh their sentimental choice, because in an age of prissy, image-conscious athletes who slip through back doors to do their boistering, the Steelers are men's men. They have refused to resign from the male sex.

"I call them the Gashouse Gang," says Jimmy Brown, the Cleveland halfback. "I hear their coach puts beer on their bus.

Ernie Stautner was one of the NFL's toughest players in his era.

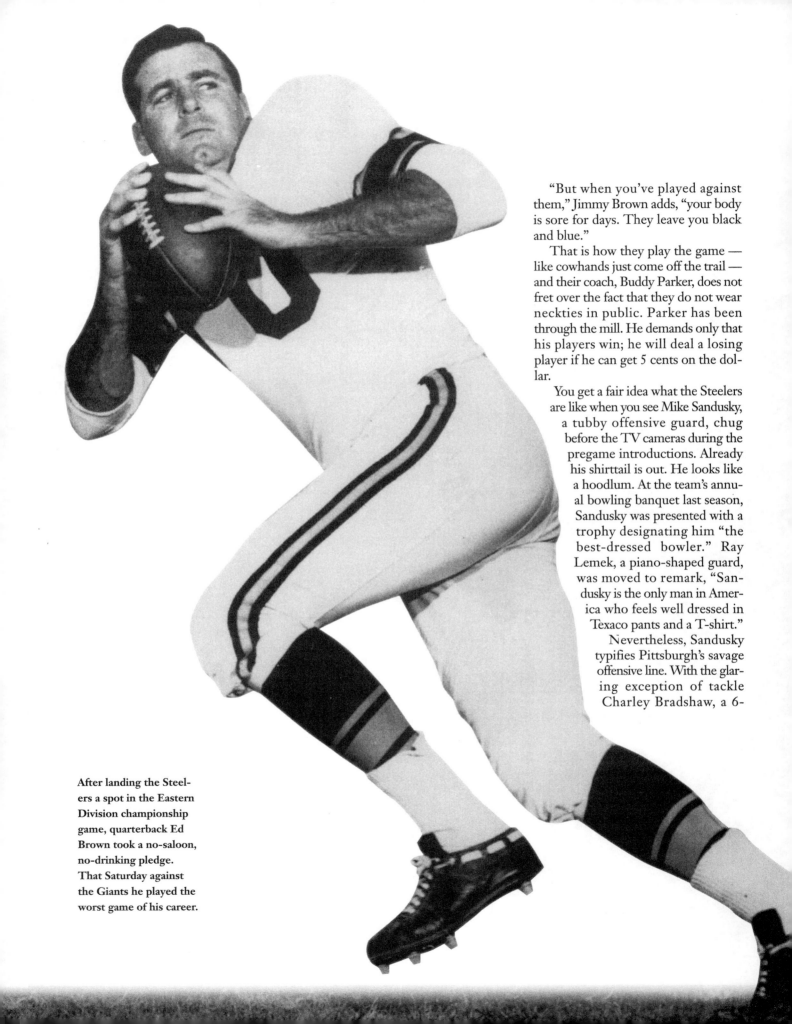

"But when you've played against them," Jimmy Brown adds, "your body is sore for days. They leave you black and blue."

That is how they play the game — like cowhands just come off the trail — and their coach, Buddy Parker, does not fret over the fact that they do not wear neckties in public. Parker has been through the mill. He demands only that his players win; he will deal a losing player if he can get 5 cents on the dollar.

You get a fair idea what the Steelers are like when you see Mike Sandusky, a tubby offensive guard, chug before the TV cameras during the pregame introductions. Already his shirttail is out. He looks like a hoodlum. At the team's annual bowling banquet last season, Sandusky was presented with a trophy designating him "the best-dressed bowler." Ray Lemek, a piano-shaped guard, was moved to remark, "Sandusky is the only man in America who feels well dressed in Texaco pants and a T-shirt."

Nevertheless, Sandusky typifies Pittsburgh's savage offensive line. With the glaring exception of tackle Charley Bradshaw, a 6-

After landing the Steelers a spot in the Eastern Division championship game, quarterback Ed Brown took a no-saloon, no-drinking pledge. That Saturday against the Giants he played the worst game of his career.

foot-6 Texan who has a face like John Nance Garner's, the line mostly resembles a collection of hot-water boilers. You can best grasp its style of play by knowing that in the offseason Sandusky is a saloonkeeper, center Buzz Nutter is a beer salesman, and fat-boy tackle Dan James is a collector for a finance company. "If you want to punch him," says Buff Boston, a Steeler front-office man who frequently bends an elbow with the help, "the finance company dares you."

It suits Buddy Parker that his ball-carriers are blasters, not sneaky speed merchants. Sneers Parker, "Those fast backs go 70 yards once in a while, but they don't want contact."

Old John Henry Johnson, to name one Steeler back, has so strong a penchant for contact that a few years ago it almost resulted in his being awarded a cement bathing suit by the Chicago branch of the Cosa Nostra. Playing against the Chicago Cardinals in 1955, John Henry roared downfield and hit Charley Trippi with a ferocious blind-side block. Trippi's skull was fractured. Two plastic-surgery jobs were required to put his face back together. Surgeons had to remove one of his ribs to obtain new cartilage for his nose, parts of which had been left on the playing field.

"Which side of the river you want him fished up from?" Trippi was asked by Chicago fans wearing pearl-gray fedoras.

Fortunately, Trippi insisted John Henry be left alone. "I didn't think it would be in the best interests of professional football," he explains. Trippi's teammates, however, resolved to fix John Henry's wagon in their next meeting, but John Henry quickly let them know he doesn't frighten. He deliber-

ately ran the ball past the Cardinals' bench, inviting them to start a hey-rube. All that happened was that two Cardinals leaped of the bench and kicked him.

No man, however, reflects the essence of the Steelers so much as Ernie Stautner, who doubles as assistant coach and emergency defensive end. Martini for martini, this may be the toughest man ever to play in the NFL.

Stautner may be 39 or 42 or ready for Social Security — it is hard to say, because the records are in Bavaria, where he was born. Note, though, that he fought in the Borneo and Okinawa campaigns even before he went to college. His face, emerging directly from his shoulder without, the benefit of a neck, is about as pretty as an auto accident. His philosophy is simple, if chilling: "You got to be a man who wants to hurt somebody. You know where I'm going for? The quarterback's face. It hurts in the face. I want him to know I'm coming the next time. I want him to be scared. Those quarterbacks can't tell me they don't scare, because I've seen it in the corners of their eyes."

Stautner's 15 seasons of pro football are a testimonial to good gin. Not long ago Stautner and a journalist – this journalist, unfortunately – frightened acquaintances by drinking martinis from 5 p.m. till 1 a.m. At noon of the next day, as I lay abed writhing, my telephone rang.

"Hey, dad, you gonna make the scene with me today?" demanded Stautner, fresh as a laundered shirt.

As the reader well may have surmised, Steelers management is a tolerant sort. (Tolerant? Good Lord, the club's official program relates with undisguised glee an occasion when Stautner beat the blazes out of a trou-

blemaker in alley fight.) Club owner Art (The Prez) Rooney — a chunky, beloved Irishman who has a great shock of iron-gray hair atop a ruddy face that clenches a one-dollar cigar — got into the football business 31 years ago because he figured it would be fun. An ex-carnival fighter who made his fortune betting horses, Rooney is depressed to see lawyers overrunning the NFL front offices these days. More to the point, however, The Prez has an easy-going nature that rules out dictatorial methods. At a recent testimonial dinner in his honor, he told a vast audience of Rooney-lovers (ranging from high clergymen to Toots Shor) a story that nicely describes his modus operandi.

"A few years ago," stated The Prez, "I had a coach named Walt Kiesling, who started every game the same way — he sent his fullback into the middle of the line on the first play. The fullback was a little guy named Fran Rogel, and after a while the fans began to chant, 'Hi, diddle, diddle! Rogel up the middle!' It got pretty bad.

"So finally I went to Kiesling and said, 'Listen, Kies. This week I want you to throw a pass on the first play. Don't argue with me. That's an order.'"

Kiesling obeyed. On the first play a rangy end named Goose McClairen loped downfield, snatched a pass, and romped to a touchdown. But the touchdown was nullified because a Steeler lineman had lurched offside. "I found out later," said The Prez, continuing his account, "that Kies had ordered that lineman to go offside. Kies told the players, 'If this pass play works, that Rooney will be down here every week giving us plays.' Gentlemen, that was the first and last time I ever tried to send in a play."

JOHNSON RUNS WILD, STEELERS SHOCK BROWNS

By Pat Livingston, *The Pittsburgh Press*

CLEVELAND, OCT. 10, 1964 — JOHN HENRY JOHNSON, A 35-year-old fullback, ran last night like a frisky colt as he led the Steelers to a brilliant but amazing 23-7 upset of the Cleveland Browns before a crowd of 80,530 in Municipal Stadium.

Johnson, barging over the goal line on runs of 33, 45 and 5 yards, set a personal high of 200 yards in 30 carries. It was a club record and put Johnson into the exclusive 200 yards in one game club.

With two linebackers, Bob Harrison and Bob Schmitz injured, Coach Buddy Parker had to come up with something, and what he came up with was the same five-man line that he used so successfully in Detroit in the early 50's.

In a daring move, he replaced his regular linebackers with 200-pound Clendon Thomas, playing the defensive halfback behind the line with Bill Saul.

In the battle of fullbacks, the graying Johnson bested Cleveland's Jimmy Brown. Brown, who made a 40-yard run on a draw play to help the Browns to their only touchdown of the game in the second quarter, gained 59 yards in eight carries.

The Browns, who trailed, 10-0, as the Steelers scored the first two times they got the ball, never had a chance to exploit their vaunted balance. Trail-

SCORE BY PERIODS

Pittsburgh	10	6	7	0	23
Cleveland	0	7	0	0	7

Kicker Mike Clark accounted for the five Steelers points John Henry Johnson did not score against the Browns.

ing as they were, quarterback Frank Ryan was forced into the air and it wasn't his night.

He passed 29 times and completed only 13. The Steelers' Ed Brown, passing when he felt like it, completed nine of 11, including all three he threw in the second half.

Mike Clark accounted for the points Johnson didn't score with a 21-yard field goal and two conversions.

In the opening period, completely dominated by the Steeler offense, the visitors held the ball for all but eight plays. Taking the kickoff, they marched to a first and goal on the Cleveland 10, mainly on a 42-yard Ed Brown to Jim Kelly pass, but were unable to move beyond that point.

On fourth down, Clark booted a field goal from the 21, giving the Steelers a 3-0 lead.

Then, after holding the Browns, the Steelers embarked on a 78-yard march with Johnson and Clarence Peaks, a surprise starter in place of Dick Hoak, grabbing off great gobs of yardage.

With second-and-9 on the Browns' 35, Johnson, who a play earlier had gone 13 yards on the same call, broke through the middle, gave a shoulder to defensive back Bobby Franklin on the 20 and barreled home for the score. When Clark converted, the Steelers led, 10-0.

But Johnson wasn't to be stopped

by his first touchdown run. The next time the Steelers got the ball, the big fullback was back in action again.

Taking a pitchout from Brown on the 45, Johnson swept around his left end and cutting in and out like a halfback, stormed all the way in to the end zone, eluding Walter Beach and Franklin again as he jitterbugged home.

Clark missed the extra point and the Steelers led, 16-0.

BROWN PERKS UP BROWNS

Cleveland quickly got one of those scores back. Brown, who carried only once in the first quarter, suddenly exploded on a 40-yard draw play, and he was Johnny on the spot moments later as Ryan, breaking his pattern, started to run on third down, suddenly spied Brown by himself and threw a 12-yard pass for a first down on the Steeler 26.

Two plays later, Ryan hit Gary Collins, running diagonally toward the goal posts, with an 18-yard pass and the Browns were on the scoreboard but trailing, 16-7.

A subsequent Steeler drive fizzled on the Cleveland 4 when the visitors, moving the ball from the kickoff, marched to first down on the Cleveland 9. But Peaks banging into the middle, fumbled and Vince Costello fell on the ball at the 4.

Although the Browns drove to the Steeler 22 following the second half kickoff, the defense hurled back Ryan and on fourth down Lou Groza was wide with a 45-yard field goal attempt.

It was not Groza's only miss. With two seconds to play in the quarter, he was short and wide with a 46-yard attempt, but the Steelers had a touchdown to offset anything Groza might have kicked.

Again it was Johnson with his third

John Henry Johnson rushed for 200 yards on 30 carries and three TD's against Cleveland.

scored of the game, giving Pittsburgh a 23-7 lead. He barged over tackle from the 5-yard line, culminating an 80-yard drive that started with Groza's first unsuccessful field goal attempt.

ED BROWN GETS INTO THE ACT

While Johnson's unrestrained running was the feature of the drive, a pair of passes from Ed Brown to Gary Ballmen, one of 15 yards to the 5, and Brown's running was the talk of the crowd. The lumbering quarterback sneaked over the middle for one first down and later, leaping over linebacker Vince Costello, he raced 16 yards to the Cleveland 43.

The Steelers continued to march, even into the fourth quarter, but again after reaching the Cleveland 23, they failed to capitalize on the ground attack. This time, Clark missed a field goal from the 31.

By now, Johnson had carried the ball 26 times for 170 yards. It was the best performance of the National Football League campaign.

From that point on, it was a matter of the Steelers running out the clock. With relentless driving, with Johnson running sparingly in the closing minutes of the game, he just did make his 200 yards.

But the Steelers had the victory — and that's what counted.

LIONS HAVE NOWHERE TO RUN AGAINST STEELERS

By Pat Livingston, *The Pittsburgh Press*

PITTSBURGH, SEPT. 21, 1969 — CYNICS CAN MAKE WHAT they will of the Steelers' 16-13 triumph over the Detroit Lions at Pitt Stadium, but one inescapable truth floats in the jetsam of the National Football League's biggest opening-day upset.

The Steeler victory yesterday was a product of the Steelers' defense.

"You can't say enough about the defense," said Coach Chuck Noll after the game. "They played their hearts out. They were a very weary bunch. I don't know how they managed to do it."

Noll had hoped to have help for his front four. Lloyd Voss, Ben McGee, Joe Greene and Chuck Hinton were the stars of the afternoon — but his reserve linemen, L.C. Greenwood and Dick Arndt, were injured on the opening kickoff. From that point on, the starters had to go it alone.

"They played a ball game," Noll was remarking an hour later, after all but the stragglers had deserted the Steeler dressing room. The new Steeler coach, celebrating his first victory in his new role, was savoring the triumph.

What 51,360 fans came out to see — an improbable Steeler victory — had been accomplished three minutes before the end of the game. A rookie fullback, Warren Bankston of Tulane, made it possible, sliding around his own left end and over-running three Detroit tacklers before he hurdled into

SCORE BY PERIODS

Detroit	3	0	3	7	13
Pittsburgh	3	6	0	7	16

the end zone.

Before the Steelers could gift wrap this one, however, there was one big play left — a fourth-and-inches situation, the Lions in control of the ball, at their 37.

But Andy Russell, knifing through a web of blockers, upended Bill Triplett a hair's breadth short of the sticks.

"I had to make that play," said Russell. "I caught a lot of flak all week for missing one like that against the Giants."

While Russell's all or nothing effort was the critical play — the play that captured the fancy of the cheering spectators — it was unheralded Hinton, a somber, silent sphinx of a tackle, who engineered the victory. Twice during the course of the game, Hinton recovered key Detroit fumbles, and all during the afternoon the 260-pound

rock stood firm against the rushes of halfback Mel Farr.

Farr, a genuine running threat, was held to 35 yards by the miserly Steeler line.

Still, Farr was a factor. As the Steelers periled quarterback Bill Munson, harassing him but rarely reaching him, they put enough pressure on the Lions' passer to force him to forget his primary receivers and lob the ball to Farr, his safety valve, instead.

Munson completed 19 passes, but 13 of them wound up in the arms of Farr, Triplett and Nick Eddy, his secondary outlets. Detroit's wide receivers, Bill Malinchak and Earl McCullouch, caught only two passes downfield.

One of them, McCullouch's only reception of the game, was a 12-yard touchdown pass, five minutes before the end of the game, which put the Lions ahead, 13-9. On two other occasions, Clarence Oliver, another rookie starting his first game as a pro, knocked the ball out of McCullouch's arms to thwart long gainers.

The Detroit touchdown triggered the Steelers' most impressive march of the game, a seven-play, 71-yard drive that was climaxed when Bankston stormed into the end zone. Highlighting the game-winning drive was Roy Jefferson, who caught two passes and raced 12 yards on an end-around play to set up Bankston's heroic dash.

In a defensive game, ballcarriers are

With three minutes left in the game, rookie fullback Warren Bankston rushed 6 yards for the Steelers' winning touchdown.

rarely the stars of the show and, because of this the early scoring was a matter of field goals. For the Steelers, Gene Mingo contributed three three-pointers, connecting from the 27, 18 and 40. Mingo's counterpart with the Lions, Errol Mann, hit on two of three, both from the 23, which left the Steelers with a shaky 9-6 lead at the end of three quarters.

Detroit's big break came at the Steeler 27, as Bankston committed his second fumble of the game. After tack-le Alex Karras fell on the ball, the Lions marched in for the go-ahead touch-down, McCullouch taking Munson's wobbly toss behind the goal posts as rookie Chuck Beatty grasped desper-ately for the ball.

It was at this point that Steelers quarterback Dick Shiner, playing con-servatively until then, started gambling on big yardage-eating plays.

He made them, five in a row, and moved the Steelers down to the Detroit 6, from where Bankston, churning along like a runaway freight train, blasted into the end zone.

Artistic or not, it was a grand way to win a football game.

The Steelers weren't worried though, about the artistry of their first victory.

"It's great to win," smiled Bruce Van Dyke, the 240-pound Steeler guard who spent the day spearing his helmet into Karras' navel. "It doesn't make any difference how you do it."

STEELERS ON VERGE OF 1ST TITLE IN CLUB HISTORY

By Phil Musick, *The Pittsburgh Press*

HOUSTON, DEC. 10, 1972 — GERRY MULLINS SAT SLUMPED on the bench, sucking oxygen from a thin, green tube. He had a concussion and the flu. The last time he tried to get off the bench, his legs buckled and someone put a gentle hand on his shoulder and eased him back where he belonged.

"I got knocked goofy pretty early, but when Bruce went down there wasn't much I could do," Mullins said later. "There wasn't anyone else. I just went as long as I could stand up."

So did the rest of the Steelers, who stood pretty tall. Jon Kolb had the flu and spent Saturday night sick to his stomach. Bruce Van Dyke tore a calf muscle early. Jim Clack wrenched a leg. Ray Mansfield was hobbling. Terry Bradshaw dislocated a finger. Joe Gilliam got his leg bent. So did Ron Shanklin. L.C. Greenwood couldn't play — he later offered to trade his leg for one attached to a 135-pound sportscaster — and his backup man, Craig Hannemah, went for a half on a knee that finally gave out. Dwight White had to be dragged off, sat down for two minutes and went back in because "there wasn't anybody else."

And the Steelers, inartistically but indomitably, all spit and grit and adhesive tape, gutted one away from Houston, 9-3, in the Astrodome yesterday in a tribute to tenacity.

SCORE BY PERIODS

Pittsburgh	3	0	6	0	9
Houston	0	3	0	0	3

"I can't tell you how proud I am of these guys," said Steeler coach Chuck Noll, and if you didn't know pro football coaches are all tough guys, you might have thought there were a few tears in his voice. "Guys like Jon Kolb out there, feeling like that. We had guys out there bleeding ... bleeding ... gutting it out. Guys who shouldn't have been out there."

But for 60 desperate minutes they were and the Steelers are now just one game from the AFC Central Division title, and a sure pop for the league playoffs, and the winningest outfit (10-3) in 40 years of regrettable history. And now when people talk about the Steelers and the Super Bowl in the same sentence, nobody laughs no more.

Franco Harris didn't get the 100 yards he needed for a slice of immortality all his own — "I'm sorry for him we didn't have an offensive line," said Noll — but he got enough to become the sixth rookie to ever gain 1,000 yards in a season. And the Steelers got three field goals from Roy Gerela and a lot of unshakable cool from a kid quarterback with the poise of a flim-flam man, and the defense that won't say die, and now a win in San Diego will secure the most elusive trophy in the history of the National Football League. In the words of one Steeler, "the wildcard is made."

"This was a good opportunity for them to say, 'Well everybody's hurt,'" Noll said as his troops straggled by to the room where trainer Ralph Berlin, known to his charges as The Plumber, worked steadily. "Thank God we came out of it with one in the win column. The guys who weren't hurt carried the load."

The guys who weren't hurt could've done a tango in a phone booth. Before Garcia and Skip Butler swapped field goals to produce a 3-3 halftime stalemate, Van Dyke came up lame and joined the previously-injured Sam Davis on the bench, leaving Noll without his regular guards. Mel Holmes slid into the breech. Mullins went out early in the second half — "the guy was using a club on me and I kept getting dizzy" — and Clark, a center by trade, replaced him.

And the beat went on, as it had with

In the victory over Houston, Franco Harris became the sixth rookie in NFL history to rush for 1,000 yards in a season.

Unable to find the end zone, Joe Gilliam's offense set up three Roy Gerela field goals.

four minutes left in the half when Terry Bradshaw dislocated the ring finger on his throwing hand and it was decided he was through because Noll felt "he would have trouble taking the pounding from the snap and we didn't want to risk a fumble."

After both he and Gilliam had proven unflappable, Clark was jubilant: "I think what happened today is what really makes this a great team." What happened was, in the vernacular, everyone hung tough and Houston, playing undoubtedly its finest defensive game of the year, could not disturb the sort of unity of purpose from which champions are perhaps spun.

Led by Joe Greene, who wore out two Oiler guards, and unruffled by

replacements in the ranks — rookie tackle Steve Furness played the second half at end in his first NFL game — the Steeler defense was nothing short of magnificent. So thoroughly dominated were the Oilers in the final two quarters that they gained the startling total of 26 yards on 27 plays — 17 of which either lost yardage or produced zip.

"Joe played a great football game," said Noll. "And we went through a 47-man roster today."

Meanwhile, a "slightly anxious" Gilliam, getting the kind of protection a stripper gets from a balloon, twice steered the patchwork offense close enough for Gerela to do his thing. He completed three passes on the Steel-

ers' opening series of the second half, Frenchy Fuqua got 15 big yards on a draw, and Gerela banged it through from the 39.

Greene took it from there. In the first half, he harassed Oiler quarterback Dan Pastorini unmercifully and blocked a field goal attempt on the final play of the second quarter. But immediately after Gerela's 39-yarder, Greene turned artist. He stripped Oiler back Fred Willis of the ball on a sweep, discarded Willis like a piece of trash and recovered the ball at the Houston 13.

Three plays later, Gilliam underthrew Al Young at the goal line, but Gerela hit an easy one from the 13 to break Steeler single-season records for field goals (27) and points (113) and it

Dwight White was but one of many Steeler casualties against Houston.

was 9-3.

"I missed him ... period," sighed Gilliam. "Maybe I could have run it in." It's doubtful, Gilliam was — what else? — hurting. "I didn't think I was going to make it," he said. "I got my leg twisted up under me early. But there wasn't anyone else." It had a familiar ring.

Houston's last and best chance at its second win in 13 games came midway in the fourth quarter, with the Steelers pinned at their own 7 after a 53-yard field goal try by Butler dropped dead at the 1 and Mike Wagner had to field it. But pressure-resistant Bobby Walden punted 57 yards — "I was thinking but one thing, get it off and hit it as far as I could" — and the Oilers were through.

Houston backup quarterback Kent Nix, working after Pastorini pulled a hamstring muscle, was buried on three of the Oilers' last four plays following another long Walden punt. And the Steelers — The Gang That Couldn't Walk Straight — stepped to within one game of their first championship.

"I'll tell you, there's a lot of guys who played their guts out," said Andy Russell. Nothing more apropos could've been said.

Although playing with a patched-up defense, the Steelers limited Houston to only one field goal.

Coach Chuck Noll enjoys a victory ride after the Steelers defeated San Diego, 24-2, to win the 1972 AFC Central Division.

STEELERS CAPTURE FIRST CHAMPIONSHIP, 24-2

By Phil Musick, *The Pittsburgh Press*

SAN DIEGO, DEC. 17, 1972 — YOU SPELL C-H-A-M-P-I-O-N-S. As in Steelers.

No more bad jokes; no more 40 years of regret. No more looking back on the smoldering ruins, or reaching for the elusive dream that was never quite within reach. The National Football League's Little Boy Lost has been found. No more history.

Just a driving stretch run to win nine of the last 10 and Art Rooney walking up the aisle, the determination to shake the hand of everyone on that wild airplane etched in the lines of his 71-year old Irish face.

Just Chuck Noll, whose devotion to discipline and detail had made it possible, abandoning both in the final minutes of play to whack people across the backside and smile away the relief like a schoolboy.

Just Ray Mansfield, "sick all the way because I was here all those years when we used to blow them." And Frenchy Fuqua, who "didn't want that last minute to ever tick away." And Andy Russell, who thought it might not ever come because "all morning I had a feeling of impending doom."

No more history. Just a lot of aching football players ... champions. Just Dwight White, standing along the sideline in those last sweet moments, mocking all that had come before with a smile you could feel in your hip pocket.

SCORE BY PERIODS

Pittsburgh	7	7	3	7	24
San Diego	2	0	0	0	2

"Same old Steelers," White leered.

And that was the bottom line, because suddenly they weren't and the holy grail was in hand, and San Diego had been whipped like a misbehaving puppy, 24-2, behind The Defense That Never Dies.

The AFC Central Division championship was, at long last, theirs, along with a chance to make it two straight over Oakland Saturday on the first step to — who would've thunk it? — the Super Bowl. And at home, baby, where they are seven and zip in this year of resurrection, and 11-3 everywhere.

And how did four decades of hard times disappear like they'd never been? Deee-fense — like they'll be screaming it from the upper tier at Three Rivers Stadium Saturday, like they were screaming it at 1 o'clock this morning at Greater Pitt — and that stuff called desire.

All that defense, squeezing the poise out of the wily, old Chargers so that they gave up the ball seven times, four of which produced 24 points and a pillow fight on the Steeler charter home.

"We had to have a great defensive effort to win," said Noll. "That's the character of this team — whatever it takes to win, they do. And they wanted it very badly — very badly."

Two minutes into the game — a half-hour after Cleveland had whipped the Jets in New York to make a win or a tie mandatory — they began to take it.

The first of four passes John Hadl shouldn't have thrown was snatched by Sticks Anderson — "Jack Ham knocked down the receiver and the ball was just there." One minute and 11 quick yards later, Franco Harris bolted in from the 2.

A Charger blitz buried Terry Bradshaw for a safety later in the opening quarter. But a defense that did not yield a touchdown in seven of the 14 games — "and I never even heard of anything like that," Russell said — didn't need the help the Jets hadn't produced.

"It wouldn't have been right any other way; we knew all along we'd have to do it ourselves," said Joe Greene, after he quit saying things like "It's beautiful, man, beautiful" and "Whooie" and "We're not going to let that bubble burst now."

If San Diego's bubble didn't burst until later, it did begin leaking badly midway in the second quarter when Leonary Dunlap bobbled a punt that Larry Brown nestled around at the Charger 34. "It was just laying there, waiting for me," Brown explained.

Terry Bradshaw threw a screen to Frenchy Fuqua for 28 yards, and two plays later when Fuqua punched in from the 2 it was 14-2 and history was about to get an offer it couldn't refuse.

"The hardest thing of all for us to overcome was the history thing," Mansfield said.

"But it makes you feel proud of guys who played hurt like that, and that feeling we have might carry us farther."

Art Rooney Finally Has His Day

By Pat Livingston, *The Pittsburgh Press*

The big plane had scarcely lifted its wings over the snow-capped peaks of the Sierra Nevadas when Arthur J. Rooney, the 71-year old owner of the Steelers, rose from his seat and started down the aisle.

A round little man with a shock of unruly silver hair, a prototype of a political campaigner, Rooney made his way from seat to seat, thanking his football retinue. From Chuck Noll on down to the groundskeepers at Three Rivers Stadium who had accompanied the Steelers as his personal guests, Rooney shook the hand of everyone aboard.

He accepted their congratulations hesitantly.

"Why congratulate me? Those fellows up there," said he, pointing toward the front of the cabin where the players and coaches were seated, "are the ones who should be congratulated."

Art's protest could not deny him his hour in the sun, however. The triumphant trip home belonged to Art Rooney, the culmination of a dream of 40 years, and no one was letting him forget it. Not even the victorious players.

An hour out of San Diego, where the Steelers had clinched their first division title, Andy Russell, the defensive captain and a team spokesman of sorts, got on the intercom microphone.

"I don't want to sound maudlin or sentimental," said Russell, "but I speak for every member of the team when I say that this ball goes to a great guy. It's always been a pleasure to play for this man."

Rooney, sitting with Lionel Taylor's wife, Loren, when the presentation was made, was speechless for a moment. It was a gesture that touched him deeply, and when he finally spoke, thanking everyone again, he let the players know how he felt about what they had done.

"This is the best gift I've ever received," said he.

Rooney is a man who treasures mementos, but the football that finally brought a championship to Pittsburgh, a project he set out to accomplish four decades ago, will occupy a special niche in Rooney's trophy case. It will be suitably mounted and place, not in his office, but in his home.

"I couldn't keep it in the office," said Rooney. "Too many people are in and out of the office. I think I'll

The guys who played hurt — Ron Shanklin, L.C. Greenwood, Gerry Mullins and others — didn't have much of a choice. "There was no one to put in," said Noll. When the adhesive tape ran out, Shanklin had replaced Frank Lewis, whose collarbone was busted in three places in the second quarter, and the walking wounded remained in the breech.

"Shank probably shouldn't have played, but he did," said Noll. "The makeshift offensive line did a hell of a job. That's the way this team is."

Suddenly, with three minutes remaining in the third quarter, the crowd of 52,873 knew what it had long suspected. It was over. Jack Ham, the human magnet who four minutes ear-lier had recovered a fumble, stole his seventh pass of the year. Roy Gerela, who had a pair of field goals blocked by Greg Wojcik and shanked another wide, hit from the Charger 26 to make it 17-2.

Someone should've hung a shroud on San Diego, and when Mel Blount's interception set up Terry Bradshaw's 18-yard touchdown pass to Shanklin, it was merely a case of rubbing salt in the Chargers' considerable wounds.

"It looked like the San Diego receivers were covering Mel," said Russell. "He played one of the finest games I've ever seen a defensive back play."

After they had capitalized on Blount's theft, this Sammy Glick of a football team stood along the sideline and it was, for all the world, recess.

Henry Davis squirted the unsuspecting fan with a water bottle. L.C. Greenwood chatted with a cheerleader, and directly behind them in the stands were 200 guys from Pittsburgh who were roaring over and over, "We're No. 1" and slugging a few stadium guards who were trying to remove their banner.

Fittingly, the game ended with San Diego, which didn't cross midfield under its own steam until the final 12 minutes, chipping futilely away. The gun cracked, Jim Clack and Mansfield hoisted Noll onto their shoulders, and 40 years of gloom drowned in a champagne bottle.

keep this in my home."

Rooney is not a demonstrative man. Upon receiving the ball, and earlier as he went through the plane thanking his friends, the thick, heavy lenses that cover his eyes hid a mist that had formed around them. He used his handkerchief a couple of times last night.

I sat with Art during the game. As usual, he occasionally second-guessed the play-calling, as a fan will do, and he grumbled when the Steelers failed to convert San Diego turnovers into scores. When the Steelers ran the count to 24-2. Rooney didn't even let out a cheer. He lit another cigar.

Unquestionably, it was Rooney's day. Yet when he walked into the Steeler dressing room, where the San Diego owners, Gene Klein and George Pernicano, waited to congratulate him, Rooney's first reaction was not toward his team.

"How's the referee?" Art asked, showing his concern for the injured back judge, Ralph Vandenberg, whose knee was seriously torn up in a sideline collision with a ball player. Vandenberg will hear from Art Rooney, you can be sure of that.

Art never got a chance to congratulate many of his quick-dressing players in the locker room. As he stepped into the hallway, he was besieged by the news media, asking his impressions of the victory and inquiring how it felt to be a winner after all those years.

"If I knew so many people were going to talk to me," said Rooney, "I'd never have gone in there."

There was some surprise that he didn't seem as excited as one might expect on a day like this. "It's just my nature," said Rooney, smiling broadly. "I never show my enthusiasm."

He did agree, though, that this "is the high point of my 40 years with the team."

"I knew we'd win if I lived long enough. I did get kind of worried as it got later in my life."

Rooney said the Steeler triumph this year came as no surprise at all. He had been anticipating it since Sept. 24, the second week of the season, when the Cincinnati Bengals beat his team, 15-10 — the first of only three losses this season.

"We lost that day," said Rooney, "but that was the day I began to think we'd win the division.

"I felt last year we had the best team in the division, but I don't think the players knew themselves how good they were. That loss in Cincinnati didn't even bother them. They didn't get down on themselves at all.

"A team that can lose a game, and not worry about it," added Art Rooney, "is a team that believes in itself. And that's all this team had to do."

IMMACULATE RECEPTION SAVES THE STEELERS

By Phil Musick, *The Pittsburgh Press*

PITTSBURGH, DEC. 23, 1972 — THE GOD OF THIS GAME'S ALL-TIME losers smiled down through a ghostly gray sky yesterday, and in the last desperate second of a mean, bitterly-fought football game, did truly wondrous things.

History would have had it no other way. And after 40 endless year of spilling salt and breaking mirrors and walking under ladders, the Steelers were smiled upon by a benevolent fate.

Through the luck that could only grace a loser of standing, and through the quick hands of Franco Harris, the Steelers rudely jerked a 13-7 decision out of the hands of the benumbed Oakland Raiders and staggered into the AFC championship game here next Sunday against the survivor of today's Cleveland-Miami encounter.

It was almost unbelievable. It happened this way, and if you can't bring yourself to believe it, don't worry — neither did the 50,350 wild folk who stumbled from Three Rivers Stadium in the kind of daze they might have know had the field suddenly opened and swallowed the Tartan-Turf:

Shackled until the final 1:13 by a Steeler defense that had yielded just 21 points in the previous 21 quarters, Oakland snatched a 7-6 lead when backup quarterback Ken Stabler scrambled 30 yards on a busted pass play to cap an 80-yard drive.

SCORE BY PERIODS

Oakland	0	0	0	7	7
Pittsburgh	0	0	3	10	13

But nobody messes around with history and fate, and all the game's first touchdown brought the Raiders was titillation.

Desperation rolled up its sleeves then. The Steelers worked the ball to their own 40 following the Raider score and with only seconds left, quarterback Terry Bradshaw retreated to pass on a fourth-and-10 play. Evading the Oakland hands plucking at his jersey, he gunned the ball to Frenchy Fuqua.

Fate didn't like his choice. Oakland safetyman Jack Tatum, who had swatted down Bradshaw attempts on the previous two plays, either did or did not deflect the ball off Fuqua's chest.

We'll never know — Tatum said he didn't; Fuqua just leered — but the ball ricocheted off toward the sideline, where Franco Harris whisked it off his shoe-tops at the Oakland 42, got a partial

block from tight end John McMakin, then outran the Raiders' other safety, Jimmy Warren, to the end zone. There were five seconds left when he crossed the goal line.

He was greeted by pandemonium and some confused officials, undecided whether Tatum had touched the ball, making the play legal, or had not touched it, making it illegal.

After deliberating with the league officials and watching a television replay in a nearby dugout, referee Fred Swearingen confirmed what everyone had suspected: Sooner or later everyone gets lucky. Oakland had five seconds to reclaim the victory, but no such luck.

"Whatever it takes ... that's the story of this team, isn't it?" Chuck Noll smiled and smiled. "Whatever it takes ... even if it's a little luck. One busted play got them a touchdown, why shouldn't it get us one? An eye for an eye."

Elsewhere in the Steeler dressing room there was delirium.

"I can't believe it. I saw it, and I can't believe it," said guard Bruce Van Dyke. "When they scored, my damn brain was gone. I can't believe it."

For three quarters and change it was a wholly believable game. Noll's "magnificent defense" controlled the third-most potent running game in the AFC and choked three turnovers out of the Raiders, who had given up five when they lost here in the opener. The third one was costly.

The Immaculate Reception: With 22 seconds left, Steeler quarterback Terry Bradshaw's fourth-down pass intended for Frenchy Fuqua was deflected by the Raiders' Jack Tatum (above) and caught by Franco Harris (below), who ran 42 yards for the winning TD.

The Steelers drove 87 yards to the Oakland 11 with the second-half kickoff to grab a 3-0 lead on Roy Gerela's 18-yard field goal. After an interception by Jack Ham and a fumble recovery by Glen Edwards had stalled two earlier drives, Mike Wagner fell on a fumble by Stabler at the Oakland 35 and five plays

later Gerela was true from the 29 to make it 6-0.

The Raiders clung to life after the ensuing kickoff. Stabler completed four passes — three on third-down plays — to drive Oakland to the Steeler 30, at which point Fate went out for lunch.

The slim Oakland quarterback, nick-

named The Snake for reasons that were immediately apparent, slipped outside a hard charge by rookie defensive end Craig Hanneman and fled 30 yards untouched into the end zone.

"I don't know what I would have done if ..." sighed Hanneman, who had just entered the game to replace Dwight White. "I put an arm out, but he did a reverse pivot. I was outside because we had a safety blitz going and I closed down. I should have smelled a rat."

Down by one with just 22 seconds left, Noll sent in a pass play with rookie receiver Barry Pearson.

"The pass was called to Pearson," explained Noll, who said he "could've kicked myself" for a fourth-and-1 gamble from the Raider 32 in the second quarter that misfired.

"Pearson got hung up and Frenchy adjusted his route and Terry went to him.

Tatum hit the ball and Franco made a fantastic catch. Franco had been blocking on the play and then went out. He was hustling ... and all good things happen to those who keep hustling."

Harris was hustling and so was McMakin, whose partial block got him some precious running room. "I just fell down in front of somebody," said McMakin. "I can't believe it either."

The rest — and in reality there wasn't anything else but those final five frantic seconds — read from a mundane script. Neither team could control the line of scrimmage; consequently neither could sustain a running game.

Possessed of the second best ground

The referee watches intently as Franco Harris makes a miracle catch just before the ball hits the turf.

'72 STEELERS: NEVER SAY DIE

By Pat Livingston, *The Pittsburgh Press*

No team had ever been closer to defeat.

Trailing 7-6, the result of a heartbreaking 30-yard touchdown run by a reserve quarterback, the Steelers had fourth down, 10 yards to go and they were on their own 40-yard line, 20 yards short of field-goal range.

Not only that, but the clock was running out. Only 22 seconds remained in the game when quarterback Terry Bradshaw squatted behind the center. At the snap of the ball, the Oakland Raiders came through in a vicious, aggressive charge.

One of the Raiders got to Brad-shaw, high around the shoulders, but somehow he twisted out of his grasp. Downfield, Barry Patterson, the primary receiver, was running a post pattern toward center of the field and Frenchy Fuqua was curling into the hook zone, deep enough to make the sticks if Bradshaw had to cut the pattern.

But as Bradshaw broke from the pattern, all signals were off. Fuqua stretched out downfield and Franco Harris, held in to block, suddenly started looking for an open spot. They raced toward the goal line to Bradshaw's left.

It was then that Bradshaw spied Fuqua and fired. The ball and an Oakland safety, Jack Tatum, were on a collision course, reaching Fuqua at precisely the same instant. The ball flew out of Fuqua's arms, or was pushed as the officials ruled, and bounced high into the air.

"Oh, no," groaned Harris as he saw the ball flying loose.

But suddenly it was flying toward Harris and, with a crouching grasp just before the ball hit the turf, Franco grabbed it at his ankles and took off down the sideline.

By the time the big fullback reached the end zone, fans had already swarmed out of the stands, mobbing the rookie. It wasn't until referee Fred Swearingen checked with the instant replay, however, that he raised his arms to signal the wild, incredible touchdown.

It came with five seconds to play.

game in the league, the Steelers rushed for only 108 yards, and a game plan built around throwing to the backs wasn't successful with the exception of the third quarter march that brought Gerela's first field goal.

Armed with one of the more versatile offenses, Oakland got a meager 216 yards total offense, and Mark Hubbard, a 1,000-yard-plus back, was held to 44 yard in 14 attempts. And Daryle Lamonica and Stabler, who entered with 11 minutes left and the Raiders plodding along, completed only 12 of 30 passes for just 78 yards.

Oakland was wedged into poor field position throughout the game by the Steeler defense and the punting of Bobby Walden, who got off pressure punts of 59 and 62 yards, both of which set AFC playoff records.

SINATRA CALLS

The man obviously takes his rank seriously.

His telegram arrived about 45 minutes after the Steelers defeated Oakland, 13-7, yesterday.

It read: "The following is an order, Attack, Attack, Attack, Attack."

And it was signed Colonel Francis Sinatra (of Franco Harris' Italian Army).

Eight of the Raiders' 12 offensive series began inside their 22-yard line,

and until they scored their deepest penetrations carried to the Steeler 47- and 44-yard lines.

Losing a first-round playoff game for the first time — and dropping its fourth straight post-season game on the road — Oakland suffered at the hands of the Steeler secondary. Fred Biletnikoff, who has led the AFC in receiving the past two years, made only three receptions and was just one of several Oakland receivers to drop good passes.

"Our coverage was just fine and we pressured them," said Noll.

Terry Bradshaw was more articulate. "There aren't any words for our defense," he smiled.

"Luck? Sure we were lucky. After 40 years, why shouldn't we be? Who deserves it more?"

Who, indeed.

"No, I didn't see it," said a grinning Bradshaw later in the dressing room. "All I saw was Franco running with the ball. I figured, man, I must've hit him right on the numbers."

Seething on the sideline, Joe Greene didn't see the touchdown either.

"But I saw Franco with the ball and that was good enough for me," said Greene, the leader of a defense that once again had come up with an utterly brilliant game. Only a broken play, a 30-yard touchdown run by Ken Stabler, who got outside the Steelers' containment, marred an otherwise perfect game.

"When I saw Franco with the ball," explained Greene. "I knew we were in field-goal territory. I figured he had to be down around the 5- or 10-yard line."

The happy Steelers weren't taking full credit for yesterday's victory, however. They knew there was another force somewhere that enabled them to snatch victory from the jaws of defeat.

"Do you have type big enough to report a miracle?" asked Bob Adams, a veteran who has spent the season on the taxi squad. "A miracle, that's what it was."

"A cheap one for a cheap one," said a beaming Terry Hanratty, who was as happy over the victory as if he had thrown the game-winning pass. "I'm glad we had the last one."

Hanratty, of course, was alluding to Stabler's touchdown, which had given the Raiders a 7-6 lead with only 1:13 left on the clock. The heartbreak of what apparently was a gamelosing score would have been enough to shatter an earlier Steeler team, the

Steelers of a year ago perhaps, but it didn't affect this scrappy team.

"All year," said Coach Chuck Noll, "they've been doing what had to be done. They did it again against the Raiders."

Bradshaw was a leader who felt no discouragement, even though the clock was running out on his dream. There were no pep talks in the huddle, he said. "I didn't have to pep 'em up," said Terry. "They all knew what we had to do.

"All we needed was the field goal. I figured we could get the field goal."

There were the critics, though, who tried to dash cold water on the Steelers' victory. Blind luck, they muttered. But the Steelers have been victims of bad luck too often in the past to look askance at a stroke of good fortune, even if it has taken it 40 years to arrive.

MIRACLES RUN OUT IN AFC CHAMPIONSHIP GAME

By Jack Sell, *Pittsburgh Post-Gazette*

PITTSBURGH, DEC. 31, 1972 — THE MIRACLE OF THREE Rivers seemed about to be repeated yesterday afternoon.

Trailing the Miami Dolphins in the last quarter by 11 points at 21-10, quarterback Terry Bradshaw, who had been shaken up and sidelined in the first half, came off the bench for a brilliant display of aerial fireworks.

The blond bomber hurled the Steelers 71 yards in four plays, the last a 12-yard touchdown loss to wide receiver Al Young, who made a brilliant one-handed catch, and the Black and Gold was back in contention. That required only 2:04 and there was still 5:15 to go.

But the run of good fortune that had brought eight straight home victories without a defeat finally ended. The defense got the ball back for two late tries but Bradshaw tosses were intercepted to the disappointment of a sell-out crowd of 50,350.

So it's on to the Super Bowl after a hard-earned 21-17 victory for Coach Don Shula's Dolphins. They are now 16-0 for the season. Coach Chuck Noll's finest team in local history closed out at 12-4.

Each winning player collected $8,500 while the Steelers wound up $5,500 richer as they headed for home. Of course, Miami became the American Conference champion.

Later yesterday, the Washington

Score by Periods

Miami	0	7	7	7	21
Pittsburgh	7	0	3	7	17

Redskins defeated the Dallas Cowboys, 26-3, for the National Conference championship and the right to meet Miami in the Super Bowl Sunday on Jan. 14 in Los Angeles.

There was some more good luck for the losers when they gained their first lead because a fumble by Bradshaw that rolled into the end zone was covered by tackle Gerry Mullins for a TD.

Bradshaw's pass to Young got the other local six-pointer while Roy Gerela booted a 14-yard field goal and added the PAT's.

Jim Kiick, whose father played for the Steelers in the 1940's, went across from 2 and 3 yards out while ex-Steeler Earl Morrall passed 9 yards to Larry Csonka for the other score. Garo

Yepremian took care of the conversions.

Bradshaw, who left Divine Providence Hospital Saturday after a bout with intestinal flu, made way for Terry Hanratty in the second, third and the early part of the fourth quarters.

Terry Bradshaw's fumble near the goal line was recovered by tackle Gerry Mullins in the end zone for a Steeler touchdown.

Morrall played the entire first half, which ended in a 7-7 deadlock. Bob Griese, injured early in the season, took over after the intermission and sparked the Eastern Division champs.

One of the key moves by the victors was a 37-yard, fourth-down gallop by punter Paul Seiple who caught the home defense asleep. That led to the tying TD.

In a curious statistical showdown among 1,000-yard gainers, the Steelers' Franco Harris and the Dolphins' Mercury Morris each carried 16 times and each gained 76 yards. The other

After returning in the fourth quarter, Bradshaw found few openings in the Dolphins' defense.

member of the trio, Larry Csonka of the Dolphins, rushed 68 yards on 24 trips. The Steeler defense contained Paul Warfield with two catches for 62 yards but one for 52 yards was crucial.

In any game — especially an important game such as this — there are several turning points. You could pick a dozen in yesterday's contest by way of an argument.

There were those who thought Bob Griese replacing Earl Morrall did it. Griese was great but I though the 38-year-old Morrall did very well.

Quite a number of Pittsburgh people believed the injury to Terry Bradshaw was a big factor. It could have been, yet one couldn't fault the bench-rusty Terry Hanratty the way he pitched and ran the Steelers' offense while he was in there.

There were dropped passes and penalties that hurt. The Steelers fumbled four times, turning the ball over twice. There was Roy Gerela's blocked kick on a 48-yard attempt on which the Dolphins capitalized.

Oh, there were many turning points.

I would guess, however, that the vote would favor Seiple's unexpected play which caught the Steelers napping.

RAN LONGER THAN HE KICKED

It was mentioned here one morning last week that the Steelers had an edge in punting. Larry Seiple couldn't match Bob Walden's long boots.

He didn't. Walden was superb, as usual, averaging 51.3 on four punts to Seiple's 35.5. The irony of the Dolphin kicker's figure is that his run on the fake was longer than his kicking average.

Seiple raced 37 yards on a fourth-and-5 situation from the Pittsburgh 49 to the 12. Two Steelers, unknowingly, helped lead the interference for Seiple. They were downfield, looking for the ball to come down and somebody to catch it.

Pittsburgh was ahead, 7-0, at a time on a semi-miracle play. Bradshaw fumbled trying to score from the 2. Gerry Mullins saved the situation by falling on the ball in the end zone for six points.

The two teams punished each oth-

er physically all though the game. While the Steelers appeared the stronger in this department they suffered the most casualties. They also suffered from overeagerness, a sophomore trait that cost them a few precious yards at most embarrassing moments.

Griese took over with Pittsburgh leading, 10-7. He led the Dolphins on two touchdown marches to make the score read, 21-10.

Did the Steelers have any miracles left?

It seemed that way. The injured Bradshaw came off the bench in the last period to throw four straight passes, the last a touchdown to Al Young. Young made a great catch.

With 5:13 left, the Steelers could win. Didn't they win with five seconds left last week?

It wasn't to be. They had two opportunities. Both ended in interceptions of Bradshaw's passes.

I told Don Shula last Thursday the Steelers would win.

"See you at the Super Bowl," he said, "where we'll be 17-0."

STEELERS STAGGER PAST BROWNS FOR DIVISION LEAD

By Phil Musick, *The Pittsburgh Press*

PITTSBURGH, OCT. 20, 1974 — THIS STORY DOESN'T BELONG here. It should be back there somewhere between Peanuts and Dick Tracy with the rest of the funnies.

The Steelers (4-1-1 and teetering) beat (survived?) Cleveland, 20-16, yesterday, before 48,100 suffering souls at Three Rivers Stadium to stagger a half-game ahead of Cincinnati and take the lead in an AFC Central Division race that no longer concerns the Browns (1-5).

While Cincinnati was getting clipped, 30-27, in Oakland, the Steelers were involved in a Marx Bros. affair that further raised the question: If they are a contender, how come they look so much like the Houston Oilers?

The Steelers fumbled five times. They passed for a net 66 yards, rushed for 3.7 yards a pop. They lost the battle of statistics to a disorganized mob that earlier in the week fired one-third of its regulars. And it took a couple of gutty field goals from a guy with a bum leg to get them past a 17-point underdog.

The script was unchanging. The defense did the work, and against a club that had given up 143 points in five previous games and a week ago would've

Terry Bradshaw struggled all afternoon against Cleveland. All of the Steelers' points were created by the defense and the kicking game.

SCORE BY PERIODS

Cleveland	0	13	0	3	16
Pittsburgh	7	7	3	3	20

been hard-pressed to stop Bethel Park High, the offense stood around a lot. Mostly wasted was excellent field position, which saw the Steelers begin four series inside the Cleveland 37 and two more beyond their own 40.

"We haven't played as well as we think we can," said Chuck Noll, who along with many other less-partial observers may be guilty of overestimation. "We were pleased with the way our defense stopped their rushing game, but the offense is still struggling.

"This is the age of the mistake. We get a drive going, a penalty hurts us. Mistakes just continue to plague us."

Struggling would seem adequate to describe a Steeler offense that had both of its touchdowns yesterday set up by the defense and which now has gone 18 quarters without mounting a scoring drive from its own territory.

The Steelers' first touchdown was set up courtesy of Mike Wagner, who recovered a Hugh McKinnis fumble. The second came after Joe Greene sacked Brown quarterback Mike Phipps at his own 6, forcing an end zone punt.

The argument might be made that the Browns dragged the Steelers down to their level of incompetency, which is such that by the time you read this Coach Nick Skorich may have qualified for unemployment.

After failing to breach midfield in the first 28 minutes of the first half — and after scoring but one touchdown in losing all of the four games they've played at Three Rivers — the Browns managed to score twice in 1:54. They were aided by a roughing the passer penalty against L.C. Greenwood in the first instance, and a Franco Harris fumble in the second. Thus they were in mortal danger of winning a game they weren't in until the two-minute warning in the first half.

So inspired, the Browns ceased struggling only when Glen Edwards made his fourth interception of the year and third in two games. After Cleveland had moved to the Steeler seven with 2:30 to play, Edwards stepped in front of McKinnis and raced 59 yards with a pass the valiant, but beleaguered, Phipps tried to throw with Greenwood and Greene busy leaving their fingerprints on his helmet.

"One mistake killed us," Phipps said. "Maybe I should have thrown sooner." Perhaps, but that would've cost Roy Gerela a game ball, and he deserved one.

Gerela, whose field goals of 31 and 26 yards provided the margin of victory and came after he badly strained a thigh muscle in pre-game warmups, and Bobby Walden — who was forced to kick off for "the first time since high school" and whose punting was such that Cleveland began seven of its 13 possessions inside its 30 and four inside its 15 — literally kicked the Browns to death.

"Tremendous" and "fantastic" were two adjectives Noll heaped on Gerela, who warranted them. Attending to his usual pre-game loosening up, Gerela "tapped the ball" three times. The fourth time he tapped it, his right thigh made the sort of noise usually associated with broken guitar strings. Later he attributed the injury to overwork.

"A kicker's like a baseball pitcher," he explained. "You can only do so much in any one period of time. Then you lose your rhythm, your timing." To say nothing of your thigh muscles.

"Maybe I put too much of a load on my leg during the week," agreed Gerela, who had spent extra time practicing because he "hadn't been sharp as a I thought I should."

Against the Browns, whose offense was Phipps, Gerela was sharp enough. Kicking a bit gingerly — "I just wanted to get some height on it; I only half hit it" — Gerela nudged a 31-yard field goal just inside the upright midway through the third quarter to give the Steelers a 17-13 edge.

Then, four minutes into the final quarter with the Steelers perched shakily atop a 17-16 lead, a parlay of Franco Harris feet and Gerela's foot bought another field goal.

"I don't know how I hurt my leg,"

FRANCO: STIRRING THE ARMY AGAIN

By Phil Musick, *The Pittsburgh Press*

Franco Harris was happy. The Tartan Turf hadn't yawned open and amputated one of his legs.

It's been that sort of season, and that sort of two years, for Harris, who yesterday in the Steelers' 20-16 win over Cleveland gave the world a peek at the guy who two years ago needed an army of fans to do him justice.

"I hope my luck's changing," he smiled softly after running for 81 yards in 14 carries while playing just about half the game. "It just seems like the first five games every year."

What happens the first five games every year is that the sky falls on Harris. A year ago, knee injuries suffered early in training camp kept him from starting until the sixth game and he completely missed two others. Even en route to becoming the Rookie of the Year in 1972, injuries held Harris to only 79 yards in his first four games.

A private man, he tries to shrug off his problems. "I try not to let it get to me," he says. "After Denver this year, I felt I was ready. Then, boom."

Boom was a sprained ankle, suffered on the first play of the Oakland game three weeks ago. Harris didn't play against Houston or Kansas City,

Gerela said. "When I put something on the opening kickoff. I felt a real sharp pain."

So did Chuck Noll, every time he saw a penalty flag. And, in keeping with the rest of the proceedings, the officiating was so lousy that both coaches were bitter.

In Noll's estimation, it was at its lousiest just prior to Cleveland's first touchdown. On a first down play from the Steeler 45, Phipps, whom the Steeler sacked six times to tie a season-high, hit Milt Morin for 12 yards only to have L.C. Greenwood wind up in his lap as he released the ball.

It was not an uncommon sight — on the previous play Greenwood had dealt Phipps "a pretty good lick" — but it did constitute roughing the passer. On the next play, Phipps scrambled 18 yards to score.

"The turning point was the roughing the passer penalty," Noll deadpanned. "We're giving the game ball to the officials. If their intent was to intimidate our pass rush, they did a hell of a job."

Moments after Phipps' touchdown, Harris fumbled to Nick Roman, and

Steeler linebacker Jack Lambert wraps up a Cleveland ballcarrier.

Phipps threw 46 yards to Gloster Richardson and 14 yards to Morin for a touchdown. But an indignant Greenwood ticked Don Cockroft's conversion attempt wide, and in the second half the officials and Harris conspired to save the Steelers.

Midway through the third quarter, Ron Shanklin caught a Joe Gilliam pass, took two steps, was hit and fumbled at the Steeler 35. The Browns' John Garlington recovered. But the officials ruled Shanklin had not had possession of the ball, to which Cleveland's Bob Babich replied, "That's a lot of crap," a theory smilingly substantiated by Shanklin. "I had it," he said. "It should've been called a fumble."

On the following series, Lynn Swann fielded a Brown punt he should've just watched, and fumbled when hit by Van Green. Brown rookie Mark Ilgenfritz recovered. Forget it, said the officials, penalizing the Browns for a man leaving the line of scrimmage too soon.

"That was cheap," Andrews thought. So did Skorich, who said, "The officiating took the big play away from us twice when we needed it."

But the Browns had ultimately taken themselves out of it earlier in the fourth quarter, driving to a first down at the Steeler 7 only to have to settle for a Cockroft field goal.

"We're happy with the victory," Noll said, and he wasn't laughing.

and didn't start yesterday.

"It's just a mental thing. I put it out of my mind," he said. "You just tell yourself to forget it, do whatever it takes. It felt pretty good today. I just said, 'Hey, I'm going to forget it.'"

Apparently Harris did. Twice he burst off tackle and ran down defenders the way he did as a rookie, and in general ran well.

Maybe Harris' luck is changing. One thing: it couldn't have gotten much worse.

Harris said he would like "to play

the whole game. When you get warmed up, you don't like to be taken out. You can't turn it on and off. It worked today, but you have to be more in the groove to bust a few things."

Joe Gilliam cashed only 5 of 18 passes for 66 net yards, by 40 yards his lowest production of the year.

"We had the lead, so we tried to get something going on the ground," Chuck Noll said. "When we did try to pass, we didn't connect."

Noll said he didn't plan to use Harris the whole game. "We want-

ed to give him a feel for it; we hoped we'd get him through without getting him hurt."

Notes: Ray Mansfield, a place-kicker in college, was next in line of succession to kick off if Bobby Waldon would've had problems.

... L.C. Greenwood attributed his roughing the passer penalty to having hit Mike Phipps hard the previous play. "The officials tell you they're keeping a close eye on you after that happens," Greenwood said.

... Phipps has now been sacked 24 times.

BRADSHAW, STEELERS LOOKING SIMPLY SUPER

By Phil Musick, *The Pittsburgh Press*

PITTSBURGH, DEC. 22, 1974 — IT MUST HAVE FELT SOMETHING LIKE getting mugged by your Aunt Ethel or having your thumb chewed off by Baby Tender Love. In a moment of sweet, sweet retribution yesterday, the Steeler offense sprang to life, fell upon the stunned Buffalo Bills in the second quarter like some awful medieval plague, and went streaking off into the AFC championship game Sunday in Oakland, trailing a wake of open mouths and arched eyebrows.

The mighty O.J. was left for pulp by the Steeler defense, but on a day given over to vengeance, it was the Steeler offense, that onetime child of misfortune, which brought about a ridiculously easy 32-14 victory over Buffalo in the quarterfinals of Peter Rozelle's annual tournament.

When it was over, no one said it better than Ray Mansfield: "They were good; we played super football." No pun intended.

Before 48,321 of the faithful gathered on a crisp, lovely afternoon to watch the Steeler defense duel O.J. Simpson to the death at Three Rivers, Terry Bradshaw authored "the best game I've ever had here."

When that half had ended, the Buffalo Bills were dead, and Terry Bradshaw had triumphantly scaled a year of

Terry Bradshaw had his greatest game as a young Steeler against Buffalo, completing 12 of 19 passes for 209 yards.

SCORE BY PERIODS

Buffalo	7	0	7	0	14
Pittsburgh	3	26	0	3	32

----

bad times to know his finest moment as a professional.

True, others of the Steelers were valiant. The Steeler defense buried Simpson, who got only 49 yards on 15 carries, eight of which produced just two yards or less. And there were individual Steelers who gleaned a full measure of personal satisfaction.

Larry Brown, for instance. For weeks the world had been saying his hands were really waffle irons in disguise, but yesterday he made a brilliant, leaping stab of a Bradshaw pass to set up the last of four Steeler touchdowns in the second quarter, the one that sucked the final drop of intrigue from the proceedings.

And there was Lynn Swann, the

Steelers' No. 1 draft pick who caught eight passes in his first 10 games and had half the scouting department hiding in the men's room when the coaches were around.

Yesterday, he was magnificent, running 25 yards on a reverse to set up one touchdown; making a diving catch to set up another.

Certainly, the entire offense deserved the game balls it was awarded, lifting its eyes to the defense with a leer. "We carried you guys today," Mansfield told Jack Ham, who said simply, "I know it."

But, mostly, the day and the triumph belonged to Terry Bradshaw and you could at times see in his amused expression the question. How dumb am I now? And the only honest answer was like a fox, baby, like a fox.

Adversity's handmaiden, Bradshaw had lost his job in training camp and again following the loss in Cincinnati, but yesterday he prevailed.

"The thing I pride myself on is that I've been able to come back," he said. "It's a great feeling to face adversity, overcome it, and rise to the top."

Poised like a prima ballerina, Bradshaw did it all. He was 12 for 19 for 203 yards in his finest passing performance in 29 games and almost three years. But it was his composure rather than his arm that was the most impressive.

He threw a 27-yard strike to Rocky Bleier to give the Steelers a 9-7 edge early in the second quarter only because he had the cool to move to the fringe of the pocket for a better view and an extra second that let him loft a strike over Buffalo linebacker Doug Allen.

Six minutes later, his passing to Swann accounted for another score. In the next minute, Mike Wagner left-hooked the ball from Bills running back Jim Braxton, Ham recovered and Bradshaw threw 35 yards to Swann. Zap, another touchdown.

Then, Buffalo's hopes fading as quickly as the halftime clock, Bradshaw calmly passed the Steelers 54 yards in 85 seconds for their fourth touchdown of the quarter, which set a playoff record.

However, Mansfield was more impressed by a 5-yard lob Bradshaw

completed to Franco Harris with Buffalo defensive end Earl Edwards hanging on him like a shirt.

"A year ago you know he wouldn't have dumped that pass off to Harris, he'd have run," said Mansfield. "I can't say enough about Terry. He just seems a lot more mature. He ignores criticism now. He seems almost cocksure in the huddle now."

Bradshaw agreed. "I've just gotten so much more confident the last few weeks," he said. "And that's the key to winning. You start believing in the things you can do."

Ironically, it was Bradshaw's I.Q. that did in the Bills as much as his passing. Early on, being chewed up by the Steelers' inside running game, the Bills

junked their normal three-man defensive front alignment. They switched to their "80 defense," which is a 4-1 alignment, and Bradshaw, hacked it to bits with good, old reliable P-10.

Although its sounds like some jazzy World War 2 fighter plane. P-10 is bread and butter — Harris up the gut.

The blocking is straight-ahead, Harris reads the movement of the defender over the center and the bodies begin to fall. "That's the play we go to when we're in trouble," Mansfield said.

The Steelers were not in trouble after the mortar-shell second quarter brought 26 points. It also put to rest the theory that Bradshaw possessed a million-dollar arm and a 40-cent head.

BRADSHAW KEEPS FAITH, INSPIRES TEAM

By Phil Musick, *The Pittsburgh Press*

Six weeks ago, he was the Job of the quarterback fraternity. His marriage had dissolved amicably, but there isn't any such thing as a painless divorce. And he had lost his job, twice.

Terry Bradshaw's life was a three-leaf clover. The black cats of America put him on their coats-of-arms. Ladders did deep kneebends when they saw him coming.

So Bradshaw did what he's been doing since he was witnessing for Christ before large audiences at the age of 15. He reached out for the sort of strength you get from your faith.

"It's been a very big part of my life," he was saying yesterday, his voice pitched low even in the emptiness of the Steeler dressing room. "One day I was siting in my apartment and I kind of got all choked up. I couldn't take it anymore.

"I decided to get back with it ... go back to reading the Bible. Everybody needs something. Things go bad, you go someplace to somebody."

Bradshaw doesn't like to talk about his faith or wear it on his sleeve, which — religion being the most personal experience of all — is understandable.

"I haven't said anything," he was saying, the words coming slowly. "I don't like to talk about being 'religious.' I'm not. I'm just a Christian ... with a commitment. The last six weeks, I've gotten back to it."

Consequential or not, in the last six weeks Bradshaw has also gotten with his professional football code, reclaimed his job and in Sunday's playoff win inspired the Steelers offense to heights only Chuck Noll dreamed it could attain.

"I'm not saying that I'm playing better because of getting back in my faith," Bradshaw says. "It's just something I believe in; it helps me accept the good and the bad.

"Things were going so bad and being from a Christian family, well, I'd kinda gotten away from it. I'm a Christian, but I wasn't living like a Christian."

Bradshaw's divorce and his professional problems were compounded by his failure to tap a source of personal strength that he has counted on since adolescence. His faith.

"The divorce blew my mind," he says softly. No drama; no self-pity. A flat statement.

"It all goes back to Terry," said Mansfield. "If there was anything our offense needed it was his leadership."

Nobody had to tell Bradshaw, who had seemingly proven that no longer is he the guy who in a game three years ago became so rattled when the crunch came that he couldn't call a play and had to have someone else do it.

"If I ever had a problem," he was saying, "it was in pushing too many things."

The biggest of those things was his apparent need to prove his leadership capabilities from the day he signed. At an informal barbecue held by one of the veterans shortly after Bradshaw signed, some Steeler veterans spotted a lack of confidence. "It was a fiasco,"

said one. "It was like he thought he could prove himself to us by telling a lot of jokes and smiling."

Bradshaw is no more the smiling young man of naiveté who last season after suffering a painful injury and being booed as he left the field, waved to a group of teenagers while driving home and got an obscene gesture in return.

"I think I can provide leadership by what I do on the field," he said quietly. "In the past, when I didn't play well, I'd worry and it would fog my mind. I'm trying to flash that stuff out of my head now."

Apparently, Bradshaw has succeeded in becoming less anxious. Yesterday he "slept a solid 13 hours" and arrived

at Three Rivers just an hour and 20 minutes before the game.

"I tried not to get too high for this one," he said. "In the past, I took too much responsibility. Now I just let things roll. I think that comes from not playing. It gives you a sense of awareness."

Obviously, there is a difference in Bradshaw's play. "We handled everything like a championship team today," he said. "I never felt so much in control. I've had great games in the past, statistically speaking. But I was doing that searching here, searching there thing. It was different today. I was in complete control."

Because Bradshaw was, so were the Steelers.

"I'd gotten away from it," Bradshaw says. "That bothered me and I said to myself, 'Shoot, I can't handle this alone.'"

A friend helped steer Bradshaw back to his beliefs and seemingly, they sustained him to the point that if he is not more mature, more confident, he is fooling a lot of his teammates.

"I'm not saying that the answer is my belief, but if things don't go my way, I can accept it," Bradshaw says. "Before, I'd fight it.

"It's kind of relaxed me. And the key is to go out there relaxed."

Noll has helped Bradshaw in a couple of ways. He has condensed what is called the short list — 20 or so plays which a team plans to rely on a majority of the time for a particular game. He also stuck with Bradshaw after he had a poor game in the loss to Houston here a month ago. But, perhaps most important,

he has broadened the communication between them. And there was a time not very long ago where Bradshaw's confidence was suffering because of a lack of such communication.

"Chuck has really been a great help," Bradshaw says, and then peers into your eyes to make certain you understand he is not being sarcastic. "Staying with me after Houston really helped my confidence. Listen, Chuck Noll had a tough decision about the quarterbacks."

Bradshaw jerks a thumb toward Joe Gilliam's locker. "That guy was playing great."

Now it is Bradshaw who is playing great. He figures that just might continue. For two more games. "I have the ability," he says. "If I keep my head clear, I'll be OK.

"You know, I had a hard time sleeping Sunday night because I was amazed at how it all fell into place."

An old Bible student like Bradshaw shouldn't have been alarmed, as it says in Romans 1:16, " ... it is the power of God for salvation to everyone who has faith ..."

Notes: The Steelers had only minor injuries from the Buffalo game. Gerry Mullins (ankle) and Franco Harris (toe). Mullins had another superb game against the Bills.

... Preston Pearson worked the special teams Sunday and will be ready for Oakland, which remains a five-point favorite in the AFC title game.

... Says Noll of Bradshaw's recent performances and their importance to his team: "I can't say enough about it. It's a big thing."

... The home team won all four of the opening-round playoff games.

STEELERS PLAY SUPER, PICK UP 1ST AFC TITLE

By Phil Musick, *The Pittsburgh Press*

OAKLAND, DEC. 29, 1974 — THE PITTSBURGH STEELERS, those one-time children of despair, went and won the big one.

They knocked off, swept past, burrowed under, roared through, leaped over and generally outclassed the Oakland Raiders, who had been expected in New Orleans on Jan. 12.

In so doing, they won the American Football Conference championship — and ain't that something ... the Steelers?

They also sent 10,000 delirious souls screaming to Greater Pitt, qualified for the Super Bowl against Minnesota, and proved that a trite phrase can be mightier that a broadcast.

Outlined against a blue-gray sky, the Oakland Raiders ran afoul of a cliché. The collision proved fatal.

"Whatever it takes." Words more powerful and meaningful than all of the X's and O's that contributed to the Steelers' 24-13 whipping — and no lesser word would be accurate — of Oakland yesterday.

And what might the "it" stand for.

"Faith," Chuck Noll said. A faith that ultimately proved more important to the outcome than a tackle-trap used on Raider Art Thoms with devastating effect. More important than Jack Ham making two interceptions from a pass coverage the Steelers were scared to death of using. And more important

SCORE BY PERIODS

Pittsburgh	0	3	0	21	24
Oakland	3	0	7	3	13

than jerking the rug from under Oakland's running game so severely that in 21 pops it produced 29 yards. Which ain't many.

"Faith," Noll went on. "Faith in one another. Faith that you can do it. Faith when the offense isn't scoring and when you're getting bad calls and when you're fumbling all over the field, you don't chuck it."

The Steelers didn't. They were grittier than a mouthful of sand. Even though a horrible call cost the Steelers a touchdown when it was ruled John Stallworth had caught a Terry Bradshaw pass in the end zone, out of bounds, although an instant replay seconds later made head linesman Ray DoDez look like Mr. Magoo.

Even though Roy Gerela blew a chipshot field goal in the first quarter.

Even though fumbles by Terry Bradshaw and Rocky Bleier and Lynn Swann, all of whom later became heroic, ruined drives.

In the pragmatic sense, however, "it" was several things. Ham's interceptions, the second of which erased the last of two Oakland leads (3-0, 10-3) and led to the killing touchdown that put the Steelers on top to stay at 17-10. A third interception by J.T. Thomas that came with a minute left and led to a final Steeler score. The Steeler coaching staff spotting a weakness in Oakland's defensive line that could be exploited and was, for critical yardage and both of Franco Harris' touchdowns.

And, more importantly than any of these, victory came from beating the Raiders physically at the line of scrimmage. So much so that Andy Russell's first words of exultation were, "Did we beat their butts? Did we?"

"They just beat our butts," agreed Oakland coach John Madden, who had unwittingly contributed to his club's downfall earlier in the week when he said of the Raiders' opening playoff game with Miami, "When the best plays the best, anything can happen."

Gathering his troops last Tuesday following their win over Buffalo, Noll couldn't contain his anger at Madden's remark.

"He had his teeth bared," Russell laughed. "He told us, 'Well, they're not the best. And neither one of them's

Wide receiver Lynn Swann (88) stretches the Oakland defense as he reaches for a pass from Terry Bradshaw.

going to be in the Super Bowl.' Man, did he fire us up. Joe Greene leaped up and started talking it up. We were ready for them."

Explained Greene a bit indignantly: "We were overlooked. We're a football team of pride. We knew we had it ... even if no one else did."

The Steelers had the Raiders largely because of Ham's interceptions. They came from a coverage the Steelers call "Cover Four," in which Ham must come across the field to cover the second back leaving the backfield on a pass play.

"We've always been leery of it," Russell said, "because he has to come so far. A couple of times we've almost been burned but the receivers have dropped the ball. When he came across today, the quarterback (Ken Stabler) never saw him."

"Stabler read a blitz and he was just trying to dump the ball off to Charlie Smith," Ham said of his key steal.

But those were the technical details of the win, and they were relatively simple. The Steelers controlled the ball on the ground — Harris getting 111 yards, Rocky Bleier a career-high 98 — and when the crunch was at hand, they trapped Thoms.

"We saw something on the films from the way Thoms played," explained veteran center Ray Mansfield. Figuring Thoms could be trapped, offensive line coach Dan Radakovich huddled with his troops for a half-hour Saturday afternoon.

"Rad took us in that room and we went over every conceivable angle of the tackle-trap. We didn't call it in the huddle. Terry called it from the line," Mansfield said.

Perhaps the major factor in the Steeler win and Oakland's fifth straight loss in an AFC (or AFL) title game, however, was simply muscle. The Raiders, who

John Stallworth's apparent touchdown catch was overruled by a referee who claimed Stallworth had stepped out of bounds.

did it at Three Rivers to win 17-0 earlier in the year, tried to overpower the Steelers. And they didn't quit trying until it was too late. Before it was, their efforts made you think of a guy trying to cut down an oak tree with a breadstick.

"They thought they were going to blow us away ... run us right out of there," Russell chortled on the bus going to the Oakland airport while a few of his teammates were hiding trainer Ralph Berlin's medical bag and punctuating the ride with cries of wild exuberance that later gave away to what Ham described as "a feeling like I never had before. Something that's almost too much."

"Sure, that's what they thought," Russell continued, a huge grin making him appear to be a sophisticated 17-year old. "That's why they kept trying to run

... stayed with their game plan so long."

The Raider game plan was as basic as dirt — blow the Steelers off the ball. It failed so miserably that Marv Hubbard, a thousand-yard back, got 6 yards in seven pops, or about 2½ feet a try.

When Stabler abandoned the run, it was too late. A classic case of too little, too late, although he threw 38 yards to Cliff Branch for a short-lived 10-3 lead that was buried under the Steelers' 21-point explosion in the final quarter.

" If you have to go to the air on us, we'll beat you," L.C. Greenwood smiled softly. "We'll bend some, we never break."

The Steeler defense didn't, and immediately following Branch's touchdown, Bradshaw, calling what Noll described as "a masterful game," drove the Steelers 61 yards in nine plays to tie it, 10-10.

Before the crowd of 53,515 at sunny Oakland Coliseum could even be made uneasy by the deadlock, it ceased to exist. Ham made his second steal and three plays later, Swann made a nifty end-zone catch and got both feet down inside the end line. It was all over, save for one final Oakland gasp and Noll's hard-hitting clichés.

Gathering themselves, the Raiders drove back to a third-and-5 from the Steeler 7, but Stabler, who had resurrected Oakland against Miami, couldn't work his trick again. Mike Wagner came roaring through on a safety blitz and Stabler had to throw the third-down pass away.

George Blanda came on to kick a field goal, but you could almost see the life run out of the Raiders. In their final three series — one eclipsed by Thomas' interception and Harris' ensuing touchdown — the Raiders didn't breach their own 40 until the final play of the game.

When it was over, and the Steelers had their first conference championship and the most meaningful win of their 42 years, Noll's clichés glittered like frozen diamonds. Whatever it takes.

"We put it right here," he said, tapping a forefinger over his heart. "I keep saying the same trite things, over and over. But they're just tried truisms.

"We had some bad breaks early that could've disheartened a team. But we weren't going to let that happen. We were of a mind where we couldn't be disappointed."

On the way home, Ham and Greene sat slumped in a jump seat at the tail of the United charter. Forward, Art Rooney was saying warm things and people looked at him and smiled for all they were worth. And Andy Russell talked about "waiting 12 years for this. I've played with a lot of great guys here who played their guts out. I wish they could've been here to share this."

Ham nodded. Someone said something about "Whatever it takes." With a straight face.

"All of his clichés ... they all came true," Ham said.

Notes: Andy Russell said he "was really surprised how easily we stopped their running game. But we knew going in that would be the key. And we thought we could do it. The feeling of personal satisfaction I get from this is beyond belief."

ROCKY ROAD LEADS TO SUCCESS

By Phil Musick, *The Pittsburgh Press*

Rocky Bleier remembers the day in 1971 when he though he was done with pro football. Remembers driving home from Three Rivers after practice ... the tears hot as his face.

Chuck Noll had called Bleier to his office after practice one afternoon just a few days before final pre-season squad cuts. Bleier had a foot full of shrapnel, compliments of the war in Vietnam. He couldn't break 5.0 in the 40, which would've been OK if he had been an offensive tackle. But he was a running back.

"I told him I thought he should retire," Chuck Noll was saying yesterday after Bleier had run for 98 hard yards and, because he had, the Steelers had thrashed Oakland and qualified to spend a week on Bourbon Street. "That's the closest I ever saw Rocky to a panic.

"But he had problems with his speed. The substance of his reply was, 'I don't want to retire. I think I can get back. I want to give it a try. I think I can lick it.'"

Dan Rooney put in a plug for him with Noll and it was agreed that Bleier would spend the 1971 season on the special teams. He did, becoming their ace. The following spring, he worked with weights two or three hours a day, did special stretching exercises geared to increase his speed, spent afternoons running up and down a fire escape at the Chicago building where he was working.

Speed was a problem, but even when he was slow, he had great ability to pick his spots, cut.

Bleier hung tough. "I was crying that day on the way home after Chuck said I ought to retire," Bleier says. "My whole idea that year was just to be part of a team. I just wanted to hang around. I didn't want to be out of football."

Noll had a change of heart and Bleier stayed to work the kicking teams and try to build his speed. "Two years before he'd run a 40-yard dash in 5.0 seconds. In 1973, he got it down to a 4.65. And he's like having a guard in the backfield. He just knocks the hell out of people," Noll said.

"I figured my career was over," Bleier was saying, "but I finally got it together."

Yeah, and because he did, yesterday Oakland fell apart.

STEELERS ON CLOUD IX WITH SUPER WIN

By Phil Musick, *The Pittsburgh Press*

NEW ORLEANS, JAN. 12, 1975 — IT SHOULD BE INSCRIBED on their Super Bowl rings and on the Minnesota Vikings' tombstone. Whatever it takes. Forevermore, when they hear those words, their eyes will automatically dart for the ring.

Whatever it takes, Chuck Noll's thought for the day. Any day. If there are epitaphs for the losers in this game, a suitable one for the Vikings would be "killed by a cliché."

Three little words. Whatever it takes. Never again, in good conscience, will they use it loosely, in a bawdy, locker room way. Now they believe. As one of them said, rather reverently, "I bet he has that embroidered on his shorts." And maybe he has. But more than anything else it thrust Minnesota aside yesterday in the ninth coming of Pete Rozelle's favorite fantasy. Whatever it takes.

It took a lot of things, really, for the Steelers to thwart Minnesota, 16-6, in Super Bowl IX before 80,997 fans who filled Tulane Stadium. And because the Steelers were new to this and were exciting, the place sounded like Three Rivers.

It took Dwight White. He lost 18 pounds last week in the hospital "living on water and sleep." But he played, as defensive line coach George Perles put it, "Like a guy going into a burning house after his family."

SCORE BY PERIODS

Pittsburgh	0	2	7	7	16
Minnesota	0	0	0	6	6

It took Joe Greene to play so dominantly that his boss, defensive coordinator Bud Carson, could only shake his head later and say. "I'll tell you Joe Greene is ... the best I ever saw. I just didn't think he could be any better. Only he was."

It took some soul-searching. By a guy like Andy Russell, who tore a hamstring muscle in the third quarter and let his head overrule a heart that told him to do what he had been taught to do ... suck it up. Go back in.

"I kept begging the coaches to put me back in," he said, "but they'd ask how I

Pittsburgh's Jack Ham (59), Mike Wagner (23) and T.J. Thomas (24) triple-team Vikings halfback Chuck Foreman.

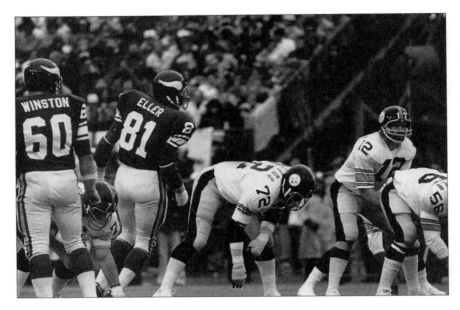

felt. I'd say, 'I shouldn't be in there.' I didn't want to play the hero and then get isolated on (Chuck) Foreman or (John) Gilliam and get beaten for a touchdown. It ate my heart out."

It took flawless performances from two young backup linebackers, Russell's replacement, Loren Toews, and Ed Bradley, who replaced middle linebacker Jack Lambert, after we went out late in the first half with a sprained ankle.

"When they saw me coming on the field," Bradley said, "they were saying

Terry Bradshaw's cadence causes Carl Eller (81) and the Vikings' defense to jump offsides.

GREENE 'WASN'T PREPARED TO LOSE'

By Phil Musick, *The Pittsburgh Press*

This was before the hoopla of television. Before any of it had really sunk in. Before they gathered their thoughts and tried to be glib or sentimental or slick.

Joe Greene was sitting in the training room, on a packing case. Dwight White on some kind of foot locker. There were maybe three reporters from Pittsburgh there, smashed with them into a corner.

Greene wore a glazed look. White the pallor you might expect of a guy who'd spent Sunday night through Friday in the hospital with pleurisy that had turned into pneumonia.

You could've made an argument that they, more than any other two Steelers, had been responsible for Minnesota dying kind of ingloriously in Super Bowl IX.

"Who's No. 1?" Greene grinned at a guy. "Who's No. 1? Who's No. 1?"

There was only one answer — a grin. The evidence was all in. The Steelers had won, decisively, 16-6, on the strength of a defense that never quite dies when the crunch is at hand.

"Championship games are won like that," Greene was saying, glancing at the exhausted White from time to time like some sort of an anxious mother hen.

"You do what it takes. We played good football; we got some breaks."

Greene — and none of his teammates — had thought the result was going to be anything but what it was. "I wasn't prepared to lose," Greene said. "A great part of me would've died if we had lost."

By appearance, some part of White had died in the victory. He spent all but three small portions of last week in a hospital; ate nothing solid from Sunday night until Wednesday noon. He left the Steeler victory celebration before midnight, ate a cheeseburger at a diner across from the hotel and went to bed. In tote, he looked as though he had lived the week in a coffin.

"Dwight's a real toughie," Greene smiled. "He convinced everyone he could play."

And so White had. He got out of the hospital Thursday, returned 12 hours or so later, got out again Saturday. Back at the hotel, a guy asked him how he was feeling. "I'm alive," he said.

But Saturday night, he spent three hours calling the room of defensive line coach George Perles. "He wanted to know if what had been in the paper was true ... he couldn't play," Perles said. "I told him, 'If you can

'Who's this turkey?' They came right after me, then."

They didn't get Bradley. "He was masterful ... made big hits and big plays," said Noll.

It took Terry Bradshaw keeping the cool a lot of his teammates thought he didn't possess. Like the one who a year-ago said, "If we ever got to a Super Bowl, Terry will be so shook up we won't get a first down."

Only Bradshaw was also masterful. He guided a Steeler offense that missed by a mere 25 yards of breaking Green Bay's total offense record for this proceeding. An offense so in control that when Minnesota's Bill Brown mishandled the opening kickoff of the second

half Marv Kellum scooped it up to trigger the Steelers' first touchdown drive, only the Viking diehards didn't know it was just a matter of time.

It took Glen Edwards hitting John Gilliam with such force that a Fran Tarkenton pass he had in his hands was deflected to Mel Blount in the end zone. Instead of a Viking first down at the Steeler 5, Minnesota got zilch.

"That could've been the thing that made the difference," Jack Ham said. "Glen and Gilliam had a little feud going earlier. That one play might have done it."

And it took so many other things. If things is the word. Franco Harris driving for Super Bowl records for rushing

yardage (158) and attempts (34) with a kind of indomitability Winston Churchill would've admired.

He got the most valuable player award, an automobile from Sport Magazine, but he got something else he'll probably remember when the car is rusty junk.

"You are the best bleeping back in the whole wide world," Lynn Swann told Harris quietly as they slipped through a parking lot to skirt wild Steeler fans at the team hotel. Whatever it takes.

What do you call the "it?" Faith, as Noll has? Dedication ... determination ... pride? All of those hoary, old clichés that sophisticated football fans chuckle over.

go when we tee it up, you can play.'"

Whether or not White could go wasn't determined until the pregame warmups, when Perles had him go against Greene in "a couple of live hits."

White hit. Pneumonia and all, he got it together and hit Greene two good shots. "The second time, I really gave him a shot," Greene grinned. "He's tough. I said it all week, 'If Dee-wit could walk. He'd play.'"

White played, batting down a pass, shutting down the Viking ground game on his side and deflecting a second pass that Greene intercepted to ruin a Viking drive, ate in the third quarter.

"I felt like I had to play," White explained as the television troops milled about, anxious for him to explain it all to the 70 or so million viewers. "It's hard to describe how you feel when you work so long and so hard for something ..."

White had during the regular sea-

son worked hard and long without what he felt were sufficient results. "I'm not crying over spilled milk," he reflected. "But I felt 1974 was going to be my disaster year."

Yesterday, against Viking tackle Charlie Goodrum, of who he made a light snack, White certainly redeemed himself for any past transgressions.

"Dwight was great," Greene said. "It got to be head to head and everything went crunch ... crunch ... crunch. They didn't give us much; but we gave them less."

When the interviews were over and the dressing room had cleared and they were the only two guys not dressed, White asked for a stocking cap Greene had been clutching.

"Anything, Dee-wit, anything at all," Greene said. And then the impact of what had happened finally reached him. "I may become a very obnoxious person because I'm so proud," he grinned. So wide you would've thought his mouth was in

mortal danger of disappearing.

"I'm going to show it. To everybody. Let them know it ... that I'm on a ... a championship team."

For a week or so, Greene didn't think he would be a member of such a team. Not this year, at least. "After the second Houston game (a loss in Pittsburgh), we scraped bottom. That's why this feels so good. We had problems.

"Chuck told us that championship teams don't run smooth, that it's rocky. After the Houston game, some truths came out. I wouldn't ... don't want to ... discuss them.

"But we own it now. We own it. It's going to make us want to come back here."

And then somebody said that the Steeler defense had allowed a total of 99 yards rushing in the three playoff games. "In three games — 99?" Greene asked incredulously.

"That's unreal. Unreal. Unn-real."

And it wasn't anything less.

Whatever it was. Alan Page, the Viking defensive tackle and foremost tower of strength, could feel it. Gave way to it, finally. With three minutes to play, Bradshaw rifled a 4-yard touchdown pass to tight end Larry Brown that relieved the intrigue and accounted for the final score. The pass was thrown with such force that offensive backfield coach Dick Hoak said, "It was buried in Brown's stomach."

Page knew it was over; that the Vikings had lost in this game for the third time in six years to a team that didn't know it should be beaten on its maiden trip here.

He threw his elbow pads in the air and turned to Steeler guard Jim Clack, who'd played him to a standstill, and said, "Hell, Clack, I'm all through."

Maybe, as Noll says, it is faith. The kind Art Rooney had. Has. He presented the trophy to the winner of the Super Bowl Handicap Saturday at the Fairgrounds race track. The horse's colors were purple and white, which the Vikes wore yesterday.

"My wife said it was a bad omen in Irish folklore," Rooney said. But, earlier, he had said, "I knew we were going to win it."

The reasons that the Vince Lombardi Trophy will go back to the Steeler offices to serve as reminder that 42 years have been tucked neatly into the dusty pages of history go on and on.

There was a Steeler front four that was magnificent, that's all. Ask Tarkenton, whose fine Viking offense could get a total of only 123 yards, or 2.6 a play. Which ain't enough. Ask him about Minnesota getting 21 yards rushing. On 20 pops. Really, you spell that Deeefense.

But the Steelers don't, didn't win on statistics, but rather intangibles. Like yesterday. When, with the Steelers up 9-6, and driving deep into Minnesota territory, backup quarterback Joe Gilliam made a critical suggestion. Throw to Brown, he told Chuck Noll. Bradshaw rifled the pass into the vicinity of Brown's pancreas and Super Bowl IX became a

Franco Harris (32), right, outraces Minnesota's Jackie Wallace to the goal line for a Steeler touchdown.

Bradshaw (12) sweeps for 11 yards around right end in the first quarter.

STEELERS: DEPRESSION TO PROSPERITY

The Pittsburgh Press

The Pittsburgh Steelers' 42-year trek to the Super Bowl was a voyage during which loses outnumbered victories, disappointment overshadowed hope and failure smothered success.

It was a voyage marked by tragedy and despair, by anticipation and unfulfillment, by dreams that never materialized, even though the architects of those dreams included two of the finest coaches in the land.

Until Chuck Noll arrived, the elusive bauble that symbolizes the championship of pro football had been beyond the Steelers' reach.

It was so frustrating at times that even loyal, patient, intelligent fans were known to throw down their tickets and despair.

For the Pirates, the name by which the Steelers originally were known, it all started in 1933, the year the country was starting its climb out of the Great Depression by repealing Prohibition and modifying Blue laws that outlawed sports on Sunday.

The NFL that year was in the process of reorganization. It had divided itself into two divisions and when it needed a 10th team, Art Rooney, well-known as a sponsor of sandlot teams, was talked into buying a franchise for $2,500.

The Steelers were not an instant hit. Rooney's incursion into big time football came at a time when Pittsburgh was college oriented. Carnegie Mellon (then known as Carnegie Tech) was a national power. Duquesne, which within the decade

was to become one, was on the rise. But the city belonged to Pitt and the remarkable coach of the Panthers, John Bain (Jock) Sutherland.

Generating mild excitement among a limited audience, the Steelers played those early campaigns in relative obscurity, part of which was self induced by poor management and listless football. Rooney, though he had invested in the franchise, had other interests that prevented him from making his football team a full-time operation.

The team itself was in the hands of Joe Carr, its only employee, whose duties ranged from clerical work to selling tickets.

While the college teams, Pitt, Tech and Duquesne, were standing the town on its ear, the Steelers labored in vain, even in 1936 when they could have won their first championship. After 11 games that season, that Steelers still had a crack at a division championship, but that dream went up in smoke through an act of scheduling.

With an open date before their season's finale with the Boston Redskins, Rooney had scheduled a meaningless exhibition game on the West Coast, mainly to accommodate a friend. By the time they concluded the trip, a transcontinental voyage by train, the Steelers were in no condition to play football.

The Redskins walloped them by a score of 30-0 before a crowd so slim that George Preston Marshall, the

owner of the Boston franchise, decided in disgust to move the championship game to New York City, and his franchise to Washington.

Before the Steelers started another season, Rooney had fired the man who had brought them a semblance of respectability, Joe Bach, and hired an old vagabond, Johnny Blood, and his sidekick, Walter Kiesling, to replace him. That pair was to have a telling impact on the Steelers for another decade.

Blood, who regarded the players as a supporting cast for his own center stage performance, immediately wrecked what was left of the team. When its final destruction was accomplished, not even the easy going Kiesling could re-assemble the carnage.

And Rooney was so fed up with what had been going on that, in 1941, he sold the team to a cosmopolitan playboy, Alexis Thompson, the heir to a cosmetics fortune, who was looking for a hobby. After seven seasons, pro football, to all intents and purposes, was dead in Pittsburgh.

Almost as quickly as he sold out, however, Rooney realized that he missed the old scene.

Fortuitously, another of those friends, Bert Bell, was suffering a parallel failure in Philadelphia. Strapped for cash, he caught Rooney in a commiserating mood and suggested that, together they might be able to make a go of a football team. Rooney agreed, if they could run the team in Pittsburgh.

Bell sought out Thompson, a man whose social traits traversed the Atlantic seaboard cities from New York to Washington and suggested that they exchange franchises. Thompson was delighted.

Before bringing football back to Pittsburgh, Rooney and Bell decided to return with a new image — a new name, a new green and white uniform, a new training site, a new coach, Bell himself, and an imaginative new system, the T-formation.

At this time, the Chicago Bears had called the attention of the country to the T. The previous December they had walloped the Washington Redskins, 73-0, resurrecting one of football's earliest formations and loosening it up by putting a man in motion — a halfback running toward the sidelines. In Bell's T, the flanker ran toward the backfield.

It was in Hershey that year that Art Rooney, sitting on the sidelines with a Pittsburgh Press sports writer, Claire Burcky, made a statement that was to haunt the ball club for the next 30 years.

"We have a new name, a new coach, a new system and new uniforms," said Rooney, "but they look like the same old Steelers to me."

World War II demolished the Steelers. The victims of a manpower shortage, the Steelers were forced to merge with the Philadelphia Eagles in 1943 and the Chicago Cardinals in 1944. They tried it alone in 1945, but the talent was so thin that by the last game of the season, with the ground at Forbes Field frozen solid, a Steeler running back, Johnny Grigas, decided to quit the team rather than play, even though he had a chance to become the league's leading rusher that year.

The post-war era had some promise, though. Bill Dudley, who had been a sensation in his rookie

year in 1942, was coming back, but even bigger news broke in January of that year.

Jock Sutherland, who had become a legend at Pitt, signed to coach the Steelers.

Sutherland was an organizer as well as a coach. An efficient office was set up. In the best two years of drafting the Steelers ever had, Sutherland quickly built a team into a sell-out attraction. In 1947, they tied for the Eastern Division title but, with their top tailbacks, Johnny Clement and Walt Slater, out with injuries, the Steelers lost the playoff, 21-0, to the Eagles.

Within three months, Sutherland was dead, the victim of a brain tumor.

Sutherland had thrown out the T-formation and for six years the single wing Steelers were one of two teams in football playing with a tailback as the dominant figure in its offense. The other was the New York Giants.

For Pittsburgh, the modern era of football started in 1952 with the hiring of Joe Bach, the coach who re-installed the T. Walt Kiesling served another hitch, until he was replaced by Pittsburgh's second qualified coach, Buddy Parker, who ushered in the Bobby Layne era, in 1957.

Parker lasted through the 1964 season and while he made the team respectable, he never did quite grasp the brass ring. He came close, however, finishing, second in 1962 and losing out to the New York Giants in the final game of the 1963 season.

Parker, after the ill-advised retirement of Layne, finally quit in 1965, starting another stretch for a coach which lasted until 1969 when Chuck Noll arrived.

warm memory in Pete Rozelle's heart and a chunk of Pittsburgh folklore for all of time.

"Our quarterbacks hang in there together," Noll smiled.

And maybe it took something else — the sort of affection a town can lavish on a football team. Maybe it's no big thing. Maybe.

Only with two minutes left and panic deep in Viking hearts, Clack turned to Ray Mansfield and grinned hugely, "I bet The Burg looks like Hiroshima."

A few million words were written about Super Bowl IX. A lot of them said it was a bizarre game. There were seven fumbles and three interceptions, and it wound up turning on Kellum's recovery of a fouled-up kick return. And a few times one official wound up pointing in one direction and a cohort in another. So you could say honestly that it wasn't

Time runs out on Minnesota coach Bud Grant and his Vikings.

Cinderella Steelers of '74

By Pat Livingston, *The Pittsburgh Press*

It took 42 years, and Art Rooney's boundless faith, and a miracle that came to be called the Immaculate Reception, and Chuck Noll's diligence, and a busload of what they call young studs, but it happened. The Steelers got their act together, and in 1974 they were a Cinderella team in the truest sense of that overworked adjective.

Cinderella came out of hard times, got it turned around, almost blew it, but would up in a happy ending. And so it was with the 1974 Pittsburgh Steelers, children of four decades of despair who came to the Super Bowl.

The season started badly in one sense (the player strike), and amazingly well in another — the Steelers swept the six-game exhibition schedule and blew Baltimore out, 3-zip, in the regular season opener.

All of which made Chuck Noll seemingly something of a prophet. A dozen times during training camp, with the veterans walking the fringe of the St. Vincent campus carrying picket signs on their shoulders and a decreasing resignation in their hearts — Noll made the same statement.

"We're not so interested in winning the division," he said repeatedly. "We want to go a littler farther ... see what it's like at the end of the rainbow."

But, like Cinderella, the Steelers lost their slipper. Their midnight began looming in the second game of the season. Joe Gilliam, the young quarterback whose passing had been awesome during the exhibitions, cranked it up a half-hundred times against the Broncos and produced 35 points. Alas, Denver picked the Steeler defense apart as it had not been probed in two-plus years and the result was a 35-all dead heat.

Roy Gerela duckhooked a field-goal try into a Bronco lineman's face mask with three seconds left and the National Football League wound up celebrating its very first regular season overtime game. Naturally, nothing was settled by the fifth quarter.

Despite his passing brilliance — he completed 24 passes — Gilliam was ultimately doomed in Denver. Running the Steelers to a 4-1-1 record — the loss against visiting Oakland to later be ever-so sweetly revenged — Gilliam's reliance on the pass cost him his job. And fired the season's biggest controversy.

"We've got to have more balance in the offense," explained Noll, whose team had reached the playoffs the two previous seasons almost wholly on the strength of its defense.

Balance was achieved by installing Terry Bradshaw at quarterback in place of Gilliam. From phffft the Steelers went to pow. Eschewing the pass, Bradshaw sent Franco Harris and his other backs crunching over Atlanta and Philadelphia. The Steelers led the AFC Central with a 6-1-1 record. They turned into a pumpkin the next week in Cincinnati, losing 17-10 in a game highlighted by safety Glen Edwards' one-tackle TKO of Bengal quarterback Ken Anderson, which became a national cause celebre because of some naive telecasting.

The following week, Noll stripped the all but forgotten Terry Hanratty of his brown and raggedy clothes and installed him at quarterback, benching Bradshaw, who for a day or so later talked some of a desire to be someplace else.

Hanratty lasted one game, a staggering 26-16 win in Cleveland in which he went 2-for-15 and was intercepted three times. That, as it turned out, was the Steeler midnight.

"We seemed to get it straightened out there," Bradshaw thought in retrospect. And so the Steelers did. They battered New Orleans, staggered briefly in a home loss to the onrushing Houston Oilers, and the following week clinched the AFC Central title with a 21-17 win in New England. In the finale, they crushed injury-depleted Cincinnati, 27-3, to totally exonerate Noll's actions throughout the season.

In reality, and despite the fact he denies it, Noll had been a gambler. Before the season began, he had cut loose, mostly through trades for medium-round draft picks, almost a dozen veterans. When the year ended, 14 of the 47 Steelers were rookies. This from a team that had made the playoffs two years running.

"It wasn't a gamble," Noll insists. "We knew what sort of talent we had and what we had to let go."

History will record Noll correct. The Steeler talent played itself individually and collectively. The Steelers — their defensive image never stronger — still managed impressive offensive statistics. They were one of only four AFC teams to score more than 300 points (309). Behind Harris' second 1,000-yard (1,006) season, they were the AFC's top rushing team.

But it was defense that carried the day and sent them rushing into Super Bowl IX. They led the NFL in six defensive categories: total yards, passing percentage, sacks, takeaways and fumble recoveries.

The front four were generally acknowledged the NFL's most feared. Glen Edwards, Jack Ham and J.T. Thomas, who in his first year as a regular performed so admirably, each had five interceptions, which tied Ham for the league lead in thefts by a linebacker.

That defense shoved Cinderella back into the Prince's arms in the playoffs. The Steelers easily handled Buffalo in the first round, 32-14. The feared O.J. Simpson carried the ball 15 times, and made two yards or less on eight attempts. He was not a factor in the game. Said Simpson afterward, "Their defense is the best."

The offense wasn't bad, either, racking up considerable yardage against Oakland in the AFC title game, as it had against the Bills. But the Steelers won, 23-14, mostly because they shut down the Oakland running game.

The Raiders got 29 yards on 21 pops. As their coach John Madden, put it. "You have to be able to both pass and run against them, or you lose."

Because Oakland could only throw, the Steelers sallied forth once more to the Grand Ball, which the NFL knows as the Super Bowl.

something that would've thrilled Amos Alonzo Stagg.

But they'll take it to The Burg, baby. In spades. Because it was triumph come by honestly. By, as Noll said, "outhitting them." By wanting it just a little bit more. By being unwilling to accept anything less than Art Rooney getting paid off for 42 years of playing the fall guy.

And after those millions of words were written, nobody said it better than The Man. He stood there in a dressing room that was something less than revelry and something more than restrained, where the joy was all in looks that passed back and forth among the players, silently. And he grinned like a school kid kissing his first love for the first time.

The words — synonymous for love of a team that the coaching manual forbids — just poured out. "I keep saying the same things, over and over," he said.

"This game is what this team is all about," Noll said. "The doctor told us

there was no way that Dwight White could play this game. I said, 'We'll let him on the field for warmups and then when he keels over, we'll drag him off.'"

And he smiled, wider, because the words were cold and what he felt wasn't. "You could see it in their eyes on the field," he said just before he got on the team bus. "They wouldn't let themselves be denied."

On that same bus, going to Tulane Stadium before the game, he sat next to a guy and twisted his hands until they began to look as wrinkled as a newborn baby's bottom.

"I unclenched them with 30 seconds left to play," he smiled.

"They demonstrated ... an attitude. All year. Any time things went bad, they didn't panic. They made things happen. That was my biggest satisfaction. They gave that little extra. It made the difference."

That and a cliché, of course.

Pittsburgh coach Chuck Noll is presented the game ball following the Steelers' 16-6 Super Bowl victory over the Vikings.

STEELERS DUST OFF COLTS WITH DEFENSE, 28-10

By Phil Musick, *The Pittsburgh Press*

PITTSBURGH, DEC. 27, 1975 — THE SLIPPER DIDN'T FIT. THE coach turned into a pumpkin at about a quarter to 4. The ugly sisters took off with the prince. The gown became a dust cloth. And Cinderella? That's her over there by the chimney, wondering what the hell happened.

Chuck Noll knew what had happened to the young and airy and tough Baltimore Colts. Simply said, they got their lunch eaten by a Steeler defense playing the way it did back then in 1972 when the Steeler offense was mostly a figment of Noll's imagination.

All thumbs and turnovers, waiting for Terry Bradshaw to grow up. Which, by the way, he did yesterday. In spades.

So it was that the Steelers hung very tough and outlasted the Cinderella Colts, 28-10, before 49,053 convinced fans of Three Rivers in the opening round of Peter Rozelle's annual joust.

If a quorum can be put together — the Steelers suffered a handful of injuries in hitting, which Noll termed "as fierce as I've seen in a long time" — the Steelers will meet the Oakland-Cincinnati survivor here next Sunday for the right to face the NFC champion in the Super Bowl Jan. 18 in Miami.

But the Colts — resilient 12-point

SCORE BY PERIODS

Baltimore	0	7	3	0	10
Pittsburgh	7	0	7	14	28

----

underdogs who wouldn't fold despite losing quarterback Bert Jones early on and having Lydell Mitchell finish an embarrassed second to Franco Harris in their individual duel — took an awful lot of convincing.

Leading by three points with seven minutes gone in the third quarter and trailing by only four with eight minutes left in the game, they were convinced.

By Jack Ham and Mel Blount and Dwight White and then Ham again, and finally by Andy Russell, who scooped up a Jones fumble caused by Ham and rumbled no less than 93 yards on a bum knee to nail it down at 28-10 and end a nine-game winning streak put together by the AFC East champions.

And, lest you misunderstand just

how many positive adjectives are owed to the Steeler defense, understand this: Terry Bradshaw hobbled about on a right knee all but torn from its moorings late in the first half; Baltimore began five series inside the Steeler 47, two at the winners' 19; the Steeler offense turned the ball over four times and played perhaps its poorest game of the year, limited almost entirely to Franco Harris' playoff record 153 yards rushing.

"We had a hell of a lot of pressure on our defense," Noll said in the dressing room displaying the sort of quiet celebration the Steelers reserve for all games except the Super Bowl. "They were on the field almost all day.

"We could've kept the offense home."

If Noll had, the Steelers still would've let the air out of the exuberant Colts. The defense accounted for three touchdowns.

A Ham interception set up Harris' 8-yard touchdown burst that gave the Steelers a 7-0 lead late in the first quarter. Colt cornerback Lloyd Mumphord intercepted a Bradshaw pass and returned it 58 yards to help the Colts tie it on Marty Domres' five-yard pass to Glenn Doughty.

And Baltimore took a 10-7 edge seven minutes into the third quarter on Toni Linhart's 21-yard field goal following Colt cornerback Nelson Munsey's recovery of Harris' second

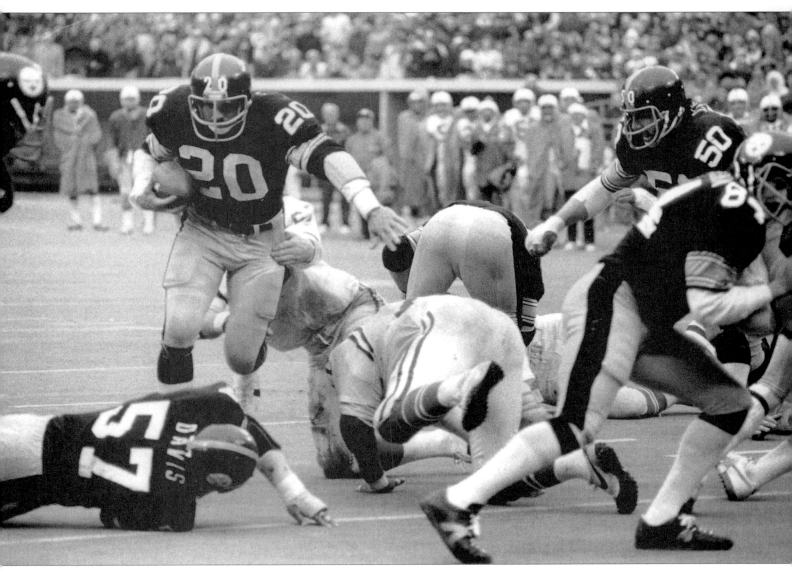

Rocky Bleier (20) hurdles through the middle of the Baltimore line for the Steelers' second touchdown.

fumble of the game.

But, as Ham later explained it, "We hang in. We've been there before. We don't fold. If you're going to beat us, you better make damn good plays."

The Colts, who managed just 154 total yards on 68 plays for a 2.3 average, didn't. Trailing 10-7, the Steelers did.

Although it was later lost in the welter of gaudier plays, the big one was probably made by L.C. Greenwood. He knifed through to belt Mitchell with a tackle you could feel in the soles of your feet and the fever set in.

"The defense got excited then," Ham said. "Everybody was up."

Certainly Mel Blount was. Two plays later, he leaped into the air and picked off a Domres pass intended for receiver Roger Carr on an interception Ham termed "the greatest I ever saw."

"A great play ... a great play," Noll said of the theft that led to a 7-yard touchdown dash by Rocky Bleier, which gave Steelers a 14-10 edge late in the third quarter.

"That was the one that turned it around."

Bradshaw Bit the Bullet, Hobbled

By Phil Musick, *The Pittsburgh Press*

His right leg was numb. They dragged him, literally, 75 yards to the dressing room. His leg was hanging there like a tired snake. Some of the 49,053 fans at Three Rivers sat transfixed and stared for a while before turning away.

The score was tied, 7-7, at the half. But the young Colts were coming on and you wouldn't have bet your mother-in-law's mouth that Bradshaw could play the second half. Or next month.

"I couldn't feel it at all," Bradshaw said after returning, his right knee taped like some forgotten pharaoh, to lead the Steelers past Baltimore, 28-10, in the opening round of the playoffs.

"There must've been some nerve damage. When I was leaving the field at the half, I thought I'd really torn it up. I was just hoping I could walk."

And that's about what Bradshaw can do right now. And maybe all he'll be able to do in next week's AFC championship game. The Steelers didn't know.

No one was more candid about his immediate future than Bradshaw, who in the second half threw four passes and ran once, or as he put it, "hobbled."

"It's no secret," he said. "I won't be able to run." It also won't be much of a secret that Bradshaw can't get all of his weight on the foot he plants to throw on. The right one.

"I started to feel my feet during the halftime," said Bradshaw, who was 8-for-13 on a slow day for the Steeler offense. "But they strapped it up and I could walk. I didn't get a shot. They just strapped it up."

Among those who couldn't believe Bradshaw would return were Chuck Noll and the Steelers.

"They taped him up ... tight," Noll said. "I thought he'd go one series and that would be it. But the doctor came over and said, 'He can go.'"

Bradshaw went, and hopes to next week. "I'm going home and lay down and ice it up," he said. "I'll be OK."

Fats Holmes, who had an outstanding game, clogging the middle, thought Bradshaw was more than that.

Terry Bradshaw suffered a sprained knee during the second quarter.

"Terry's a hell of a player," Holmes said. "I knew he'd come back and play the game."

If Bradshaw hadn't, Terry Hanratty would have played the second half. He is now the No. 2 quarterback.

Notes: Lydell Mitchell, who rushed for 1,193 yards and caught 60 passes for 544 more, had a 2.4 average rushing yesterday. He got 63 yards in 26 pops and caught four passes for just 20 yards. "The field was 150 yards long," he said.

... "In the playoffs," one Steeler veteran noted, "you try anything you can get away with."

Which brings us to Gordon Gravelle, a Steeler offensive tackle, and Baltimore's Fred Cook, a 247-yard defensive end.

Cook was intent on taking out Gravelle with one punch late in the first half as a protest to being shoved by Gravelle from behind after the whistle.

"I told him about it one time and boom! I got hit again," Cook protested.

"A cheap shot on my part," admitted Gravelle, who claimed to have committed the foul deed only once. He simply decided to fight fire with fire.

"On some plays, I'm supposed to hit him then slide off and get the guard," Gravelle explained. "He was holding my jersey, so that I couldn't reach the guard. I got ticked off, so I pushed him.

"I kept telling the referee about it and he told me, 'Shut up and play the game.'"

... Ted Marchibroda, the first-year coach who took General Manager Joe Thomas' rebuilt Colts and put together a 10-4 season, was buoyed by their surprising record.

"I told my guys they got beat by a better football team," he said. "With the Super Bowl, there's only one winner, but this year, there's two winners.

"We accomplished what everybody thought couldn't be done (reaching the playoffs). We're going home winners."

... The Steelers kept intact their streak of not having a touchdown scored against them in the first quarter this year ... Both Jack Ham and Andy Russell, bothered by injuries earlier in the week, said they came out of the game in good shape ... Lloyd Mumphord, who had two interceptions and made the tackle on which Bradshaw was hurt, was cut by Miami the final week of the pre-season.

... Marty Domres, who replaced injured Colt quarterback Bert Jones in the middle two quarters, was 2-for-11 for only 9 yards and had two intercepted.

Lynn Swann caught just two passes, but had an outstanding day blocking.

... Noll was still livid after the game about some Colt tactics. Baltimore defensive lineman, said Noll, were guilty of holding Steeler offensive lineman to set up the Colts' three sacks. The Colts were pulling Steeler linemen inside to let the defensive tackles get free outside.

"I told them (the Steelers) to scream like hell," Noll said. "But the officials said, "Shut up and watch your hands.""

No less enthused was Ham, who yesterday was to the art of linebacking what Hugh Hefner is to girlie magazines.

"It was the best interception I ever saw," Ham said. "A good receiver comes back for the ball and Carr did but Mel beat him back and jumped and reached around ... it was the best."

"I just read the ball all the way and beat him back to it," said Blount, aided by a nifty play by Russell, who forced Carr unusually wide as he came off the line of scrimmage.

"Mel was hanging inside," Russell explained. "My job was to widen him (Carr). I just kept him from getting a quick release inside and Mel made a super play."

Obviously, but not any more super than one by Ham after what seemed like a lack of playoff experience began to tell on the Colts.

Mumphord — who'd made the earlier interception and then low-bridged Bradshaw on a scramble that caused the Steeler quarterback to play the second half with a tightly-strapped knee that could keep him out of the championship game — made a major gaffe.

He interfered with Dave Brown, who was trying to field a punt, and the 15-yard penalty gave the Steelers the ball at the Colt 29. They scored on Bradshaw's 2-yard sneak in five plays and then Ham made the prettiest play of the game to assure the win.

It was one of those plays that deserve a setting like, oh, a 10-carat emerald. Jones, who had missed the middle two quarters of the game after being hit by Dwight White on a scramble and hurting his passing arm, had engineered a drive that advanced to the Steeler 3.

It went like this ...

On third down, Jones sets up to pass. Ham and Russell, on the line in a goal-line defensive set, blitz. Ham is blocked, only he hooks Jones' arm as he goes by and Russell fields the fumble waist-high on the hop.

Ham doubles back and screens Jones as Russell ... ah ... lumbers away. A convoy forms, Donnie Shell throwing the final block, ironically enough on Jones, as Russell goes 93 yards to the promised land.

And, later, it's mostly for laughs. Russell's buddy, Ray Mansfield, talks about "Andy trying to run the clock out." Ham giggles something about "delay of game."

But then it turns serious. Ham glances over towards Russell, the spiritual leader of a defense that, even without Joe Greene, made the difference.

"The best," Ham says as people check to see if his tongue's hung up on a molar. "Like that gentleman across the room there. Day after day, he's the best.

"I don't know how old he is, but ... Andy would go out there on crutches and a cane if he had to."

Crutches and a cane. Next week, they may be embossed on the Steeler coat-of-arms.

Greene is out and probably will be for the duration. Bradshaw may have suffered nerve and ligament damage to his right knee. Harris ducked the post game interviews, probably because he had trouble walking on an ankle he reinjured. And there are several more injuries.

Noll took note of them.

"You're depressing me," he said as someone ticked them off.

"But our guys have a way of doing it, hurt or not."

And so they do.

STEELERS' DEFENSE CRUSHES RAIDERS, 16-10

By Phil Musick, *The Pittsburgh Press*

PITTSBURGH, JAN. 4, 1976 — OUTLINED AGAINST A GHASTLY gray January sky, the Four Horsemen rode again. You remember them. Lambert, Wagner, Russell and Holmes.

Al Davis will remember them. They will be in the nightmares of the Oakland Raiders' owner forevermore. The resilient inner core of the Steeler defense played so well that you knew up there on some heavenly vista, Vince and Knute and Granny and the boys were smiling, nodding and nudging one another in the short ribs.

Defense? No deee-fense. Like the Stalingrad winter. The stuff that cut Oakland's rushing average in half and made Ken Stabler a 42 percent passer.

What you play when a team such as Oakland tires of being destiny's doormat and recovers an onside kick with enough time left to win it, and guys like Andy Russell remembering "you can't start thinking it's not your day."

Defense. The primary reason the Steelers put it on Oakland, 16-10, yesterday to win the AFC championship in the wildest, gut-wrenchingest, slam-bangingest football game that you, or I, or the 49,103 screaming cases of frostbite at Three Rivers Stadium ever saw.

A suck-it-up, shut 'em-down Valley Forge of a defense that zapped the Raiders nine of the 11 times they

SCORE BY PERIODS

Oakland	0	0	0	10	10
Pittsburgh	0	3	0	13	16

crossed midfield to win a long-running, playoff war in which the combatants have met four successive times, the Steelers taking three.

A defense that set up 10 of the 16 points that pushed the Steelers in search of immortality; a chance to become only the third team ever to win consecutive Super Bowls if they can slip Dallas' foot out of the slipper Jan. 18 in Miami.

And, most pertinently, a defense that broke the heart of Al Davis and anyone else who thought Pride and Poise was a letterhead slogan and not what you had to have when it was late, and the wind was in your face, and the other guys were howling back from the dead.

And lest you think all of this is over-

Mel Blount (47) recovers a fumble by teammate Mike Collier (44) on the Raiders' opening kickoff.

done, consider: The Steelers have now survived no less than 12 turnovers in these playoffs. Which lets Mike Wagner say without a trace of cockiness, "It was a playoff game and we're a playoff team, and we just got together and did a number on them."

And a number is precisely what the Raiders had done on them. They got to the Steeler 42, 30, 21 and 34 on their first four series. They got zip. Later, they got to the Steeler 36, 16, 30, 46 and 15 on separate occasions. They got some more zip.

"There was a lot of cash flying around out there," Jack Ham explained. "We were ready. We thought we could shut them down."

The Steelers did, and even the dumbest guy in the place knew exactly why Chuck Noll, obviously among the brightest, had at least 11 reasons.

Squinting into a klieg light, and trying to forget the stricken look on Raider coach John Madden's face and the tears he was fighting to contain when he'd come into the Steeler locker room minutes before, Noll let loose those reasons in a stream.

"Dwight White was magnificent ... Andy Russell made great plays ... Jack Lambert was outstanding ... Mike Wagner was fantastic ... Ernie Holmes was ... "

Adjectives momentarily escaped Noll, backdropped by a sea of his smiling troops, who celebrated as they always do, by whacking each other on the backsides and trading outrageous insults and talking about the next one.

But, indeed, all of Noll's soldiers had been worthy of the adjectives he normally hoards for the Super Bowl.

Lambert recovered a playoff-record three fumbles. Two choked off Oakland drives at the Steeler 27- and 30-yard lines, the third triggered the Steelers' first touchdown drive and some

Jack Lambert (58) takes the high road in stopping the Raiders' Marv Hubbard (44) for a short gain in the first quarter.

candid observations.

"I don't realize what happens with fumbles," said Lambert, who leaned against his locker, blood on his hands and pants, and let waves of reporters wash up at him.

"I'm not especially good at it. The key is simply pursuit. We get as many black jerseys around the ball as we can and someone is bound to come up with it."

Wagner twice filched Stabler passes, the first of which set up a Roy Gerela field goal that gave the Steelers a 3-0 edge with 8:22 left in the first half and set the tone for a game so savagely-contested that Lynn Swann wound up hospitalized with a concussion. No less than seven different players had to be removed from the field for repairs, including Terry Bradshaw, who spent the final minutes in the

dressing room holding a battered head.

But even an incredible 13 turnovers would not rattle Noll's conviction that "it wasn't sloppy ... when you have hitting like that, you have mistakes, no matter what the field's like."

The field looked like hell probably would if the devil was cold-natured — 15 degrees and 20-mph wind produced a minus-10 wind chill factor — but it was ironic that the adverse conditions were critical to only the Raiders' aspirations.

The field did not thwart Franco Harris. Improvising on a play called 33-trap, intended to go between guard and tackle, Harris rode wide behind a dike of a block by John Stallworth and ran through Neal Colzie, the obviously-hexed rookie cornerman, for 25 yards to the touchdown that gave the Steelers a 10-0 edge one minute into the final quarter.

"I block 'cause it's my job," grinned Stallworth, whose crackback shot picked off Raider free safety Jack Tatum and inside linebacker Monte Johnson. "It's nothing I enjoy, like I enjoying catching passes."

In any case, Harris was grateful. "A hell of a block," he allowed. "They closed the trap, so I just kept bouncing it to the outside." Once there, Harris ran over Colzie. "Most of the time you think you can make them miss one-on-one," he explained.

Which brings us to what Stallworth enjoys. And fate. And the tundra-like field, which fairly cut the heart from an Oakland rally so furious and so desperate that later Joe Greene watched Madden congratulate Noll and then turned his head "because I couldn't look at him."

Down 10-0 after Harris' run, the Raiders drove back to within three points on Stabler's arm only to be undone by Colzie's feet. Trailing 10-7 with 12 minutes left, the Oakland running game, which Stabler had given up on after it produced only 3 yards a pop in the first half, visited disaster on the Raiders.

L.C. Greenwood shackled Marv Hubbard, J.T. Thomas stripped the ball loose, and Lambert did his thing. Two plays later, Stallworth, who earlier told Bradshaw he could beat Colzie, did.

Guard Sam Davis, peeled a blitzing Ted Hendricks off Bradshaw's neck, the pass went up, and Colzie went down, the victim of a patch of end zone ice. Stallworth put the ball away behind a frantically-lunging Jack Tatum and the Raiders' torturous death dance began.

With 9:31 to play and tension so thick Russell thought "you could've cut it with a knife," the Steelers suddenly lost their grip on the ball, and almost on the game.

Rocky Bleier fumbled, the Raiders recovered, but had to punt. Three minutes later, Harris fumbled, Hendricks recovered. Stabler — who was 6-for-18 in the first half and had a miserable day despite Fort Knox protection — hit three passes, including one for 19 yards to Cliff Branch, and Madden made a tactical move Ham later called "brilliant."

With 17 seconds to play and trying to conserve the clock in order to give his club a chance at recovering an onside kick and enough time to throw for a winning touchdown, Madden had George Blanda kick a 41-yard field goal on third down.

And, as might've been expected in a series capable of an Immaculate Reception, the onside kick was muffed by Reggie Harrison and recovered by Hubbard.

"I tell you, gentlemen, I was shaking from the time I walked on that field until I walked off," was the way Fats Holmes summed up the Steeler situation with seven seconds remaining.

The Raiders had their final, albeit slim opportunity and the Steeler defenders trudged back out one more time. But it wasn't in the cards or tea leaves or whatever it is that Al Davis reads when he's trying to figure out why his Raiders have been bumped out of six AFC title games and have fallen seven times in eight playoffs.

Stabler hit Branch for 37 yards to the Steeler 15, but Blount bulldogged him inbounds with "the best tackle" Russell ever saw and clock went to zero.

"I wasn't worried," grinned Russell. "They only had seven seconds and they had a long way to go."

Too long.

Defense.

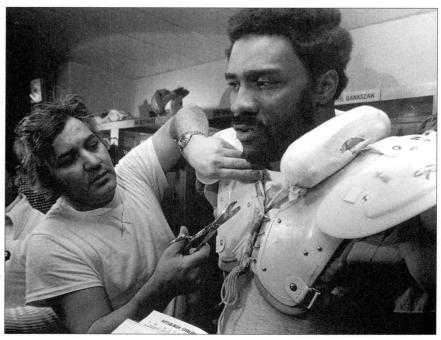

After the battle, Joe Greene gets some assistance from equipment man Tony Parisi in removing his shoulder pads.

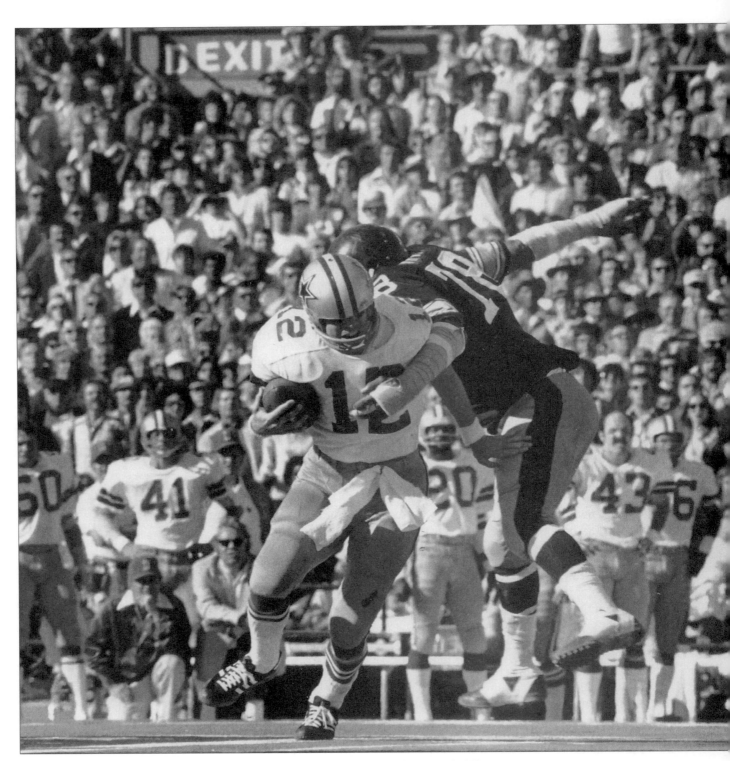

Dallas quarterback Roger Staubach (12) attempts to elude the grasp of the Steelers' Dwight White.

STEELERS' 2ND STRAIGHT TITLE WAS JUST SUPER

By Phil Musick, *The Pittsburgh Press*

MIAMI, JAN. 18, 1976 — EVEN THE SEAGULLS MIGHT HAVE found this one interesting.

Yessir, about Thursday they're going to have to break Pete Rozelle's jaw in six places to get the smile off his face. The Super Bowl — formerly a long-running ad for No-Doz — is finally a smash.

Thanks to the Steelers and a cliché, at least a temporary halt has been called to nine years of games following which it was necessary to wake the crowd up, explain the teams had spent 60 minutes trading midfield fumbles and point to the exits.

Yesterday, the Steelers did whatever it took, along with marvelous things for cardiac arrest to outlast game Dallas, 21-17, for a second straight Super Bowl trophy and the right to bill themselves as the latest thing in NFL dynasties since Green Bay turned the trick in 1966-67 and Miami duplicated it in 1973-74.

For once, ennui did not edge tedium. All the world — really only an Orange Bowl crowd of 80,017 and 70 or so million people not watching "I Love Lucy" re-runs — saw the Steelers wilt the Dallas flex, twist Tom Landry's shotgun into a granny knot, and reduce "playing them one at a time" to second place on the list of your favorite football clichés.

SCORE BY PERIODS

Dallas	7	3	0	7	17
Pittsburgh	7	0	0	14	21

Right there at the top — etched deeply into the frontal lobes of every Steeler fan — stood those words which someday may rank right up there in historical importance with "To the best of my recollection" and "How's your cow, Mrs. O'Leary?"

They would be, of course: Whatever it takes. Words that must be inscribed on Chuck Noll's scivvies. You know Chuck. Vince Lombardi with couth? What Don Shula was before Larry Csonka took the money and ran?

A CLICHÉ TO LIVE BY

Whatever it takes. A cliché to live by. And yesterday, as the gulls soared in a sky bluer than Big D's heart, it took a whole lot of things.

A pair of gut-shot field goals by a kicker who shanked his first two tries. And a 59-yard punt by a guy whose insides were quivering because, at 37, he'd made the biggest gaffe of a long and honorable career.

And it took a play called 333, which Noll had stuffed at the bottom of his playbook to be lifted up on just such a day, and another called 60 flankerpost.

And it took a blocked punt by a reserve fullback and Jack Lambert starting fights and breathing inspirational fire on his teammates.

And it took, as usual, those old Steeler heroes — Franco Harris (27 pops, 87 yards) and Terry Bradshaw (9 of 19, 209 yards and critically zero interceptions) and defense like the Russians played it in that long ago Super Bowl against Napoleon.

What all of that produced was a game that ... was ... well ... super. And forget the eight fumbles and three Steeler interceptions and the Cowboy offense giving its swell imitation of the Maple St. Tigers at their flee flickeringest.

Ultimately, what prevailed were talent and staying power and pure skill and luck. What dropped by the wayside were Dallas' untimely errors, Landry's reputation as an innovative genius, and such gadgetry as the flex and the shotgun.

However, not before Dallas acquired leads of 7-0, 10-7 and 10-9, and not before there had been played all but nine minutes of Big X. At which point, knock-them-out-of-their-jocks football took precedence over gimmickry.

"I ate Ralph Neely's lunch," exulted Dwight White, referring to the Dallas guard who was frequently guilty of holding. The Cowboys' use of plays such as the one in which Roger Staubach handed off to Preston Pearson, who lateraled back to Staubach, who got smeared, hurt the game's esthetics.

"They tried to fool us," White sneered mightily. "All that stuff is junk. And they stayed with it all the way. You can't play catch-up with junk stuff."

SITTING ON THE LEAD

"At the half, they led, 10-7, but they were trying to hatch those 10. All that really had happened was that we made three mistakes. We gave them field position with the opening kickoff return (a 53-yard gain on a reverse), we fumbled on the punt and we just blew a pass coverage.

"They hadn't done a damn thing but run junk and they wanted us to lose our cool. But at the half, we didn't get nervous, eat at each other. We knew sooner or later we'd score some points.

"And they'd be in bad trouble."

Before that happened, two errors had given Dallas 10 points, one by punter Bobby Walden. Reaching nervously for a cigarette as Andy Russell was peering into the kleig lights and announcing Lynn Swann and Art Rooney had been given game balls, Walden talked about mishandling a

After missing a pair of field goals early in the game, Roy Gerela rebounded with a pair of critical three-pointers in the final quarter.

Roger Staubach fumbles as Steelers defensive lineman L.C. Greenwood drives him into the Orange Bowl turf.

center snap that led to a Staubach touchdown pass to Drew Pearson and a 7-0 Dallas lead in the first four minutes.

"I just took my eyes off the ball. It happens to every punter once in a while," Walden said, the butterflies still alive in his eyes. "You have to forget it.

"You try not to press after something like that. Sometimes you don't succeed."

Later, Walden swallowed hard and succeeded.

So did good, old dusty 333 and Randy Grossman, who combined with Bradshaw on a 7-yard pass for the 7-7 equalizer.

For all of Noll's seasons, the Steelers, when close to the goal line, have run from their three tight end offense. Guard Gerry Mullins lines up as a third tight end and the Steelers run inside. Yesterday, they passed. For the first time since even Noll couldn't recall when.

"I'm like the Lone Ranger — leave the silver bullet and split," smiled Grossman as he slipped from a subdued locker room scene hyped frostly by television technicians tripping over one another.

"Early in the game, we'd run on that play to give them a look at it. Then we threw the pass."

LAMBERT TAKES OVER

Enter Jack Lambert and his angry nature, jumping at Cowboy free safety Cliff Harris when he tried to embarrass Gerela after a miss, and exchanging swipes, and then grins, with ex-teammate Preston Pearson. And, when the Steelers were behind and the clock was running, playing like a linebacker possessed.

"Lambert was the guy who sparked us," Joe Greene said. "When it wasn't going good for us, he held it together. He spearheaded us. He made the 3-4 licks that got us going. You could just feel it."

After Lambert got the Steeler heart beating, Reggie Harrison — caddy to Franco Harris — headed Super Bowl X in the right direction. With his tongue.

With Dallas up, 10-7, four minutes into the final quarter, Harrison, Walden and Noll pooled their finest efforts for the play which everyone later agreed prevented the Cowboys from matching their 1972 Super Bowl win over Miami.

First, Walden punted 59 yards to back the Cowboys into the proverbial goal-post shadow. Then, Noll ordered up an uncommon 10-man rush as Dallas punter Mitch Hoopes' heels rested on the goal-line.

Hoopes took the snap, stepped up and ... let's let Harrison tell it. "I don't know what happened," he said. "I just came up the middle. I was going to block that one ... it was mine. I was always scared to block one before because I'd get kicked."

Harrison did, on the tongue, as the ball bounded out of the end zone for the safety that made it 10-9.

"Look," Harrison opened his mouth hugely. "Man, cut my tongue. I'm going to put a $1,000 bill on it and see what happens."

What happened after that was Gerela finally finding the range, nudging one barely over the crossbar for the points that gave the Steelers their first lead, 12-10, and three minutes later converting a Mike Wagner interception into three more points.

All day it had been raining on the Cowboys; the deluge was about to fall. "They'd had the lead, but the pressure was on them," said Greene, who shared

An injured Terry Bradshaw leaves the Orange Bowl after the Steelers' 21-17 win.

playing time with Steve Furness.

Gerela's second field goal triggered an ending that even Rozelle couldn't have written.

With three minutes to play, the Steelers scored for the fourth time in 480 seconds. Swann, who'd been doing a number on Dallas cornerman Mark Washington all day — four receptions for 161 yards — went deep on a ditty called "60 flanker post." Bradshaw scrambled, and wearing blitzing linebacker D.D. Lewis as a twin-knee brace, pumped it into what by now had indeed become the wild blue yonder. Swann took it in stride and went the distance.

It, at that point, was over, save for the last-minute attempt to provide heart failure for anyone who'd missed it earlier.

In the final two minutes, Staubach hit rookie Percy Howard for a 34-yard touchdown to make it 21-17, and then the Steelers failed in trying a fourth-

down run at midfield to prevent a punt block, setting the stage for what football coaches perceive as character.

Three times Staubach fired bombs into the Steeler end zone, one just tricking off Howard's desperate fingertips. The game ended when the last pass was intercepted by Glen Edwards, who ran out of harm's way as the clock expired.

"We did what we had to do," Greene said. "That is what this football team does. This is the best damn team in football."

Dressing slowly as the room cleared, Noll tended to agree. There had not been a particular turning point, he felt. Unless it had occurred some years before in the building process.

"You make mistakes and it can crush you mentally," he said of his troops' errors. "But this team does not crush."

Pittsburgh coach Chuck Noll gives Jim Allen (45) a victory ride as the Steelers head for the locker room.

Don't Mess With Jack Lambert

The Pittsburgh Press

It was, Jack Lambert thought, bad enough that Dallas had been leading all day and had been acting as though the Steelers didn't really invent defense back there in 1972.

That was injury enough.

But accept insults? Never. So, when Dallas free safety Cliff Harris came up and waved the football in Roy Gerela's face after he missed his second field goal try of the game, Lambert took what he deemed proper action.

He tried to unscrew Harris' head from his shoulders.

"I felt he jumped up in Roy's face, and that it was uncalled for, and someone had to do something about it," Lambert said.

A brawl was averted, so Lambert did the next best thing. He started tearing up a Cowboy offense already plagued by the ineffectiveness of the shotgun.

On the ensuing series, Lambert made three tackles, two of them resounding enough to register on the

Richter scale, and the Steeler defenders caught fire.

"We were getting intimidated and we're supposed to be the intimidators," Lambert said, incredulity creeping into his voice at the thought of it. "So I decided to do something."

Earlier, Lambert had taken the situation less intensely, swatting at ex-teammate Preston Pearson, who'd objected to Lambert trying to bury him in the poly-turf surface on an incompletion.

"I felt him on my neck, and I just swiped at him," Lambert said. "Then he smiled at me and I smiled at him. He's a heck of a competitor and so am I."

Although Joe Greene credited him

with being "our spark ... our spearhead," Lambert denied he sought to be an inspiration.

"I wasn't trying to get anyone fired up," he said. "I just play emotionally. Jack Ham plays and never says a word. I yell and scream a lot.

"Sometimes they don't pay any attention to me."

But had he felt a change after his outburst at Harris and trying to singlehandedly dismantle the Cowboys on the next series?

"After that, we had some hitting," Lambert allowed.

He has a very definite idea of the game's purpose. You try to knock the other guy's head off; you do not in any way attempt to humiliate him.

"I tackle somebody as hard as I can and then I get up and go back to the huddle," he said. "I don't like the idea of people slapping our kicker or jumping up in his face and laughing when he misses a field goal.

"That stuff you don't need."

If Lambert wouldn't admit he had provided a Steeler defense that held Dallas to a paltry 108 yards rushing with an inspirational lift, he hinted at it rather broadly.

"Sometimes it's like in hockey," he smiled. "You need to take a penalty to get things juiced up."

What really irritated Lambert were Cowboy insinuations he had taken a few cheap shots at Dallas players. He implied he had given tit for tat.

"I'll play it clean if you want to play clean," he said. "If you don't, I'll play it that way. But I don't care what they're saying.

"I'm sitting in the winners' dressing room, they're in the losers'."

A reporter gingerly approached the player he obviously figured was the real Steeler meanie. In fact, Lambert plays the game fearlessly, but is a good-natured young man stuck with an unfortunate stereotype as some sort of ogre in shoulderpads. Which, occasionally, he seems to foster.

"I play the way I think it should be played," he said. "It's nice to be able to take your frustrations out on a football field and stay out of trouble at home."

HIGH-FLYING STEELERS CRASH COLTS, 40-14

By Glenn Sheeley, *The Pittsburgh Press*

BALTIMORE, DEC. 19, 1976 — LOOK, UP IN THE SKY. IT'S A bird. It's a Terry Bradshaw pass. It's the Steelers, soaring toward Oakland with a 10th straight win.

No, it's a plane.

"I thought it was a kamikaze pilot from Oakland," laughed Ray Mansfield.

Presumed John Banaszak, "It was a guy who bet his plane on the Colts and was trying to to collect the insurance on the thing."

Actually, it was a guy named Donald Kroner who had been buzzing Memorial Stadium all week and finally flew his single-engine Cherokee into the upper deck about 19 minutes after the Steelers crashed on the Baltimore Colts, 40-14, in yesterday's AFC divisional playoff game before 60,020 fans.

Bradshaw, throwing over the barren turf, commonly referred to as Astro-Rock, put on an air show that flew the Steelers into the AFC championship game against the Raiders in the Oakland Coliseum next Sunday.

Franco Harris, rambling for 132 yards before Joe Ehrmann butted his ribs early in the second quarter, an offensive line that decided to conduct it own All-Pro balloting and Lynn Swann and the Steeler defense provided the remain-

Terry Bradshaw's three touchdown passes doomed Baltimore.

SCORE BY PERIODS

Pittsburgh	9	17	0	14	40
Baltimore	7	0	0	7	14

----

ing ingredients in the shocker.

Baltimore quarterback Bert Jones wished he was Kroner's co-pilot. Chuck Noll, a pilot whose team has now been given clearance to land on Al Davis' strip, moaned about several critical injuries, but couldn't help smiling. Not nearly as broadly as he did when Mansfield place-kicked for the first time in 14 years and converted on an extra point, but broadly enough.

Asked about his passing game at a press conference last week, Noll answered. "What passing game?" Yesterday Colt coach Ted Marchibroda or cornerback Jackie Wallace, who was burned like a new bride's toast, knew the answer to the question. Bradshaw, injured and frustrated much of the season, completed 14 of 18 passes for three touchdowns and 264 yards and bombed a Colt defense that never recovered from his 76-yarder to Frank Lewis on the opening series.

"People were wondering where our passing game was," Noll smiled.

Bradshaw, who is the passing game, could also laugh. After a regular season of watching rookie Mike Kruczek hand off to Harris and Rocky Bleier, Bradshaw set new individual completion percentage and yardage records.

"It feels good," Bradshaw said in the locker room, spitting tobacco juice into a paper cup. "It was one of those games where you say, 'Hey, I really need a good one, and you go out and get it.' "

Noll said the Steelers had presumed the Colts' secondary was vulnerable. But even Bradshaw was shocked at Coach Conservative's call that sent Lewis on a fly pattern and the Colts into a fatal nosedive.

"Never since I've been here, have we ever opened up with a bomb," he said.

Bradshaw, shaky in the Central Division clincher at Houston last week, his first start since spraining his wrist three weeks before, admitted his problems were still more mental that physical.

"I had my mind off worrying about getting injured," he said. "Chuck took a big gamble last week, and it helped."

What also helped yesterday was his offensive line, providing him sufficient time to spot even secondary receivers. "The protection was outstanding," Bradshaw said. "526 yards? ... In a playoff game ... That's phenomenal."

Equally phenomenal were the Steelers — who use the run like Bert Jones usually uses the pass — imitating the Colt offense. Their 40 points were the most relinquished by Baltimore this year and the Steelers' highest ever in post-season play.

"We stuffed 'em," Mansfield said with considerable accuracy.

Said cornerback J.T. Thomas, who combined with the rest of the Steeler secondary to limit Jones to 11 completions in 25 attempts, "Man, I wouldn't have wanted to play against our offense today."

Swann, who caught three touchdown passes and faked cornerback Lloyd Mumphord out of his sanitary hose on a 11-yard TD pass in the fourth quarter, finished with five receptions for 77 yards. With the offensive line blowing the Colts halfway to Towson, Md., the Steeler passing game performed as Harris did until bruising his ribs. Noll inserted three new plays, used one on a single occasion and bagged the other two.

"I knew we had a super football team, but I didn't know we had anything like this," said guard Jim Clack. "I knew we could score like that, but I didn't think we would."

Said Noll, "That's the best Terry's been in a long time."

Harris had also been doing his predictable playoff number until Ehrmann, on a late hit, jammed his ribs with 10:22 left in the third quarter. For the Colts, the hit was about two periods too late. Breaking outside on a 50-yard run aided by a Swann block in the second quarter, Harris took the Steelers to the Colt 3. Ironically, Reggie Harrison, who replaced Harris superbly by rushing for 40 yards and two TD's, fumbled on the 2.

But that was about all the Steelers botched. Rookie Theo Bell returned a first-quarter Toni Linhart kickoff 60 yards and set up Harrison's 1-yard TD early in the second quarter. The game

was over at the half, when the Steelers led, 26-7, and the Colts were about to be eliminated by the Super Bowl champs for the second straight year.

With Noll's offense clicking with unusual explosiveness, the defense, which shut out five of its last eight opponents, rested and ravaged. Colt running back Lydell Mitchell, a 1,200-yard man, was granted only 55 yards on 26 carries. Jones threw two interceptions and was sacked five times.

Defensive end Dwight White, fuming about Colt defensive tackle David Taylor calling him a "bush-leaguer," was awesome.

"They bleeped me off," White said. "He called me a bush-leaguer. Now, do I play like a bush-leaguer?"

Defensive tackle Joe Greene, who had vowed to play his finest game of the season, promised the Steelers "would put it together," and said "the best team will win," emerged as a sound prophet. Several Colts thought it particularly humorous when Steeler rookie Ernie Pough was hurt on the opening kickoff and Greene and crew seethed.

"The best team won," Greene smiled, smelling the scent of Super Bowl cash.

Greene pointed to Bradshaw's locker. "We ain't gonna lose when he's hot," Greene said.

And quite naturally, Steeler thoughts turned to the nemesis Oakland Raiders and Sunday's AFC championship game which threatens to blow the needle off the Richter scale.

Said Clack, "It would be the biggest Christmas present you could have. Three little wins is all it takes to win the Super Bowl."

Bradshaw fires a 76-yard touchdown pass to wide receiver Frank Lewis on the third play of the game.

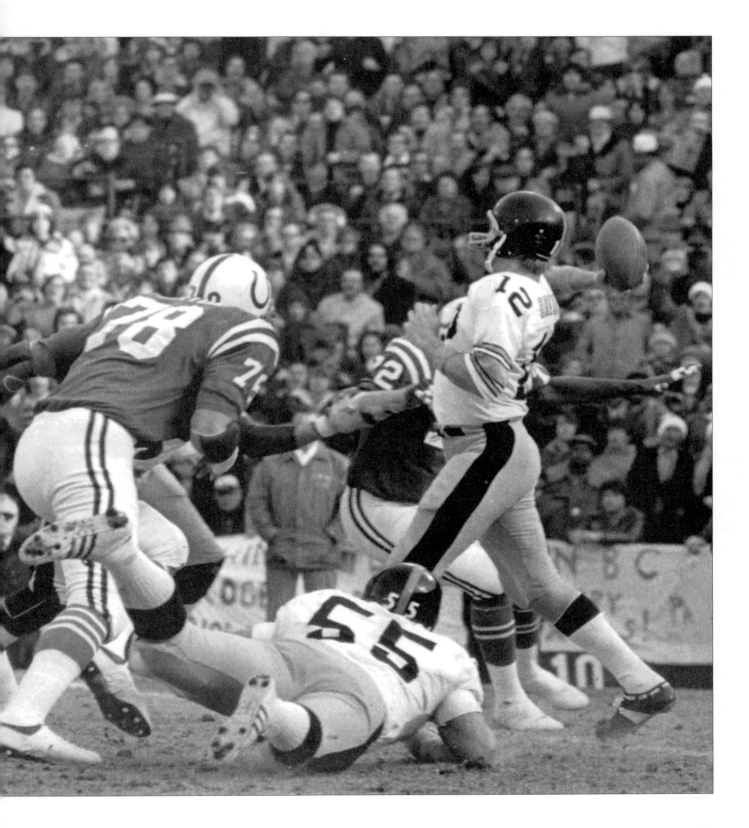

Roy Gerela's 36-yard field goal tied the score at 9-9 and sent the game into overtime.

STEELERS SCORCH BROWNS WITH GADGET PLAY

By Glenn Sheeley, *The Pittsburgh Press*

PITTSBURGH, SEPT. 24, 1978 — MAYBE CHUCK NOLL WILL show up at his weekly press conference today wearing a white, three-piece velour suit. Maybe he'll come out for ERA. Maybe he'll abandon all his former traits of conservatism by instructing Dan Rooney to outfit cheerleaders for the Steelers' next home game and call them Charley's Angels.

After what happened yesterday in Three Rivers Stadium — when a meat-and-potatoes coach whipped up a souf-flé in overtime — nobody would be surprised.

What happened, of course, was that the Steelers hit the gutsy old Cleveland Browns with their neutron bomb, stunning them, 15-9, with 3:43 gone in overtime on a play that caused 49,513 to spray their Iron City all over the North Side.

It was a play that was as uncommon in the Noll tradition as it was thrilling, and if there's a more electrifying way to win a football game it hasn't been invented yet. Yeah, Terry Bradshaw called it, but there it was, in Noll's play-book.

The Steelers used the trickiest of flea-flickers to overcome a Browns team that seemed to have forgotten it had never won in Three Rivers Stadium. With Roy Gerela having forced the game into the extra period with a 36-yard field goal that made it 9-9, the

SCORE BY PERIODS

Cleveland	0	6	3	0	0	9
Pittsburgh	3	0	0	6	6	15

Steelers won the toss and had a sec-ond-and-9 at the Browns 37.

That was when Bradshaw said in the huddle, "This is it." It was something

Bennie Cunningham catches the game-winning 37-yard touchdown pass.

known as Fake 84 Reverse Gadget Pass, which looks like a reverse but, as the Browns will admit, is far more lethal.

Bradshaw handed off to Rocky Bleier, who handed off to Lynn Swann. The Browns, thinking a reverse was as tricky as the Steelers or Noll ever get, pursued for the run.

But, of course, they were wrong. Swann lateraled the ball back to Brad-shaw and before Cleveland safety Thom Darden could realize what doom was coming, Bennie Cunning-ham was open in the right corner for the winner — a 37-yard pass, and the Steelers were 4-0, all alone in the AFC Central lead and the conference's only undefeated team.

"It's called 'High School Right,' " Noll said, grinning as he walked into a room full of shocked reporters. "It was getting so dull around here, we figured we had to give somebody something to write about except up the middle."

Stating that "we couldn't get any-thing done offensively," Noll admit-ted the Fake 84 "is not your run-of-the-mill play. But it was set up as part of our game plan. Terry was just wait-ing for the right situation."

The Steelers had practiced the play about four times last week and when Noll met with reporters Friday he was asked, curiously, if Cleveland would be an ideal team on which to run such a gimmick. Noll said only, "Sssshhhh."

Perhaps it explained why a Cleveland writer who was in town at mid-week was not allowed to view the Steelers' practice session.

Surely though, it was the right situation. After all, the Steelers had successfully pulled off an on-side kick during the afternoon, Tony Dungy nearly returned an interception all the way, and they saw a referee's decision go in their favor in the overtime period. Rookie Larry Anderson fumbled on the kickoff, which began the overtime, but the officials had already ruled the play dead.

The television replays did not totally explain the controversial play, but it was not clear that Anderson was down when the ball popped loose. The official may have blown it with a premature whistle.

"At first I thought I fumbled," said Anderson, who had lost a kickoff fumble in the second quarter and set up the Browns' second field goal. "I didn't know whether my knee touched or not. The only thing I could think of was, 'I've blown it.' Then somebody said to me, 'Don't worry about it — you were down.' "

Anderson did not hear a whistle, but Noll said he did.

"I heard the whistle blow," Noll said, "and when the ball came out the referee had no choice but to call it dead."

Browns coach Sam Rutigliano would only say, "I don't get paid to comment on officials' decisions."

The Steelers, of course, figured the score had been evened, since Cleveland cornerback Clarence Scott appeared to have interfered with Lynn Swann on a pass at the 2-yard line.

Terry Bradshaw's touchdown pass in overtime surprised the Browns, who were looking for the run.

But the Fake 84 Gadget Pass transcended everything else. Said Bradshaw, late to arrive at his locker because of treatment for a hip pointer, "That was a pass me and the boys put together in the hay field one day."

The play almost fell through. Bradshaw had trouble gripping the ball — "Swann was sweatin' when he gave it to me; it was soppin' wet" — and safety Darden had recovered slightly by the time the ball was thrown for Cunningham.

"I thought Darden was going to knock the ball down," Bradshaw said. "If I would have had a good grip, I would have fired the ball in there sooner."

Darden was shocked at the Steelers, those up-the-gut people, attempting something so wild.

"It looked like a run ... a reverse. The next thing you know, Bradshaw has the ball and Cunningham is open," Darden said. "I got caught. It was a damn good call and they did a good job executing it, but no, they don't usually run the flea flicker ... it's the only way they were going to beat us."

All Cunningham knew was that the ball was on the way as the crowd rose to its feet. "I was just waiting," he said. "I just wanted to make sure I caught it."

Cunningham's orders were to jog out into the secondary and serve as a decoy for the run. "As soon as I saw Darden come up, I took off. If they had guarded me, then I could have cleared out the zone for John Stallworth."

It was, all in all, a rather fortunate day for the Steelers. They were outplayed offensively in the first half and still remained undefeated and the Browns had two touchdowns taken away through penalties.

Said Rutigliano, who wound up losing on a flea-flicker, "I don't feel like the captain of the Titanic if that's what you mean."

UNSTOPPABLE STEELERS DRILL DENVER, 33-10

By Glenn Sheeley, *The Pittsburgh Press*

PITTSBURGH, DEC. 30, 1978 — FRANCO HARRIS, WHO IS known for speaking softly and not known for originating rallying cries, sat at his locker after it was all over and declared: "I think our only problem would be if we would stop ourselves. If we don't beat ourselves, we're gonna be tough."

It was something that the Denver Broncos did not have to be told, having been thumped by the Steelers, 33-10, yesterday at Three Rivers as 48,921 waved their Terrible Towels, even when they became soaked with rain.

They watched the Steelers force the Broncos to eventually throw in any orange towels they might have brought along and they'll watch the Steelers host the AFC championship game next Sunday against the winner of today's Houston-New England game.

It might be trite to suggest that the Steelers looked super as they took a giant step toward a possible third Super Bowl appearance, but they were certainly nothing less than that. Terry Bradshaw, John Stallworth, Lynn Swann and Harris took the Broncos' highly respected defense and turned it into scrap iron.

The Steelers erupted for a 16-3 lead in the second quarter and poured it on

Lynn Swann snags a mid-air catch for a 38-yard touchdown, despite the coverage of Denver's Bill Thompson.

SCORE BY PERIODS

Denver	3	7	0	0	10
Pittsburgh	6	13	0	14	33

as they mixed 425 yards in total offense with a defense that reminded followers of those days in 1974 when Chuck Noll's people first became known for digesting the enemy.

Not even reserve Denver quarterback Norris Weese could be Craig Morton's fireman this time. The Steelers, after allowing one Weese touchdown drive in the second quarter, burned him up, too, eventually finishing the game with six sacks.

But the story was the offensive explosiveness of the Steelers. In particular, Bradshaw's ability to find Stallworth 10 times for 156 yards — establishing an NFL divisional playoff record — and a 45-yard touchdown as the Steelers' "other" wide receiver outjumped cornerback Steve Foley. Exploiting Denver's choice to double-team Swann,

Bradshaw undressed Foley with considerable help from Stallworth.

"It was my plan to get it to Stallworth," said Bradshaw, who completed 16 of 29 passes for 272 yards and two TD's, a personal postseason high. "I don't know if it was Chuck Noll's, but I knew Swann was going to draw a lot of double coverage and I wasn't going to beat my head against the wall trying to force it to Swann."

Stallworth's biggest catch was for the TD in the fourth quarter, when the Steelers put the game out of reach and knocked the defending AFC champions out of the playoffs. Less than a minute later, following a Dirt Winston recovery of a Rick Upchurch kickoff return, Swann contributed a similar TD reception, leaping up for a 38-yarder with Denver's Billy Thompson.

It was a day during which the Steelers certainly appeared to be the team to beat in the AFC. It was a day during which even Roy Gerela overcame his early problems. After missing the extra point following the Steelers' first touchdown on a 1-yard run by Harris, who carried 24 times for 105 yards and achieved his fifth post-season 100-yard game, Gerela put forth field goals of 24 and 27 yards.

Any win would have buoyed the Steelers' hopes of visiting Miami for Super Bowl XIII on Jan. 21. This one, because of Denver's defensive reputation, made them very hopeful.

John Stallworth (82) gets past Denver's Steve Foley for a second-quarter reception.

Asked if the Steelers are unstoppable, center Mike Webster didn't exactly term it an unreasonable question.

"We can be if we play with the effort we played with today," he said. "That's the key, not turning the ball over. We turned it over one time and they got a touchdown, which was ridiculous. Our attitude is that we're not going to be denied. Houston and New England both have great running games, so we'll just have to run the ball better than them."

Webster indicated that the Steelers' performance yesterday, the complete opposite of last year's at Denver in the first round, was an example of the confidence the Steelers gained having finished the regular season with the NFL's finest record.

"Because we got in the playoffs the way we did built a lot of confidence," Webster said. "I think there is a genuine affection for everyone on this team. We don't want to shortchange each other. We're having a good time playing. We just want to keep it going. We're just looking forward to next week."

The Steelers' offensive stats were as impressive as Denver's were dismal. Morton, who left midway through the second quarter, completed 3 of 5 passes for 34 yards. Weese, who nearly engineered a win over the Steelers in the 16th game of the regular season, was limited to eight completions in 16 attempts for 118 yards. Weese, as an indication of the Steelers' defense, was Denver's leading rusher with 43 yards on four carries.

With a 19-10 halftime lead, the Steelers came out in the third quarter and immediately received an emotional lift as Joe Greene blocked Jim Turner's 29-yard field goal attempt. Later in the quarter Bradshaw was intercepted by linebacker Bob Swenson, but the

Wide receiver John Stallworth (82) outleaps Denver's Steve Foley for a 45-yard touchdown.

Steeler defense forced a Denver punt by limiting the Broncos to 3 yards. Included in the series was a 5-yard sack of Weese by Greene.

The fourth quarter, which the Broncos say is usually theirs, certainly wasn't yesterday. The lofted touchdown passes to Stallworth and Swann took care of any thoughts Denver might have had about a miracle comeback.

Bradshaw seemed to imply that he expected such a performance from the Steelers. The Broncos were admittedly riled at statements the Steelers had made earlier in the week, saying they were glad it was Denver and not Miami coming to town, and there was a midweek practice scrap between Mike Wagner and Theo Bell.

"I know that when our guys are talking," Bradshaw said, "the other guys are in trouble."

It was the Broncos who led initially, 3-0, on a 37-yard Turner field goal, but the Steeler defense dug in on a first-and-10 from the 11 and gave the Broncos zero yards on three tries.

From then on it was a struggle for the Broncos. Starting from their 34, the Steelers completed a 66-yard, eight-play drive with Bradshaw hitting Stallworth for passes of 19 and 16 yards, Harris going in from a yard out with 12:27 elapsed in the first quarter.

After burying the Broncos again, the Steelers took over from their 43. A 22-yard Stallworth pass set up Harris' powerful 18-yard TD run around the right side.

"The play was designated to go to the right," Harris said, "but things got kind of clogged up, so I went inside. Then when I went outside again, no one was there and I couldn't believe it."

Before the first half ended Gerela had contributed his two field goals and the Steelers had given up what was to be Denver's only touchdown of the day.

Aided by a block from Rocky Bleier (20) against Houston's Gary Bingham (54), Franco Harris (32) hits off tackle for a first-quarter touchdown.

STEELERS STOP CAMPBELL, PUT OILERS ON ICE, 34-5

By Glenn Sheeley, *The Pittsburgh Press*

PITTSBURGH, JAN. 7, 1979 — IS DALLAS READY FOR THE Steelers in Super Bowl XIII? Is the city of Miami ready for the Terrible Beach Towel?

These are the only remaining unanswered questions. The Steelers took care of the previous unknown yesterday in Three Rivers by wilting a Tyler Rose, otherwise known as Earl Campbell, changing a coach's first name to Bummer and burying the Houston Oilers under an icy wave of water, 34-5, in the AFC championship game.

Thus, it will be the Steelers vs. the Cowboys in the Super Bowl on Jan. 21, as the Steelers return to Miami against the same opponent they defeated there three years ago. The Cowboys won the NFC title yesterday with a 28-0 win over the Los Angeles Rams.

As the Terrible Towels were twirled by 49,917 Three Rivers fans who survived the dreadful afternoon enjoying defense by the home team, Oiler turnovers and the contents of flasks, the Steelers slid into their third Super Bowl in the last five years. The Oiler dream year went slip-slidin' away, with Houston battered and bettered and not quite ready for what Chuck Noll's team can do when a portion of Pete Rozelle's gate receipts are there for the sacking.

If Bum Phillips would have had one of his old ropes, he would have hung himself. The Oilers might have been

SCORE BY PERIODS

Pittsburgh	14	17	3	0	34
Houston	0	3	2	0	5

gushers before, but yesterday they were slushers. The Steelers went into the playoffs with the best record in the NFL and go into the Super Bowl playing like the best team in the NFL.

That was about the only point the Oilers and the Steelers agreed on yesterday after the final stats showed that there may have been more fights than fumbles. There were 12 fumbles in the game, breaking the NFL record of 10, which was established 45 years ago when the New York Giants and the Chicago Bears kicked it around in a title game. But yesterday, the record was broken before the first half ended.

"I don't see how anybody can beat them in the Super Bowl," said fallen quarterback Dan Pastorini, who the Steelers made feel as though he were back in the old AFL. The Steelers canceled the Earl Campbell Running Show, so Pastorini, trying to throw and merely getting thrown, was intercepted five times.

"To get to the Super Bowl is a thrill in itself," said Steeler defensive end L.C. Greenwood, who was literally a pain for Pastorini. "It is business, but it's a real thrill ... I think we're the best team in the NFL. Coming into this season, I told Joe Greene that if we got a little bit of help in certain areas, like from the coaches, we were going to be unstoppable."

With less than one quarter gone in the game, the Steelers were up, 14-0, on touchdown runs by Franco Harris and Rocky Bleier. On that field, that day, that was about it. The Steelers didn't need the 17 points they scored in a period of 54 seconds just before the end of the first half on three consecutive Oiler fumbles. No less than 14 of the points came in a 19-second span.

As Jack Ham, who ended the game with four tackles, a sack, an interception and two fumble recoveries, said, "When you get behind like that, you can throw those play-action passes out the window. Everybody knows it's going to be a pass. At that point, Earl Campbell's no good to you anymore."

Yesterday's game was Terry Bradshaw, supposedly ailing from the flu, making the Oilers look sickly by completing 9 of 15 passes for 187 yards and two touchdowns in the first half. On a dry field, those would have been phenomenal statistics.

"I felt weak. But when I walked out on the field, I got so pumped up I never even knew I was sick," Bradshaw said.

The Steeler quarterback likes his team's chances for an unprecedented

Houston quarterback Dan Pastorini can't escape from the Steelers' L.C. Greenwood (68) and Steve Furness (64).

third Super Bowl victory. "I would say our second Super Bowl team was better than the first and right now this team has the potential to be better than the second," Bradshaw said.

Yesterday's game was Ham recovering a Campbell fumble late in the first quarter and the Steelers scoring on Bleier's 15-yard, lunging slant two plays later.

It was Ham, proving he is the finest outside linebacker in the game, stripping the ball from running back Ronnie Coleman after a pass late in the second quarter and the Steelers going up,

21-3, 25 seconds later on a 29-yard pass from Bradshaw to Swann. It was Ham intercepting Pastorini early in the third quarter and Roy Gerela kicking one of his two field goals four minutes later.

It was Ham, on the first play of the game, tackling Campbell in the backfield for a loss of 2 yards. It was an accurate harbinger of what was to be the theme of the Steelers' day. It was the exact same play in which Campbell gained 10 yards before Donnie Shell dealt him a rib-cracking tackle in the Steelers' 13-3 win at Houston Dec. 3.

On the play this time, Ham shattered

On the slippery, icy turf, Terry Bradshaw (12) slides to a halt with the help of Houston linebacker Robert Brazile (52) after a 3-yard gain.

the side of his helmet. While searching for a replacement on the sidelines, he missed two plays. The Oilers should have kidnapped the Steeler equipment manager.

"The big thing was the fact that we got up on them so fast," Ham said. "To try to play catch-up football in that weather was about impossible."

So it was. The Steelers had a 31-3 lead at halftime. Ham told himself, "The worst thing we can do is come out there in the third quarter and lie down, think we have an easy game. But I figured if they want to run Earl Campbell and take up seven minutes, let 'em."

Middle linebacker Jack Lambert, who made 11 tackles, apparently didn't give it as much heavy thought, "I never figured we were in any danger — ever," he said.

Said Greene, "If they could have made up four TD's in a half, against this defense, man, then they would have deserved (to win) it."

All the Oilers got after halftime was two points on the first safety relinquished by the Steelers in six seasons as Bleier was tackled in the end zone by Ted Washington.

"The safety was my fault," Bradshaw laughed. "I turned the wrong way."

Sure, the Steelers fumbled, too — Harris and Bradshaw each lost the ball three times in the freezing rain — but the Oilers could do nothing with the ball but fumble it back. All Houston can say is that it almost equaled the Steelers' second-half point production (2-3).

Although the Steelers are known for

accepting moments of great victory with a little shouting, yesterday's scene was perhaps more subdued. There were a few shouts when reporters were admitted into the locker room, but hardly pandemonium.

"I guess it was because we all started celebrating by the beginning of the fourth quarter," Ham said.

Surely, though, the Steelers found the moment sweet.

"I was kind of spoiled," Lambert said. "My first two years we went to the Super Bowl and won. I felt cheated the third year, but it is sure nice to go back again.

"Let's face it, there's a lot of money involved in going all the way and winning. But really, when those guys were out there today, I don't think a lot of them were thinking about money. From the beginning of the year, I really got the feeling these guys wanted to go back there again."

The Oilers' year ended with a thud. Or perhaps a splash, and with nobody to toss them a line.

Asked if he felt the Oilers look confused by it all — the weather and the Steelers' play — Lambert said, "I had that feeling, too. Maybe they talked themselves out all week."

Lambert knew the Steelers would have been looking for fights given the same circumstances. "They had to be frustrated, but I really don't fell too bad for them."

It wasn't World War III, as it had been billed, even if Oiler tight end Mike Barber was upended by Mike Wagner and declared war on the Steeler safety. It was a mismatch from the beginning. The Steelers had tanks, and the Oilers had pea-shooters.

"That's what I like about this team," Greene said. "Chuck Noll always affords us a shot at all the marbles."

A fitting remark. The game that

John Stallworth (82) gathers in a 28-yard touchdown catch over a pair of Dallas defenders.

STEELERS REGISTER 3RD SUPER BOWL VICTORY

By John Clayton, *The Pittsburgh Press*

MIAMI, JAN. 21, 1979 — HOLLYWOOD HENDERSON SAYS Terry Bradshaw would have trouble spelling cat if he was spotted the C and the T. Spot Bradshaw a seven-point deficit in the Super Bowl, he'll spell out M-V-P and G-o-o-d-b-y-e C-o-w-b-o-y-s.

Bradshaw won the spelling bee. He wrapped the Dallas defense in a Terrible Towel and hurled it in a perfect spiral to Texas.

Yes, Bradshaw, the ugly duckling, fumbling quarterback of years ago, has blossomed into the beautiful swan (no, not No. 88). Hurray for the good guy. Boo for the heavy, Henderson.

"It was like Tom Henderson always talks about — a happy ending," said fullback Franco Harris after the Steelers became the first team to win three Super Bowls, topping the Cowboys, 35-31, yesterday at the end of the rainbow, Miami's Orange Bowl.

By halftime, Bradshaw had destroyed the Super Bowl passing record (Bart Starr's 250-yard performance against Kansas City in Super Bowl I). By the end of the game, he had 17 of 30 completions for 318 yards, a career-high four touchdown passes and the MVP trophy. The quarterback whose intelligence is always questioned silenced all his critics.

"I hope this is the start of some good," said the man who has seen so much bad in his nine years in Pitts-

SCORE BY PERIODS

Pittsburgh	7	14	0	14	35
Dallas	7	7	3	14	31

burgh. "Maybe I'm learning something. I wasn't going to let one game destroy a good season. I felt we had a good season but I wasn't about to let anyone ruin it for us."

Bradshaw played like a man possessed — possessed with great talent, poise and yes, the Terrible Towel. Towel power prevailed. In the third quarter when Cowboy backup tight end Jackie Smith broke free into the end zone, it was time for the towel.

"When he broke free, I thought it was a touchdown," Steeler safety Mike Wagner said. "I just said, 'Get 'em towel.'"

His call worked. Smith, a sure-handed veteran who came out of retirement to join the Cowboys this year, dropped a low Roger Staubach pass in the end zone with the Steelers leading, 21-14. The Cowboys had to settle for a 27-

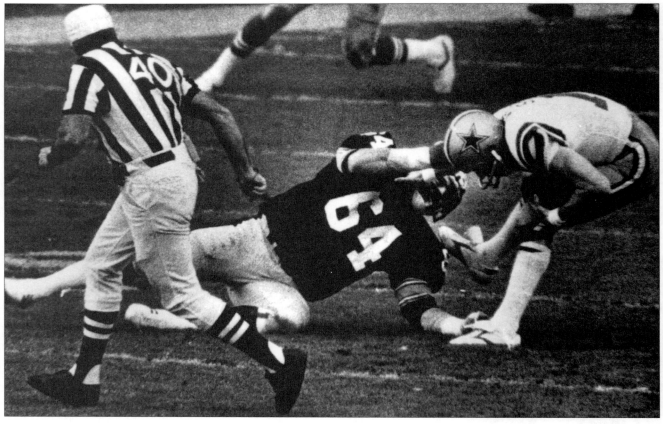

Cowboys quarterback Roger Staubach is sacked by the Steelers' Steve Furness (64.)

yard Rafael Septien field goal.

The towel later may have covered the eyes of the officials who did not see Steeler receiver Lynn Swann slip and elbow cornerback Benny Barnes.

Barnes, falling down, tripped Swann and drew a 33-yard penalty, setting up Franco Harris' 22-yard run that opened the Steeler lead to 28-17.

Oh, the Cowboys did rally from a 35-17 deficit, but surely this fairy tale belongs to Bradshaw, who said, "The game is the most important thing. You have to play the game. You don't win the game with words."

Speaking of words, Thomas Henderson will have quite a meal of them this week. His week-long promotion off his own ability and demotion of the

Steelers' talents backfired.

First, reserve linebacker Dirt Winston decked him on a first-quarter punt return and later Harris, angered at a rough Henderson tackle, rambled for the game-winning touchdown with vengeance in his eye.

"As you can see, I'm a little sad," said Henderson his face moistened by a combination of tears and sweat. "I want to keep the competitive spirit in football and any time I don't, I'd get out."

It was easy to see that this was to be Bradshaw's day. A local sportscaster talked Coach Chuck Noll into letting center Mike Webster wear a Terrible Towel for two plays.

Webster kept the towel on the whole day. And Bradshaw wiped his hands on

it, grabbed some magic and started completing passes.

Dallas took the opening kickoff and raced into Steeler territory on three Tony Dorsett runs for 38 yards. But the Cowboys abandoned the run and spoiled the offense. Drew Pearson fumbled a handoff from Dorsett on an end around double reverse and John Banaszak recovered.

"I think they may have been getting a little too cute with that flea-flicker," analyzed Steeler linebacker Jack Ham. "They tried to outsmart themselves."

Bradshaw then marched the Steelers upfield 53 yards in seven plays for a touchdown, lobbing a 28-yard strike to John Stallworth, one of two TD catches for Stallworth.

"On the first touchdown, we exploited a weakness we noticed on film," Stallworth said. "We saw the corners do some jumping. I took a slant, went back to the outside and Bradshaw (who pumped once) lobbed the ball."

But Bradshaw was grabbing the spotlight yesterday, so he also assumed the role of goat. He overthrew Stallworth and linebacker D.D. Lewis intercepted a pass.

On the next possession, Bradshaw, chased by Ed (Too Tall) Jones and Harvey Martin, lost the ball and Jones recovered, giving Dallas possession on the Steeler 41.

On the last play of the first quarter, Staubach hit Tony Hill for a 26-yard score. Safety Donnie Shell jammed Hill too closely at the line and fell behind. It was the first touchdown scored against the Steelers in the first quarter this season.

The first half was filled with exciting plays as both teams gambled on offense and defense. With the score tied, 7-7, Bradshaw faded back to pass from his 48, was pressured and grabbed by both Henderson and reserve linebacker Mike Hegman, who stole the ball and ran 37 yards for a touchdown.

With 1:43 remaining in the half, the Cowboys led 14-7. Bradshaw bruised his left shoulder on the play, but soon returned to action.

He passed to Stallworth near the sidelines at the Steeler 35 and Stallworth raced through the Cowboy defense for a 75-yard score, tying a Super Bowl record.

With the ball at the Steeler 44 and 1:41 remaining in the half. Bradshaw worked a two-minute drill. He hit Swann on 29- and 21-yard passes that moved the Steelers to the Cowboy 16. Three plays later, he rolled right and

Franco Harris celebrates the Steelers' fourth touchdown.

105

lobbed a high pass into the end zone that Rocky Bleier plucked from the air for a 7-yard touchdown to give the Steelers a 21-14 halftime lead.

"I think the Steelers and the Cowboys have played the two most exciting games ever to be played in the Super Bowl," Bleier said. "I give credit to Dallas because they didn't quit today."

Bradshaw had picked the Dallas secondary for 253 yards and two touchdowns while Dallas had only 102 yards total offense in the first half.

"I was surprised how relaxed I was," Bradshaw said. "I was able to stay relaxed and not worry so much."

Little did he know at halftime that Stallworth would miss the rest of the game because of leg cramps. But injuries were a big part of the hard-hitting game.

Dallas defensive end "Too Tall" Jones missed a few plays because somebody stepped on his ankle. Steeler guard Gerry Mullins pinched a nerve in his neck and had the wind knocked out of him.

Martin twisted an ankle and linebacker Jack Lambert was injured while trying to jump over running back Scott Laidlaw. All in all, a very physical third quarter.

Staubach finally got his Cowboy offense moving midway through the third quarter. Using short, quick runs by Dorsett and some short passes, Staubach drove to the Steeler 10, setting up a key third down and 3. That was when he found the right formation, isolating Smith in the end zone. But Smith dropped the low pass.

"I was just wide open and I missed it," Smith said.

"We weren't sure who was supposed to be covering on that pass," Steeler safety Mike Wagner said. "All four defensive backs came off the field wondering what happened. We held a meeting but still couldn't figure it."

Septien kicked his field goal, cutting the margin to four, 21-17. Bradshaw kept the Steeler offense moving, but was helped by the 33-yard interference call on Barnes, who said he was elbowed by Swann.

Harris scored the touchdown and upped the Steeler lead to 11. The Cowboys fell out of the game when Randy White fumbled the kickoff. Steelers Tony Dungy and Dirt Winston wrestled for the ball, with Winston pulling the ball away from Dungy in a pileup.

Two plays later, Bradshaw hit Swann for an 18-yard touchdown. Staubach rallied for two scores, a 7-yard pass to Bill DuPree and a 4-yard pass to Butch Johnson.

"I wasn't sure we were in control until I fell on the ball at the end of the game," Bradshaw said.

Now, that's a happy ending.

Irate Franco Stings Dallas

By John Clayton, *The Pittsburgh Press*

Mild-mannered Franco Harris was irate.

Dallas linebacker Thomas Henderson had just tackled quarterback Terry Bradshaw despite a delay-of-game penalty that stopped a play before it really got started in the fourth quarter. But the referee's whistle didn't stop the Cowboy linebacker as he proceeded to twirl Bradshaw to the turf.

To the rescue came Harris, nicknamed "Stingbee" by satirical teammates about his gentlemanly way of blocking. He jawed at Henderson for a few seconds before angrily strutting back to the huddle.

Seconds later Harris got revenge, racing 22 yards on a perfectly executed trap play that enabled the Steelers to open a 28-17 lead en route to a 35-31 victory in Super Bowl XIII yesterday.

"He ran so hard, so fast. It was awesome," said Bradshaw of Harris' 22-yard touchdown burst. "I've never seen him run so hard. He wasn't going to be stopped. He'd run through a brick wall if the brick wall would have kept him out of the end zone."

There was no stopping him. Harris grabbed the ball from Bradshaw, spotted a big hole on the left side and outran the flat-footed Cowboys for the score.

"The only thing I saw was goal line," Harris proudly recalled. "It was a tackle-trap play and we caught them in a blitz.

"I was kinda upset because of what Henderson was doing. It was after the whistle had blown and he just kept coming. That kind of defense is uncalled for."

Harris, who annually wins the nice

Joe Greene (75) assists in carrying Steelers coach Chuck Noll off the field following their third Super Bowl win in five seasons.

guy award for blockers, is usually not one to fight.

"Franco was mad for what Henderson had done to me," Bradshaw said. "When I called the play, he wanted it to be his number."

His eyes were burning as the fire of anger grew within him, and his ears opened wide to hear the play selection.

"When he (Steeler coach Chuck Noll) called the play, I just felt it was the right play at the right time to the right person," Bradshaw explained. "Everything was all set, because it was going against the right defense. I just felt so good about it."

And Harris' legs never moved so fast. As quickly as you could say, "Take that, Hollywood," Harris crossed the

goal line for the score. He was congratulated by Bradshaw, who embraced him in the end zone for almost a minute.

It was a fitting climax to what had been a rough day for the Steeler fullback who normally thrives on post-season games. He had gained only 46 yards on 19 carries before the score and had been limited to 6 yards on six carries in the second half.

"They played us to the outside," Harris said. And played well. His outside sweeps were whisked away quickly by the Dallas defense.

Credit Henderson for inspiring the new spring in Harris' legs. But it's the post-season and Harris rarely needs inspiration. Does Reggie Jackson need

lessons on how to swing at a fastball in the World Series?

Earlier in the game, Harris became the all-time Super Bowl ground-gainer, surpassing former Miami star Larry Csonka. Now he has 1,276 in 15 post-season appearances.

"You have to do it in the big games," Harris said. "I've been down to Super Bowls twice, so I know what to expect when I get down here. I just try to rest and keep away from the masses of people.

"I got a lot of rest the week before the game. Oh, I did get later calls at 2:30 a.m. and 3 a.m. People just don't know."

There really is a mean streak, a vengeful steak in Franco Harris. Just ask Thomas Henderson.

THE ULTIMATE THRILLER, BAHR NONE, FOR STEELERS

By Jim O'Brien, *The Pittsburgh Press*

PITTSBURGH, NOV. 25, 1979 — MATT BAHR MIGHT HAVE BEEN the only Steeler hero who could have kicked up his heels at a victory dance last night.

The rest would have been too tired to move off their chairs. Most of them were numb from the physically demanding battle they had been through.

They had come from behind yesterday to beat the Cleveland Browns, 33-30, in overtime to keep their hopes for another Super Bowl title intact. It may have been the best National Football League game ever played at Three Rivers Stadium.

It was the 10th year they had turned back the Browns there.

Playing five full periods of hard-hitting football, and getting frustrated throughout by the Browns' fine quarterback, Brian Sipe, had obviously taken its toll on them.

They were as happy as the crowd of 48,773, which helped rally them from deficits of 20-6 and 30-20, but were unable to show it.

Franco Harris, who scored all three of the Steelers' touchdowns, could hardly move: "I'm whipped, man," he said in a near-whisper.

The marvelous running back who is en route to the Pro Football Hall of Fame was out of moves, for a change.

SCORE BY PERIODS

Cleveland	10	10	7	3	0	30
Pittsburgh	3	10	0	17	3	33

Mel Brooks' "2,001-year-old man" could have caught him from behind.

"It was a very demanding game," said Harris. "We had no big plays. It was nothing but long drives. That takes a lot out of you."

Jack Lambert looked beat. He spent his last ounce of energy hoisting Bahr overhead after he kicked the game-winning field goal. "I'm really happy for him," said Lambert. "I had so much confidence in him. He thrives on that sort of thing."

Lambert and Harris and the other Steelers moved, almost in a trance, from their dressing stalls to the showers and back. Some were gone so long, it was feared they might have drowned.

Seeing them in transit, one would have thought there was broken glass all over the floor, they moved so gingerly. Some had to be reminded to smile.

Bahr was bright-eyed and certainly had the freshest face among those who figured the most in the Steelers' dramatic victory.

Bahr's fourth field goal of the game — a 37-yarder with nine seconds remaining in the extra period — provided the difference in beating the Browns. His 21-yard field goal with 24 seconds left in regulation tied the contest.

"There wasn't any one guy who won this game," said Bahr, on the mark once more, in the somewhat subdued Steeler clubhouse, where the dominant feeling was one of relief rather than euphoria. "You could call this game the true team effort. That's why it's so important."

The victory boosted the Steelers' record to 10-3, tying them with the Houston Oilers for first place in the Central Division of the American Football Conference, as the Browns, 8-5, fell two games back. The Cincinnati Bengals, who are fourth in the AFC Central and coming here next Sunday, beat the St. Louis Cardinals yesterday, 34-28.

The Steelers escaped with their playoff hopes intact in this thriller, but their work is still cut out for them in the three remaining games. "It's always hard, it's never easy," offered Franco.

"Today's victory did a lot for us emotionally," defensive back Ron Johnson said. "It's gonna set the tone

Matt Bahr (9) boots the game-winning field goal in the Steelers' 33-30 overtime win against Cleveland.

for us the rest of the season. It's gonna do a lot for us the next three weeks. I think the Cincinnati Bengals are in trouble."

Bahr asked about the Cincinnati score after the game because his older brother, Chris, is the Bengals' placekicker. Chris came through with two second-half field goals, so it was a big day for the Bahrs.

At 5-9, 165 pounds, Matt Bahr is by far the smallest Steeler. Jon Kolb calls him "the little guy." Others refer to Bahr by the nickname "Radar," after TV's *M*A*S*H* character and because he has been on target twice before this season with game-winning field goals.

He won the opening game in New England with a three-pointer in overtime and another comeback victory in St. Louis. This was, however, his biggest clutch effort because the Steelers would have been in a heap of trouble if they had lost this one.

Bahr had more bounce to the ounce than any of his teammates in the aftermath of a triumph many labeled "the most satisfying" so far this season.

"I'm really happy," said Bahr, the baby-faced rookie from Penn State, who hardly looks 23. "It's a great win for everybody."

By contrast, Sam Davis, the elder

statesman of the Steelers at 35 and in his 13th season, said, "I'm so tired, I feel like a zombie."

Altogether, Bahr kicked four field goals in five attempts, tying a team mark set by Lou Michaels and Roy Gerela, and was good for three extra points following touchdowns by Harris.

That's a personal high for Harris as he scored from 2 yards out on a flip from Terry Bradshaw, and from 1 and 3 yards out on marches into the line.

Harris was the workhorse who, along with Bradshaw, Rocky Bleier and John Stallworth, did the most to make Bahr's boots possible. Harris carried the ball 32 times for 151 yards — the amazing aspect of his production was

that his longest run was only 11 yards — and he caught a career-high nine passes for 81 yards.

So Harris had the ball a total of 41 times, and his body was well aware of the punishment it absorbed for the afternoon. "I'm just so tired," offered Franco afterward. "Some of us are going out to dinner, then I'm going home and go to bed."

He had earned his rest. "The way he ran, Franco ought to be tired," Lambert said in admiration.

Harris hobbled about the clubhouse. So did Bradshaw. Lambert

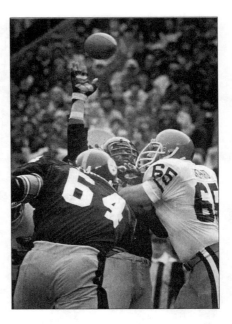

L.C. Greenwood strains to block a Brian Sipe pass while Steve Furness (64) tangles with the Browns' Henry Sheppard (65).

The Steel Curtain: That's What Did It

By Pat Livingston, *The Pittsburgh Press*

It may be ridiculous, even unconscionable, to say that the Steelers' 33-30 victory over the Cleveland Browns at Three Rivers Stadium yesterday was a triumph of defense.

Yet it was. Strange as that many seem, it certainly was.

Name your heroes. Terry Bradshaw, throwing for enough yardage to make him look like Bobby Layne suffering from a hangover. L.C. Greenwood, sacking the quarterback as though he had insulted his mother.

Listen to Joe Greene, chortling to the press: "We gave out a lot of game balls. There were a lot of super heroes out there today."

When it came down to the bottom line, the Steelers' victory over the Browns — in which the raw injustice

was that there was only one winner instead of two who might have tied — it was the Steelers' defense that won the game.

Go ahead, laugh about that. But, in the final analysis, when the computers had been programmed; when the scores had been counted; when it became understood that quarterback Brian Sipe, who fired eight touchdown passes against the Steelers' awesome defense in six previous quarters, was no mere flash-in-the-pan; when a silent, sell-out crowd, its tongue in its throat, had composed its concession notices, one truth was clear.

For 29 minutes, from the fourth quarter through the first 14 minutes of overtime, the Steelers held Sipe, the architect of the most potent offense in

the NFL, and his explosive teammates to a single field goal, three points — when anything more than that would have spelled defeat, ending, possibly, the Steelers' last hope for a role in the NFL playoffs.

It was enough to make George Perles, the Steelers' assistant head coach and the man who played such a major role in devising the complex Steel Curtin defense, cringe.

"That's my limit," shrugged Perles, his broad shoulders drooping like those of a man who had survived a death march. "That's about all I can take. I'm drained.

"That's a helluva football team," admitted Perles, the man who had urged the Steelers on the sidelines to hang in there to push themselves to another victory. For a change, he wasn't talking of his Steelers. "That's a better football team than anybody thinks. Three times during the game, I thought we were beaten. Three times, I gave up."

might still be there, sitting in front of his dressing stall.

"I'm too tired to move," allowed Lambert. "I'm drained mentally as well as physically."

Besides Lambert, Jack Ham, Harris and L.C. Greenwood were still there as it neared 7 o'clock, almost two hours after the game was completed.

To win, the Steelers had to overcome an inspired effort by the Browns, especially Sipe, and none of them stopped Sipe as well as Greenwood in the late going.

Greenwood was in on five of the seven sacks of Sipe, as three of those came in the fourth period. Steve Furness also got in on the fun twice. Two sacks occurred in the extra period, one

with Lambert's help.

"I'm so exhausted, I can barely move," said Greenwood. "I can hardly stand up. It was one of the most physical games I've played in the 11 years I've played football. The reason why it's more physical is that I played five quarters, five complete quarters.

"I guess for you guys, the sports writers, it was a very dramatic game. For us, it was a hard-fought game. We had to fight to win the game. Cleveland played great football.

Sipe and Bradshaw put on quite a passing show. Sipe completed 23 of 38 passes for 333 yards and two touchdowns — one each to Ozzie Newsome, Dave Logan and Calvin Hill — to go with field goals of 32 and 40

yards by Don Cockroft. Bradshaw set personal highs by hitting 30 of 44 passes for 364 yards. Each quarterback was intercepted only once.

In the end, however, it came down to Bahr, and his right foot, and the soccer-style swipe he takes at the ball. "You try not to think about what it means," said Bahr. "You just try to do your best."

The kick to put the game in overtime was just as important. Both of them were heart-stoppers, for sure. There was a pregnant pause at the end of the regulation game. Everybody seemed to take a deep breath.

"It seemed like our team was more relaxed in overtime," said Bahr. "And everybody was telling me to relax."

Perles wasn't the only person in the Steelers' locker room who was drained by this strange turn of events that brought the Browns, one of the Central Division teams that have been playing second fiddle to the Steelers and Houston, storming into Three Rivers Stadium yesterday. The Browns came in with their muskets loaded, fire in their eyes, their danders up and ready to play.

"There was a time, up until a year ago," said the disappointed Sipe, bitter that the Browns had lost, "when the Steelers were a better football team that we are, but we've closed the gap. I'm not pleased at all. The only thing I can say about the game is that we lost."

"It was a classic football game," said curly-haired Jim Garrett, one of Cleveland's assistant coaches, in the funeral clubhouse. "There were no losers."

There were points, however, when it was not your classic football game, particularly in the third quarter when

Bradshaw, with an opportunity to close the gap, grew uncharacteristically coy. From the Browns' 1-yard line, first-and-goal, Bradshaw decided to get cute.

Would you believe it, Terry Bradshaw — who completed 30 all afternoon, a career-high — tried to throw a pass even though his backs were running for an average of 6 yards a clip. He was sacked for a 13-yard loss.

"They were in a blitz," said Bradshaw, conceding that his original call, a running play, had been sent in from the bench. "I felt that what we had worked on all week would work. I'm embarrassed that it didn't."

Chuck Noll, of course, did not second guess Bradshaw's judgment, nor did he fly into a rage on the sidelines. He merely shrugged, which is what he does when one of his people disagrees with his strategy. If he felt strongly otherwise, Noll, who is not a second-guesser, would send in the play himself.

Sipe, who made a practice of converting third-and-8's and third-and-25's

for three quarters of the game, had no such luck in the final 30 minutes. Actually, the Cleveland quarterback was under brutal pressure, suffering four of his seven sacks toward the end of the game.

"We changed our rush," said John Banaszak, explaining how the Steelers finally started getting to the quarterback. "Earlier in the game, we had been blowing in there. But the Browns were handling us. Later, we changed the timing and we started to get to Sipe. We worked it out with George."

George, of course, is Perles.

"We didn't do anything fancy," he said. "As the game went on, we found they weren't bothering to run the ball, so we started blowing in on them. We just started doing what San Diego did to us last week.

"They might've burned us, but they didn't. When you don't have the run to worry about," said Perles, "you can knock the hell out of the passer."

FANS PUSH STEELERS PAST DOLPHINS, 34-14

By Jim O'Brien, *The Pittsburgh Press*

PITTSBURGH, DEC. 30, 1979 — "WE WANT HOUSTON! WE want Houston!"

The Steelers had defeated the Miami Dolphins, 34-14, the clock was running out, and the fans were looking forward to next week's challenge.

In a rematch of last year's American Football Conference championship, the Houston Oilers will provide the opposition here next Sunday. Two other upstarts, the Los Angeles Rams and Tampa Bay Buccaneers, will meet for the National Football Conference title in Tampa Bay.

The Steelers will be playing for the AFC championship for the seventh time in nine seasons. If they beat the Oilers, they will be shooting for their fourth National Football League championship in six years. Next week's winners will play in Super Bowl XIV in Pasadena, Calif., on Jan. 20.

The Steelers' star receivers, Lynn Swann and John Stallworth, as well as running back Sidney Thornton, all pulled up lame in yesterday's game, but they expect to play next Sunday. Swann suffered a leg cramp and is regarded as the most questionable case.

For a while, it looked as if the Steelers were trying to even up things for the Oilers, who had to go against San Diego without quarterback Dan Pastorini and running back Earl Camp-

SCORE BY PERIODS

Miami	0	0	7	7	14
Pittsburgh	20	0	7	7	34

bell, both sidelined with groin pulls, and with wide receiver Kenny Burrough a big question mark.

Asked if he respected the Oilers even more after their valiant victory on Saturday, Coach Chuck Noll said, "It would be difficult to respect Houston any more than we do."

As for the fans, they respect none of the NFL pretenders. "We want Houston!" they hollered. "We want Houston!"

The chant was first heard, however, at the end of the first quarter of yesterday's semifinal playoff game at Three Rivers Stadium. In the first 15 minutes, the Steelers scored every time they got the ball and stopped the Dolphins every time they had the ball and took a 20-0 lead.

It was never a contest after that. The roar of the crowd could have been

**John Stallworth (82) outduels Miami's
Neal Colzie for the touchdown catch.**

DEFINITELY THE TEAM OF THE 70'S

By Pat Livingston, *The Pittsburgh Press*

On the last Sunday of 1979, the Steelers left no question as to which team will be remembered as the football team of the 1970's.

Don Shula, the coach of the Miami Dolphins, the man who 11 years ago had recommended his relatively unknown assistant, Chuck Noll, as a coach of the Steelers, was the first man to concede that honor to Pittsburgh.

And three hours later as the Los Angeles Rams shocked the Dallas Cowboys, the Steelers' last serious challenger in this wild, delirious decade was finally dispatched in the upset which settled the question once and for all.

"We never challenged them," said the disappointed Shula after Miami's defeat yesterday. "We can't be proud of that.

"We had a lot going for us," explained Shula, after the Steelers had decimated the Dolphins, 34-14, at Three Rivers Stadium. "If we had won it, we could have argued about the team of the 70's. This game meant so much to us, but we never got into it.

"They totally dominated us," Shula continued. "It was an indication of their strength. We came up here to play a good football team, but we couldn't come up with the big play when we had to.

"They are a great football team," added Shula, almost as an afterthought. "They've got a fine running game, a fine passing game. The games they lost, they made mistakes. They didn't make any mistakes today."

To say that Shula was shell-shocked after the lopsided defeat, a defeat that he scarcely considered probably earlier in the day, would be an extravagant statement, but there was no doubt that the Miami coach was impressed with the manner in which the Steelers had dispatched the Dolphins. After the Steelers' first three possessions, which gave them a 20-0 lead in the first quarter, the game for all intents and purposes, was over.

If there was a turning point in the game, said Shula, it came long after the outcome was decided. The Steelers were already leading, 20-0, after a quarter of near perfect football, when the Dolphins got their initial break, a fumble by Sid Thornton at the Steeler' 9-yard line.

The Dolphins made it to the Steeler 2 but on fourth down, Griese, under a heavy rush, lobbed a blitz-control pass goalward that fell incomplete. Nobody was in the area to catch it.

"Bruce Hardy, the tight end, should have been there," said Shula, "but Nat Moore knocked him off coming out of the line. Had we scored there, maybe we might have played a better ballgame."

Shula wasn't the only Dolphin who was impressed by the Steelers.

"They're the best team in football," stated guard Larry Little, the Dolphins' 34-year-old All-Pro who said he may be hanging up his cleats after this season. "What they did, we didn't do. They outplayed us. They're the team of the 70's."

Would they compare, Little was asked, with the Dolphins of the early 70's, when Miami won two straight Super Bowls and compiled as incredible 17-0 record during that span? Little thought for a moment and then avoided an answer.

"What can you say about them?" asked Little. "They've won it three out of five years, and they're headed to their fourth Super Bowl. They've played together a long time. Of course, Pittsburgh didn't have a World Football League to contend with."

"They're awesome," said a disconsolate Jimmy Cefalo, the former Penn State star who is now a wide receiver with the Dolphins. "The Steelers do everything so well. That first drive of theirs was a piece of perfection. It seemed as if they did what they wanted to."

Cefalo, perhaps because he is so young, a second-year man, seemed the most depressed of all the players in Miami's locker room.

"It all ended so fast," the articulate young man from Pittston, Pa., mumbled morosely. "This morning, everybody was making plans, thinking of the Super Bowl. Three hours later, it's all over. It's hard to believe this happened. It was a short season."

Perhaps the happiest guy after the football game was Steve Courson, the Steelers' second-year guard who did some blocking, particularly on sweeps, that defied description. Courson, who looms larger and larger in the Steelers' plans as they move toward their fourth Super Bowl, was absolutely ecstatic.

"It's an honor to play alongside these guys," said Courson. "I remember when I was a rookie. I remember how hard it was to make this ballclub.

"But what an honor it is, what it means, when you do make it."

responsible for breaking up the gray fog that put a ceiling on the stadium and enabled the sun to slip through for the remaining three periods. The day was described as "Russian summer" by one of the tailgaters before the game.

The largest crowd of the season at Three Rivers, numbering 50,214, was in good voice. The freezing temperatures didn't numb them, even if it did seem to have that effect on the Florida visitors.

They brought their best banners — EVERYONE KNOWS DOLPHINS CAN'T SWIM IN RIVERS, and SEND THE DOLPHINS BACK TO SEA WORLD.

The Edinboro State College band brought a 300-pound "Terrible Towel," Jimmy Pol led the fans in singing the Steelers' fight song, and it was just all too much for the Dolphins. It smothered them.

When Noll said, "We were outstanding in all areas," he noted that the partisan crowd contributed to the victory as well and would be a big help next week when the Oilers came calling. The Steelers were the only favorite that wasn't upset over the weekend in the NFL playoffs.

Noll had seen the banged-up Oilers upset the San Diego Chargers in a televised game Saturday afternoon, and was pleased — if not as much as his wife, Marianne, admitted — over the outcome. Had the Chargers won, the Steelers would be playing next Sunday in San Diego, where they lost, 35-7, during the regular season. The Steelers are 7-1 in playoff games at Three Rivers, losing here in post-season play only to the Dolphins in 1972.

"We feel good about playing the next one here," Noll acknowledged. "That's part of it. It's much, much better to play at home. You saw those people out there today, they did a great

job. You have to give them an A-plus in all departments."

You'd have to do the same for Terry Bradshaw, too, but he wants the fans to be even better next time out. "The crowd means so much to the team," Bradshaw said. "I wish they were even louder. If any of these players tell you they're not affected by it, they're crazy. They get you going. And if you don't put some points on the scoreboard in a hurry, you'll hear about it."

Bradshaw & Co. couldn't have put the points on the board any quicker than they did yesterday. They had the ball three times in the first quarter and came up with a touchdown each time. And the Dolphins had it twice, and had to punt on fourth down both times. The Steelers controlled the ball for 12:51 of the initial 15 minutes.

"You're killing the clock and coming out with rewards," offered Franco Harris. "That's the kind of stuff we have to have."

The Steelers' offensive line, which included third-year pros Ted Petersen and Steve Courson starting instead of the ailing Jon Kolb and Gerry Mullins, and veterans Mike Webster, Larry Brown and Sam Davis, was driving the Dolphins backward with regularity. Mullins and Bennie Cunningham contributed to the blocking when they were at the tight end positions in short-yardage situations.

"Everyone came through with flying colors," said line coach Rollie Dotsch.

Thornton, who got the starting nod over Rocky Bleier, was running and blocking for Franco with equal ferocity, and Bradshaw was zipping the ball to Swann and Stallworth, and later to Jim Smith with ease. Thornton completed the first drive with a 1-yard trap play through the right side, with Davis delivering the key block.

On the second score, Bradshaw passed 11 yards to Stallworth, who shed one tackler, stiff-armed two others and eluded a fourth for 6 more yards and a 17-yard touchdown. Thornton had been the primary target on that play, but Bradshaw passed instead to Stallworth, who ran down the left side and across the middle to make the catch.

"I managed to slip by a few people," said Stallworth. "I don't know if I kept my feet in. It was good to see the officials' arms go up. On the play, I was going to the other side. I was running an inside curl pattern, but had to improvise."

"John adjusted well," Bradshaw said with a smile. "He adjusted all the way to the end zone. They'll call it a touchdown pass, but it was 90 percent Stallworth, all the way."

The Dolphins' left end, Vern Den Herder, blocked the conversion kick by Matt Bahr, but that didn't slow down the Steelers.

On the third touchdown, Bradshaw dropped back to pass from the Miami 20, ducked an assault by right end Doug Betters and moved up to find Swann standing all alone in the end zone and flipped the ball to him for the touchdown.

"When I brought my head back up," Bradshaw said, "I saw Lynn waving to me. Their cornerman (Norris Thomas) and safety (Neal Colzie) either stopped or came up to stop the run. No one was near Lynn." No one was within 20 yards of Swann when Bradshaw first spotted him, and they had closed to within 10 when Swann snared it.

"We almost had a perfect period, except for some passes of mine," Bradshaw said. "Any time you get 20 points like that, it certainly helps the defense."

With no receivers open, Terry Bradshaw runs for a first down against the Houston defense.

STEELERS BLAST OILERS, SET SIGHTS ON PASADENA

By Jim O'Brien, *The Pittsburgh Press*

PITTSBURGH, JAN. 6, 1980 — "HEY, MOM, PACK YOUR BAGS! We're going to Pasadena."

The Steelers had just defeated the Houston Oilers, 27-13, to win the American Football Conference championship before 50,475 boisterous fans at Three Rivers Stadium, and Dirt Winston was talking enthusiastically on a telephone to his mother back home in Marianna, Ark.

Winston wore a Steelers' uniform, a Pirates' star-studded baseball cap, and a bright, winning smile. His costume captured the championship spirit of the pro sports scene in this town.

"I've already got my bags packed," shrieked Magnolia Winston at the other end. "We knew you were going to win."

Didn't everybody?

In two weeks, the Steelers will be seeking their fourth Super Bowl title in six seasons when they go up against the Los Angeles Rams in Pasadena. The Rams beat the Tampa Bay Buccaneers, 9-0, yesterday to win the National Football Conference championship.

Each Steeler earned $9,000 yesterday and can pick up another $18,000 as the winning share in the Super Bowl.

While Winston was on the telephone, All-Pro center Mike Webster was in a hallway outside the Steelers' clubhouse, kissing his wife, Pamela, and his 3-year-old daughter Brook Winter, and slipping

SCORE BY PERIODS

Houston	7	3	0	3	13
Pittsburgh	3	14	0	10	27

them some ice cold cans of soda. "I'll be out in a while," he promised, as he returned to the team's dressing quarters.

It was a great day for telephoning your

Bradshaw celebrates the Steelers' 27-13 victory over Houston.

mother or kissing your wife and kids, or hugging whoever was next to you at Three Rivers or wherever you were when the Steelers overcame the Oilers to win the AFC title. And for drinking soda or something a little stronger to celebrate the occasion.

Save the champagne for the Super Bowl.

It was a great time to twirl the "Terrible Towel" once more, to remember the best moments of the Steelers' triumph, to toast the opposition for giving it their best shot, and to look to Pasadena for the next challenge.

Chuck Noll could not have been more pleased with his players. "In the beginning, and in the middle, and in the end, I though they showed they wanted it very badly," said the Steelers' smiling coach. "We had respect for the Oilers going into the game and it's no less now.

"So far, we've accomplished two of our goals. We won the division championship and we won the conference championship. We have one more thing to go after. I feel pretty good with two so far. I'd like to make it three out of three."

Lynn Swann, who started and suffered no effects from the leg muscle problem that caused him to pull up lame last Sunday, was looking forward to a return to his native California and a new challenger in Super Bowl XIV.

"We have an opportunity to do something that no one else has ever done," said Swann, "to win back-to-back Super Bowl titles a second time, and to win the Super Bowl four times. We truly want to make Pittsburgh the 'City of Champions.' The Rams will have the home-field advantage, but that's all right.

"The fans would have been for Tampa Bay, too, because John McKay is the coach, and all those USC fans would've turned out to root for his team. People are probably getting bored with us winning all the time. We're like the Yankees used to be in baseball."

Swann was just one of the familiar stars in yesterday's Steeler triumph.

Offensively, there was also Terry Bradshaw, Franco Harris, Rocky Bleier, John Stallworth and Bennie Cunningham, and a line that opened holes for the backs and

kept the Oilers, for the most part, from pressuring Bradshaw when he dropped back to pass.

Defensively, Joe Greene, L.C. Greenwood, Steve Furness, Robin Cole, Jack Lambert, Donnie Shell, Loren Toews and Mel Blount were the most obvious standouts.

They combined to pressure quarterback Dan Pastorini and to limit Earl Campbell, the NFL's leading rusher who was coming back after suffering a groin pull that sidelined him two weeks ago, to 15 yards on 17 carries.

The Steelers also had strong kicking contributions by Matt Bahr and Craig Coquitt.

Bradshaw threw two touchdown passes — 16 yards to Cunningham and 20

yards to Stallworth. Bahr kicked field goals from 21 and 39 yards, and Bleier bolted in for a touchdown from 4 yards out in the last minute, just for good measure.

On the Steelers' first possession; Bradshaw had them moving pretty well when Vernon Perry picked off a pass to Cunningham down the middle and returned it a record 75 yards for a TD 2½ minutes into the contest.

Perry had picked off four passes by San Diego quarterback Dan Fouts the week before, blocked a field goal try, and it appeared that he was capable of leading the Oilers to another upset victory. "I was so mad about that," said Bradshaw, who said he came away from yesterday's game with a terrible headache.

Pittsburgh's Offensive Line Shines

By Pat Livingston, *The Pittsburgh Press*

There was no question that Chuck Noll was proud of the Steelers, this remarkable football team that appears bent on changing the name of the Super Bowl to the Noll Bowl.

"Exceptional plays? We had quite a few of them," said a smiling Noll following the Steelers' 27-13 victory over their division rivals, the Houston Oilers, at Three Rivers Stadium yesterday. But the big thing he didn't want overlooked, he added, was the Steelers' pass protection.

"The protection was exceptionally good," Noll pointed out. "The offensive line did a fine job against a team that was — I don't know — one or two in the league in sacks. Terry (Bradshaw) had a lot of time to throw."

He did at that. Bradshaw, who now has thrown a record 26 touchdowns passes in playoff competition alone, rattled the Oilers with a pair of touchdown passes — to Bennie Cunningham and John Stallworth, naturally. That was more than enough to beat a team that didn't put a touchdown on the board, offensively, the entire afternoon.

The defense took over from there. With a vengeance, it took over.

Using a front that might expect to see only on goal-line or short-yardage situation, the Steelers slanted and stunted as many as eight men in a long, thin line that played in the gaps between Houston's blockers. It was a strategy that was designed to stop what Houston does best, run the football.

Playing the gaps, the Steelers were able to slither and slide through quickly enough to offset Houston's picks and cutbacks and mis-direction plays, those things that often result in game-breaking touchdowns.

That it was effective in stopping the Oilers was obvious. The strategy worked so well that Earl Campbell, the Oilers' punishing runner, was held to just 15 yards in 17 trips and it limited the entire Houston running game to a mere 24 yards in 22 carries.

But that emphasis on the running game, at the risk of leaving themselves vulnerable to Dan Pastorini's passes, was a recognition of the problems Campbell might have posed had he not been stopped as abruptly and as cold as he had been.

"We have a great deal of respect for him, obviously, to play him like that," said Noll. "We don't play every team like that."

Noll wouldn't comment, of course,

The Oilers never scored another touchdown — not one that counted anyhow — and were limited to two field goals by Toni Fritsch, from 27 and 23 yards. Dan Pastorini passed to Mike Renfro for what the Oilers felt should have been another touchdown, but the officials ruled that Renfro didn't have possession before he went out of bounds in the end zone.

"It's sad that this type of controversy has to mar the game," said Swann. His sentiments were echoed by several of the Steelers.

Bleier had a big game, starting instead of Sidney Thornton, who hadn't been able to practice until Friday after spraining an ankle against the Miami Dolphins. He made some big runs and some big catches and enabled Noll to give Thornton two more weeks to get properly recovered for the Rams.

The Steelers have never beaten the Rams with Noll as coach, losing three times, twice during the regular season in which the Steelers went on to win the Super Bowl. The Rams hold a lifetime 10-1-1 record against the Steelers.

"The key to our team is that we know we're good," said Bleier, "and that we've been there before. So we didn't panic when Perry picked off the pass and put them on the scoreboard right away.

"When you see a team like Houston turn the corner, it will be because they believe in themselves. They haven't been there, not yet. Like Los Angeles in the past. They have been one of the most dominant forces in the NFC, but they couldn't get past the Minnesota Vikings or the Dallas Cowboys. They just couldn't turn that corner and get to the Super Bowl."

Now they're there — directed by Ray Malavasi and four former Steeler assistants Dan Radakovich, Lionel Taylor and Bud Carson, who all served on Noll's staff, and Laverne Torgeson, who served three earlier Steeler coaches. Frank Lauterbur, who worked for John Michelosen at Pitt, is also on the staff.

So it should be interesting. "We're the defending champions," said Bleier, "and we're reaching for the pinnacle again."

Magnolia Winston will be among the Steeler fans in Pasadena rooting for them to do just that.

---

on whether Campbell might have been feeling the effects of his injury — "I don't know. You'd have to ask him that," said the coach of the Steelers — but, the general feeling among the players themselves was that Campbell was the Campbell of earlier in the season, coming at them as menacingly and as hard as he ever had.

He was the old Earl Campbell, according to Joe Greene.

"Campbell's a champ," acknowledged Greene. "He came to play. He did what he could do."

"He ran damn hard," confirmed a weary Dwight White, who played an excellent game. "Earl Campbell wasn't missing a beat to me. Keep giving him the ball and he's going to break one. He almost did a few times, but somebody always managed to get to him."

As usual, Bum Phillips was gracious in defeat. He felt after the game that the Oilers, who he conceded were soundly beaten by the Steelers in the playoffs last year, had contributed to their own demise in this one.

"We failed to do the things we could do," said Phillips, "and that's not taking anything away from the Steelers.

"We're proud of ourselves, but we're also proud of the Steelers," continued Phillips, manfully masking the bitter disappointment that gnawed at him. "In a way, that will be us playing against the NFC in the Super Bowl. We're from the same conference, same division, and we'll be rooting for the Steelers.

"I don't think anybody can beat the Pittsburgh except Houston," Bum added, voicing a sentiment that is not altogether unrealistic, "and we didn't do it today."

While some of the Oilers thought a controversial call by side judge Don Orr, which took an apparent touchdown away from Mike Renfro and a 17-17 tie away from the Oilers in the third quarter, might have changed the outcome of the game, Phillips wouldn't buy that hypothesis at all.

"Even after I look at the films, I'm not going to blame the officials," explained Phillips. "They're human. We had 59 minutes to beat Pittsburgh, and we didn't. The play might've changed the outcome, but the game's over now. It's done with. I don't want to talk much about it."

And so it was. And now for Noll and his Steelers, there is one more mountain to climb, and it is a formidable one.

That would be the Los Angeles Rams, who defeated the Tampa Bay Buccaneers, 9-0, in the NFC playoffs four hours after the Steelers had won their battle with Houston. It is a formidable test, for only once have the Steelers beaten the Rams and never have they done it in Los Angeles.

Surprisingly, even Noll's teams, which have met the Rams three times, have never been able to walk away a winner.

STEELERS WIN RECORD 4TH SUPER BOWL

By Jim O'Brien, *The Pittsburgh Press*

PASADENA, JAN. 20, 1980 — A MAN IN BLUE AND YELLOW attire who obviously roots for the Rams was hawking two special souvenir items outside the stadium before yesterday's big game.

"I've got Jack Lambert's missing tooth here," he hollered to all who passed by him. "You can have it for just $3.50!" And he waved a fake fang overhead.

"And I've got Terry Bradshaw's hairpiece!" he cried, twirling a mop of hay. "It's yours for $7!"

Anybody holding Lambert's tooth and Bradshaw's hairpiece has a pair of appropriate souvenirs of Super Bowl XIV.

For the second year in a row, Bradshaw was named the most valuable player as the Steelers came back three times from deficits to defeat the relentless Rams, 31-19, and win their fourth National Football League championship before a record crowd of 103,985 and a TV-audience estimated to be more than 100 million.

Bradshaw and his buddies in black and gold will get $18,000 each as their winning share, which makes for a total of $32,000 in playoff winnings, while the Rams, led by their quarterback, Vince Ferragamo, will have to settle for the runner-up share of $9,000 per player ($23,000 overall), and take pride in the fact that they gave the Steelers a real scare.

The Rams were right when they insisted they were better than they were

SCORE BY PERIODS

L.A. Rams	7	6	6	0	19
Pittsburgh	3	7	7	14	31

given credit for in the pre-game hype, and they, in general, and Ferragamo, in particular, gave the defending Super Bowl champs real fits before falling in the final period, in which the Steelers outscored them, 14-0, to pull this one out.

Bradshaw was the big offensive gun of the Steelers, firing touchdown passes of 47 yards to Lynn Swann and 73 yards to John Stallworth — and those two

Franco Harris blasts through a hole created by Sam Davis (57) and Gerry Mullins (72) in the first quarter against Los Angeles.

Lynn Swann (88) goes airborne between Rams defenders Nolan Cromwell (21) and Pat Thomas to grab a Terry Bradshaw pass.

receivers were fantastic as usual in clutch situations — while Franco Harris twice scored from 1 yard out.

Rookie kicker Matt Bahr broke the ice with a 41-yard field goal midway through the first quarter. But Bahr's extra-point kick with less than two minutes remaining in the game was an even bigger boot — at least for those fans who bet the game and gave less than 12 points to the Rams.

Lambert was the big defensive hero for the Steelers, playing well throughout and picking off a Ferragamo pass in the late going when the Rams were driving for what could have been the game-winning touchdown.

The Steeler defense had its lapses, especially in the secondary, and allowed Ferragamo to get the Rams on the scoreboard and back in the lead after nearly every Steeler score. But the defense made more than its share of big plays, too, and that was the determining factor in the outcome of the contest, perhaps the best and most dramatic of the 14 NFL classics.

Bradshaw has another MVP award and automobile and the Steelers have another Vince Lombardi Trophy, indicative of their supremacy in pro football.

"This is my most satisfying Super Bowl ever," Bradshaw said. "I felt more pressure than in any previous year because we were playing in L.A., and we had never beaten the Rams. This is our fourth Super Bowl title, and our team realized it was on the verge of setting history."

There were more mistakes, offensively and defensively, than the Steelers usually make in a winning effort, but they made the big plays when they had to and that's a point that many of the game's participants made in the post-game interviews.

Sure, Bradshaw had three passes intercepted, but he also threw two touchdown passes and picked up 309 yards through the air, compared to 194 yards passing by the Rams. The Rams outrushed the

Jack Lambert's interception in the final period sealed the Steelers' 31-19 victory.

Steelers, 107-84 yards.

Lambert felt the Steelers' defense was flat in the first half, but it came through in the second half and forced Ferragamo to hurry his passes, when the Steelers weren't sacking him for losses.

"It's not easy," said Bradshaw, who was obviously bushed by the long season and happy it was behind him now, and that the Steelers had survived a series of assaults on their exalted position. He even suggested he would have to do some thinking about returning next season, but it is hard to take him seriously on that point. He admitted later he was just tired, and needed a rest.

"Oh, I'll be back. Like a heavyweight boxing champion who has to defend his title," he said.

He was weary, but ecstatic at the same time. "Everyone has been shooting at us for the last eight years," said Pittsburgh's favorite cowboy. "It's been a tremendous strain on all of us. With everyone saying it's a blow-away game, it doesn't help. There was no doubt in my mind that the Rams would be a tough opponent."

There was doubt in Bradshaw's head, however, that the Steelers would win the Super Bowl, and that just blew his mind altogether and robbed him of sleep all week long at the team's hotel in nearby Newport Beach.

"All I could think about was losing," Bradshaw said. "I wasn't thinking about winning. That's unusual. The score 28-7 kept coming into my mind. I thought someone would win by that score."

He had a hard time getting to sleep on the eve of the game, and got out of bed at 3 a.m. and stayed up listening to tape-recorded mysteries provided him by Lou Riecke, one of Chuck Noll's assistants.

"I was just as nervous as a cat on a hot tin roof," remarked Bradshaw. "I tried to go back to sleep, but I couldn't. This is one game I'm glad is over. I'm going to the Pro Bowl in Hawaii and after that (next Sunday), I'm looking forward to getting away from this scene. I need to get charged up again. Next year will be even more difficult. If there's any one team that can win three in a row, we can

do it."

The Steelers scored on their first possession, thanks to Bahr's 41-yard boot, but the Rams roared right back. Ferragamo passed once to Wendell Tyler to get the drive going, then gave the ball to Tyler, who broke through the left side of the line for 39 yards — the biggest ground gainer of the season against the Steelers.

Lawrence McCutcheon and Tyler took it the rest of the way, on short bursts through the line, and let Cullen Bryant break through the middle for the final yard to give the Rams a 7-3 lead after Frank Corral's conversion kick.

The Steelers got a drive started near the end of the first quarter, with Bradshaw alternating handoffs to Harris and Rocky Bleier once again, this time mixing in two short passes to tight end Bennie Cunningham and one apiece to Swann and Stallworth, the latter putting the ball at the 1-yard line.

Harris took a pitchout around the right end for a touchdown that, along with Bahr's conversion, put the Steelers ahead again at 10-7.

The Rams responded with another scoring drive, with Corral kicking a 31-yard field goal to tie the game, 10-10.

"I thought Vince Ferragamo was great," Bradshaw said. "Every time we did something, or tried to take control of the game, he kept coming back with big plays. He put some fright into us, for sure. I'm more drained than relieved after this. Vince handled himself like a true champion. I didn't think a young man could play like that under these conditions."

On a first-down play, Bradshaw aimed a pass down the middle to Sidney Thornton, but it was intercepted by Rams safety Dave Elmendorf, who returned the ball 10 yards to give the Rams excellent position at the Steelers' 39.

The Rams were restrained, however, mostly because of big sacks by linebacker Robin Cole and end John Banaszak, and had to settle for a 45-yard field goal by Corral, which gave the Rams a 13-10 halftime lead.

Larry Anderson, who had returned kicks 38 yards and 32 yards in the second quarter, came back with a 37-yard return to start the Steelers off in the second half.

It took the Steelers only five plays to put the go-ahead points on the board, Bradshaw passing 47 yards to Swann for the touchdown.

Swann soared high, as only he can, for a sensational catch at the goal line between defensive backs Nolan Cromwell and Pat Thomas.

"When Swann made his touchdown catch," said Joe Greene, "that was the spark we needed."

It gave the Steelers a short-lived 17-13 advantage, but it hardly sparked the Steel-

er defense, which Greene said had been standing around flat-footed in the first half. Greene must have forgotten that the Rams replied with a quick touchdown to pass the Pittsburgh team, 19-17, on their very next possession.

The next time the Steelers got the ball, they began another good drive. Bradshaw pulled a boo-boo when he rolled right and threw back against the grain, something he often criticizes himself for doing, and Elmendorf nearly picked off his second interception at midfield. He had an open field had he not dropped the ball.

Bradshaw came back with another pass to Swann, one the Steeler receiver had to come back for, and he had his feet taken out from under him by Thomas and was knocked dizzy by the hard tackle.

Swann was stretched out on the field for a time, and then went to the sideline. He couldn't see properly out of his right eye and the doctors told him to stay out of action the rest of the way.

The loss of Swann, coupled with a first-half injury to Theo Bell, the team's punt returner, pushed No. 3 receiver Jim Smith into double duty.

On third-and-9 at the Steeler 45, Bradshaw passed to Smith, but it was intercepted by Eddie Brown. "I was so danged mad I couldn't see straight on that second interception," said Bradshaw. "That was a big one because you don't want to come away with less than three points when you get that far."

The third quarter ended with the Rams still clinging to a precarious 19-17 lead.

Early in the final period, Smith was

Two Keys: Noll, Anderson

By Pat Livingston, *The Pittsburgh Press*

While the strong arm of Terry Bradshaw and the sure hands of John Stallworth and Lynn Swann dominated the Steelers' victory over the Los Angeles Rams in Super Bowl XIV yesterday, the sharp eye of Chuck Noll and the quick feet of Larry Anderson had a lot to do with this unprecedented triumph.

Noll's aides were expressing their amazement at the man's uncanny ability to detect things on the field that other, less sharp-eyed observers would be likely to miss.

And it was Anderson's sparkling kickoff returns, following practically all of Los Angeles' scores, that kept reminding the upset-minded home team that there was still life in the old champion yet.

"Chuck Noll is an amazing man,"

said Rollie Dotsch, the silver-haired coach who handles the Steelers' offensive line. "Just having him on the sidelines is the equivalent of having an extra man on the field."

What amazed Dotsch yesterday was Noll's uncanny ability to see what was going on, analyze it quickly and come up with solutions and adjustments.

"I swear, Chuck sees everything that's going on with 22 men on the field," said Dotsch, slumped in the seat of the bus that would take the Steelers back to Newport Beach for their postgame celebration. "He's got the lousiest seat on the field, but there's nothing he doesn't see. He doesn't miss a trick.

"I have all kinds of trouble watching my people on the offensive line, but he

sees the linemen, the quarterback, the receivers and the defense all at the same time. It's incredible. It's just not real."

Anderson's contribution was more germane. Five times, he took the kickoff and, except for his final return, Anderson's dazzling feet gave the Rams fits. Three times, but for the last tackler on the field, he might have gone all the way.

The 177-pound defensive back returned the first one 45 yards, setting the stage for the Steelers to march in for their first touchdown. On the opening kickoff of the second half, he gave Bradshaw working room for another score, the remarkable pass to Swann.

"My mom was here," said Anderson, elated with himself over a performance that earned him a game ball. "She came out here to see me play, and I had to do something to please her. Last year she missed the Super Bowl because she was sick.

"Mom" is Pauline Anderson of Shreveport, La., a special education

driven backward to field a 59-yard punt by the Rams' Ken Clark, and brought it back 7 yards to the Steeler 25.

Harris hit the line for 2 yards, then Thornton dropped a pass from Bradshaw on the first two plays. Bradshaw then fired a pass to Stallworth, who caught the ball at the Rams' 32 and ran the rest of the way for a touchdown just before the three-minute mark. Bahr's kick made it 24-19 in the Steelers' favor.

Ferragamo fired passes to Preston Dennard and Billy Waddy and for a while, appeared capable of directing the Rams to another score, and possibly their first Super Bowl title.

The Steelers were nervous on the sideline. But a Ferragamo pass for Smith was snatched out of the air by Lambert, who returned it 16 yards to the Steeler 30.

With less than 5 1/2 minutes remaining in the game, the Steelers mounted one last TD drive. Bradshaw hooked up with Stallworth on the same pattern — a hook-and-go — that had resulted in the earlier TD.

This time Stallworth made a sensational catch of a ball that came directly over his head, one of the toughest areas in which to receive a ball. The play brought the ball to the Rams' 27.

Two plays later, Bradshaw's pass to Smith in the end zone was incomplete, but pass interference was called on Thomas, giving the Steelers a first down at the 1.

It took three plays before a bolt over left tackle by Harris produced the TD that sealed the Rams' fate. Bahr's kick made a lot of bettors happy and some

quite sad, depending on which way they went with a spread that started at 10 points and went as high as 13 before the kickoff.

Asked if the Steelers were the greatest team in the history of football, Coach Noll said, "I don't think I have to answer that. The casts speak for themselves. I don't have to say it. The Steelers have proven themselves."

Talking about his team's game plan, Noll said, "We tried to go deep as often as we could to get the big play because we knew they would take away the high percentage passes. This was a game between two good defensive football teams. But it was characterized by the big play. That's why it was high scoring. The Rams played well. They wanted it badly."

teacher who had to miss the team party because she had to catch a 1 a.m. plane to get back to Shreveport for her classes today.

"I'm glad she came," said Anderson, whose only glimpse of her was toward the end of the game when she came down from the stands, closer to the field.

He had such a spectacular game with the five returns and 162 yards — both Super Bowl records. The 162 yards, as a matter of fact, exceeded the career record of Miami's Eugene (Mercury) Morris, who had 123 yards in returns in three games.

"The sunshine, the grass field," said Anderson, a second-year man from Bradshaw's school, Louisiana Tech, "the excitement" of being in the game. The adrenaline started flowing.

"I'm so excited, I'm shakin," he continued. "To have a day like this, after what I'd been through earlier in the year — the fumbles, the things like that. Man, it's great to be alive."

A teammate stopped by to shake Larry's hand. "A lot of people will know Larry Anderson now," he said.

"Think so?" Anderson said. There were other heroes in the game as well — the offensive line that gave Bradshaw such fine protection, that he didn't suffer a sack by a team which prides itself in its ability to sack quarterbacks. The defense, which after being caught by surprise on Larry McCutcheon's halfback pass for a score, shut down the Rams for the last 22 minutes of the game.

And there was Bradshaw, the field general, not the passer.

"They were stealing our audibles," said offensive tackle Larry Brown. "Probably something that Bud Carson and Bad Rad (Dan Radakovich) picked up. But that worked against them a couple of times and we broke through for some big plays.

"Bradshaw told us to disregard the audible in the huddle," explained Brown. "Then he goes out and audibles anyway, the switch. And then he'd

run the original play. He crossed them up a few times."

Dotsch had some other heroes he mentioned, other than his boss. Speaking of Brown, a tight end who had been converted to tackle, Dotsch was effusive in his praise of the 6-4, 260-pound lineman from Kansas.

"Give Larry another year and he's going to be an All-Pro tackle. People are beginning to recognize that now," said Dotsch. "Did you see the way he handled Jack Youngblood? Youngblood's a player — he had something like 16 sacks — but he didn't get near Terry today.

"And Jon Kolb. I can't believe the job he did on (Fred) Dryer. In the second half, Kolb was hurting. He couldn't lift his arm above his chest, but he played a helluva game.

"These are some kind of men, some kind of men," Rollie added, shaking his head, admiration dripping from his voice. They must be. That's why they're champs.

STEELERS CRUSH JETS, CLINCH WILD-CARD SPOT

By Ron Cook, *The Pittsburgh Press*

FLUSHING, N.Y., DEC. 10, 1983 — CENTER MIKE WEBSTER needed only one word to describe the mood in the Steelers' locker room yesterday.

"Relief — I feel like the world has been lifted off our shoulders."

The Steelers' 34-7 thrashing of the New York Jets, sparked by the return of quarterback Terry Bradshaw, did that trick. It not only snapped the Steelers' three-game losing streak, it also clinched a wild-card playoff berth and all but assured them of the American Football Conference's Central Division championship, regardless of what they do in Sunday's regular season finale in Cleveland.

The loss snapped the Jets' three-game winning streak and eliminated them from the playoff chase.

"I was scared to death today," Webster said. "The last three weeks, we probably played worse than we have since I've been here. We had one foot over the cliff and the other one right on the edge.

"I kept saying to myself, 'We went to training camp in July and worked so hard. We started 9-2 and all of sudden we're 9-5. Are we going to give up and let everything slip away?'

"Even my brother called me up last week and told me my team had no character. What could I say? You can say, 'Yes, it does,' but you've still got to go

SCORE BY PERIODS

Pittsburgh	7	13	7	7	34
N.Y. Jets	0	0	7	0	7

out on the field and prove it."

To listen to the Jets (7-8), the Steelers proved it yesterday.

"We got an old-fashioned buttkicking," Coach Joe Walton said.

"We weren't just beaten," defensive end Mark Gastineau said, "we were embarrassed."

The Steelers won largely because of two Bradshaw touchdown passes, a ground game that produced a season-high 242 yards and a hungry defense that allowed the Jets only 251 total yards, including a season-low 36 on the ground.

"That's the way football is supposed to be played," Steelers linebacker Jack Lambert said. "Your offense is supposed to score points and your defense is supposed to prevent points."

"No matter how low you get, you have to pick yourself up off the deck," Webster said. "You know what they say

about a wounded tiger. If you back him into a corner far enough, he's going to come out fighting harder. I think that's what happened to us."

The return of Bradshaw, who made his first game appearance since a playoff loss to the San Diego Chargers in January, gave the Steelers a big lift.

His 17-yard touchdown pass to rookie Gregg Garrity gave them a 7-0 lead with 5:15 left in the first quarter. His 10-yard touchdown pass to Calvin Sweeney gave them a 14-0 spread with 14:16 remaining in the second period.

Bradshaw left the game after the second touchdown, complaining of a sore right elbow and forearm. Elbow surgery last March sidelined him for the first 14 weeks of the season.

"Terry showed a lot of courage today," Steelers running back Franco Harris said. "His arm's still bothering him but he gave us 14 points. That's all we needed."

Harris and backfield partner Frank Pollard, along with the Steelers defense, made sure of that. Harris carried 26 times for 103 yards — his fifth 100-yard game of the season and the 52nd of his career. He is only 49 yards shy of a National Football League record eighth 1,000-yard season.

"We played with a lot more confidence today. Instead of wondering if the passing game and the running game were going to work, we decided we were going to make them work."

Center Mike Webster, who played in nine Pro Bowl games, anchored the Steelers' offensive line during their glory years of the 1970's.

Pollard added 78 rushing yards on 15 carries and caught three passes for 34 yards.

"The offensive line made it easy today. They opened great holes against what I think is the best defensive line in pro football."

The Steelers' ground attack and the early 14-0 lead, which became 20-0 by halftime thanks to Gary Anderson field goals of 29 and 40 yards, opened the passing game for backup Cliff Stoudt.

He completed 8 of 15 passes for 83 yards and two touchdowns. His 13-yard scoring pass to tight end Bennie Cunningham gave the Steelers a 27-0 lead with 6:20 left in the third quarter.

"Cliff could have come in and said, 'The heck with it,'" Webster said. "He could have been down in the dumps because he was the starter and now he's in a backup role. But he accepted that, played well and gave us a big lift."

Stoudt and Sweeney hooked up for the Steelers' final touchdown, an 18-yard pass with 10:45 left in the game. His second touchdown reception of the day left Sweeney in a delightful mood. He and the other Steelers wide receivers were blamed for much of the offense's difficulties in the three consecutive losses to Minnesota, Detroit and Cincinnati.

"I think I was playing a little too tight, trying to please too many people. I just decided to relax and play football and stop trying to live up to other people's expectations. I'm never going to be a Lynn Swann or a John Stallworth. I'm Calvin Sweeney, and I think I'm a pretty good wide receiver."

All the Steelers could afford to feel good about themselves. They looked like a solid football team for the first time since Nov. 13, when they defeated the Baltimore Colts, 24-13.

"I'm ecstatic," Webster said.

"So am I," Harris said. "We're in the playoffs. Now, it's time to go."

BRADSHAW: TRIUMPH OF HEAD, HEART

By Bob Smizik, *The Pittsburgh Press*

On a cool, sunny afternoon in what might be the last professional football game ever played at Shea Stadium, Terry Bradshaw came back. It was like he had never been away. It was like he had taken his last snap in anger a week ago, not almost a year ago.

Terry Bradshaw came back yesterday against the New York Jets and he brought the Steelers with him. What was threatening to become an all-time great collapse has been averted. The playoffs are assured, the division championship is almost as certain. The quarterback who only weeks ago wondered if he would ever play again has, as he did so often before, made everything right with the Steelers.

In a triumph of head and heart, Terry Bradshaw returned to the starting lineup for the first time since last season and gave the Steelers the spark they needed to score a 34-7 victory over the Jets.

"It was like he never missed a game," said wide receiver Calvin Sweeney, who caught two touchdown passes. "We were lacking a leader. We needed someone to step out front. That's Brad. He did it today."

But this story has no certain happy ending. The arm that was able to deliver the ball so well in practice, found game conditions vastly different. Less than a minute into the second quarter, after throwing his second touchdown pass of the game and his fifth completion in eight tries, Terry Bradshaw removed himself from play.

"I just couldn't throw the ball anymore," he said.

His status for Sunday's regular-season finale with the Cleveland Browns is in doubt. The injury officially has been termed a bruise of the right forearm and elbow, the same elbow that required offseason surgery and kept Bradshaw on the injured reserved list until eight days ago.

"It's swollen and sore," he said. "I have no way of knowing if I can play next week."

But beyond that he is certain.

"I hope I can play in Cleveland, but I don't want to rush it. I'm hoping that in three weeks (the Steelers' first play-off game if they win the division championship) I'll be able to play. With three weeks rest, I should be able to do it."

And if he can't, the news isn't all that bad. Cliff Stoudt also came back yesterday. Stoudt, benched in favor of Bradshaw after three consecutive sub-par performances, put six points on the board before the half ended in a less-than-inspiring performance. But, in his own mind at least, he turned the corner in the second half by passing for two touchdowns.

"My confidence is back," Stoudt said. "Even though we didn't move the ball that well in the first half, I was throwing with confidence. I had zip on the ball. I felt good about the way I was throwing. Last week I had my sinkerball going. This week I was throwing with some zing. I wasn't dancing around in the pocket like I was last week.

"I redeemed myself. I got my self-respect back."

Any doubt that Bradshaw could do the job was quickly erased in the minds of his teammates and shortly thereafter in the minds of everyone else watching the game.

"Brad exudes confidence and his confidence rubs off on everyone else," said tight end Bennie Cunningham. "Before the first play, he came into the huddle and said, 'All right, boys. We're going to have fun today.' Right then I knew it was our day."

Bradshaw knew it, too.

"I was as nervous as all get-out this morning," he said, "but once I got on the field, it was like a duck hitting water. I was right at home.

"I was apprehensive about not knowing how I would handle the pass rush. I had thrown the ball well in practice but had not faced a pass rush, especially a pass rush like the Jets have."

After his first pass, an incompletion intended for Sweeney on the Steelers' third play. Bradshaw had no more apprehension about the pass rush.

He completed his next pass, a 24-yarder to Cunningham the next time the Steelers had the ball, and a masterful performance was under way. It was a drive that was the beginning of the end for the Jets and also for Bradshaw.

Scrambling out of the pocket on a third-and-10 from the 17. Bradshaw passed into the end zone for a touchdown to Gregg Garrity. But the pass put a strain on Bradshaw's arm that his eight days of practice had not prepared him for.

"You don't practice running across the field and throwing the ball 30 yards," he said.

But he complained to no one.

"It wasn't that bad. It was just hurting."

On the Steelers' next possession, Bradshaw kept the team mostly on the ground as they moved from their own 29 to the Jets' 10. He threw only once, a screen to Frank Pollard that was good for 17 yards. But on a third-and-6, he threw into the end zone, hitting Sweeney on a slant pattern. The Jets were blitzing and Bradshaw had to hurry.

"My arm isn't strong enough to throw that way. I had to throw it in an uneven way. It hurt. I couldn't throw anymore.

"I could have stayed in and directed a running attack, but there are things I wanted to do and if your arm won't let you, you better get out. It would only have made it worse."

Besides, Stoudt was ready.

"We got a good quarterback, why not give him a chance?" Bradshaw said.

But a competitor such as Bradshaw does not like to leave a task unfinished. He also left unfulfilled.

"I'm sick that I didn't finish," he said. "This was one of the greatest challenges I've ever had. I relished that. I wanted to pull it off in the worst way."

And, of course, he did.

"I believe I had the guys ready to play. I talked to them about it all week. I told them what I wanted them to do.

"I think I gave them a spark. When I turned it over to Cliff, the spark was still there."

And he left little doubt that he believes he can ignite the spark again, if not next week, then in the playoffs.

"I've proved to myself that I can do it. I know I can go into the game and throw the football. I don't think I have to throw it practice anymore to prove it to myself. I've just got to get myself involved in the mental part of the game. I know I can throw."

STEELER TRIUMPH OVER NINERS IS A BLOCK PARTY

By Ron Cook, *The Pittsburgh Press*

SAN FRANCISCO, OCT. 14, 1984 — FORGET MARK MALONE, who performed superbly and made Charles Henry Noll admit yes, he has a quarterback controversy on his hands.

Forget Frank Pollard, who rushed for 105 yards and stirred a pulse in a ground game that previously did not have one.

Forget John Stallworth, who diagrammed the game-tying touchdown play in the Candlestick Park dirt and made it work with a leaping catch.

And forget Bryan Hinkle, who outfoxed a brilliant quarterback and made the interception that won the game.

The Steelers' 20-17 victory over the San Francisco 49ers belonged to the offensive linemen.

Who would have believed those beleaguered souls would rise up and take their moment in the sun? Who would have thought they would come out on a pearl of an autumn afternoon and open the game with a 12-play, 78-yard touchdown drive? And, after they lost guard Terry Long, tackle Larry Brown and tight end Chris Kolodziejski to injuries, who would have believed they would finish their work with a 15-play, 83-yard touchdown drive?

It happened. All of it. Much to the chagrin of the 49ers, who lost for the first time in seven games.

Next Sunday, when the Steelers (4-3)

SCORE BY PERIODS

Pittsburgh	7	3	0	10	20
San Francisco	0	7	0	10	17

----

visit Indianapolis, it probably will be a different story because of the injuries. But Noll was not thinking about next Sunday. He was too busy comparing the relatively inconsequential victory — it stretched the Steelers' American Football Conference Central Division lead to three game — to his greatest triumphs.

"Super Bowl victories are great, but I don't think I've ever been associated with a victory any better than this one. We had guys playing who were beat up and hurt. They wanted it very badly."

It showed on the long drives.

The last was a thing of beauty. It came after San Francisco took a 17-10 lead, thanks to defensive end Gary Johnson, who beat guard Emil Boures and crunched Malone as he threw; linebacker Keena Turner, who intercepted Malone's pass and returned it 19 yards to the Steelers 20; and running back Wendell Tyler, who scored on a 7-yard run with 10:48 left.

The Steelers did much of their damage with Mike Webster at center, Boures and Blake Wingle at the guards, and Steve August and Tunch Ilkin at the tackles. Ray Snell limped off with a sprained ankle early in the second half, then jumped back in at tackle, and Ilkin moved out to tight end after Kolodziejski was injured. Wide receiver Weegie Thompson also played tight end in short-yardage situations.

"All I did was go straight ahead," said August, who joined the team last Thursday and still is learning the playbook.

"Ray had to go back in," Webster said. "Either that or we were going to have to put a helmet on (center-guards coach) Bill Meyers."

"It was crazy," Malone said. "We were calling plays out of formations we never ran before. Tunch kept going back and forth to the officials, reporting in as a tight end. We had guys huffing and puffing. We had guys hurt.

"Webbie is great in situations like that. He was telling the guys. 'Come off the ball. Don't make mistakes. We'll get it in.'"

"We believed him," Ilkin said. "Everyone made up his mind that we were going to overcome anything that happened."

The drive lasted seven minutes, 27 seconds. Malone called 10 running plays for 52 yards and passed 11 yards to Wayne Capers, 22 yards to Kolodziejski and 6 yards for the touchdown to

Frank Pollard's 105-yard rushing performance against San Francisco evoked memories of the days of Franco Harris and Rocky Bleier.

Stallworth, who caught the ball over cornerback Ronnie Lott with 3:21 left.

"We've always felt like we could run the ball," Ilkin said. "We just have to stick with it a little more than we have been. That was the difference. That, and the fact that we won on first down. We had some big gains on first down."

As important as the drive was, Webster said the first "set the tone for the whole game."

It lasted six minutes, 21 seconds. Pol-

Stallworth Makes the Call

By John Clayton, *The Pittsburgh Press*

John Stallworth had a secret he could not wait to unveil to 59,118 fans, 11 San Francisco defenders and Steelers offensive players.

Trailing, 17-10, the Steelers were at the 49ers 6, stalled by their mistakes and the opposition. Five plays near the 49ers' goal line failed, so Stallworth had an idea. He suggested to quarterback Mark Malone that he run a pattern toward the corner of the end zone against Ronnie Lott, the talented but lame 49ers cornerback. Malone agreed, but both decided to let the rest of the offense execute a running play.

"We're in the huddle and I hear Mark call, 'Ride, 32 trap and Stallworth, you do an I-cut,'" tackle Tunch Ilkin said. "As I'm coming up to the line, I was thinking to myself, 'What the heck are we doing here?'"

What they were doing was winning the game.

Stallworth got behind Lott for a 6-yard touchdown reception that tied the score at 17 with 3:21 to play.

The 49ers shock continued when linebacker Bryan Hinkle returned a Joe Montana interception 43 yards to set up Gary Anderson's game-winning field goal to give the Steelers a 20-17 upset over the previously undefeated 49ers yesterday.

From a raw receiver from Tuscaloosa, Ala., who came to the Steelers 10 years ago, Stallworth has become the team's all-time leading receiver, most valuable offensive player, on-the-field leader and now assistant play-caller. Even though Malone and Coach Chuck Noll shared the play calling, about 70-30, Stallworth called the two most important plays. Not only did his touchdown idea work, an earlier suggestion worked by default.

On a fourth down at the 49ers' 6, Stallworth wanted to run a crossing pattern against cornerback Eric Wright. Malone threw the pass, but Wright knocked it down with his right hand. Unfortunately for Wright, officials spotted his left hand on Stallworth's back and called him for interference, giving the Steelers a first down at the 1.

Wright, who was penalized three times for interference, did not protest, but he felt he had not touched Stallworth on that play. Yet he admitted he held Stallworth other times.

"He's one of the best receivers in the league when he's healthy," Wright said. "Earlier in the fourth quarter when he almost made a catch (an intermediate pass on second down from the 49ers' 35) and I kept grabbing him. I thought I was going to be called on that. I didn't think (the goal-line play) was a good call. When I had seen the flag go out. I didn't go toward the referee to see if he had called me. I thought it was a good play."

Stallworth caught six passes for 78 yards and a touchdown, drew two interference penalties from Wright and pulled Malone through his first victory as a starting quarterback. For the season, Stallworth has 33 catches for 656 yards, a pace that would enable him to break his team record of 70 catches and Buddy Dial's 21-year-old yardage record of 1,295.

"He's great," said Lott, who is slowed by ankle problems. "He's a Hall of Famer, or should be. He's competitive. He competes on every play. He never quits. If he's close to the ball, you know he's going to catch it. He didn't get to the Super Bowl four times for nothing. I've always said that John Stallworth is a better receiver than Lynn Swann."

To beat the 49ers' secondary, a receiver must be competitive. Lott, Wright, Dwight Hicks and Carlton Williamson have been together four years. They don't just stop receivers. They punish them.

"They like to jam receivers," Stallworth said. "I remember one guy in the films that they jammed onto the ground. They are aggressive, and you have to not be afraid to be aggressive.

"We were not afraid to get a few offensive interference calls. You have to be aggressive against their defense."

The problem, though, was being elusive. The ankle injury that has forced rookie sensation Louis Lipps out of the lineup for two weeks has taken away Stallworth's insurance against double coverage. Last week against Miami, for example, he said he received double coverage every time he was in the slot. Against the 49ers, Stallworth kept switching sides, challenging Lott one play, Wright the next.

"They had me really off-guard the first half of the game to the point where they would go deep on me to begin with, and I couldn't tighten up my coverage," Wright said. "When I was driving my intermediate routes, he would then take off. They were well prepared coming to me. They studied me real well. I adjusted in the second half."

Perhaps Stallworth's most brilliant achievement was the way he drew a 13-yard interference call on Wright when his mind was preoccupied by a cramp in a leg. Pain shot through Stallworth's leg as a high pass headed toward the sideline. Stallworth turned, leaped and was nudged by Wright, who was trying to go for the interception.

"I was more concerned about the cramp than the interference," Stallworth said.

Mark Malone connected on three passes, including a 6-yard touchdown pass to John Stallworth, in the game-winning drive.

lard carried three time for 23 yards. Thompson caught a 23-yard pass and halfback Rich Erenberg scored on a 2-yard run.

"I'll tell you why we ran the ball so well," said Pollard, who enjoyed the first 100-yard game of his five-year career. "It's because we didn't kill ourselves with mistakes like we did in the past."

That is not entirely true.

There were plenty of mistakes. Early in the third quarter, the Steelers turned a first-and-10 at the San Francisco 37 into a third-and-41 at their 32, thanks to holding penalties on Brown and Kolodziejski, a delay-of-game penalty against Malone and a 7-yard sack by

defensive end Dwaine Board, who blew by Snell.

Ilkin jumped offside three times. Wingle jumped offside at the 49ers' 1-yard line during the game-tying drive but was saved by Stallworth.

"Those things are going to happen," Webster said. "It's not a sin to get knocked down, but it is a sin to stay down. Our guys got back up today."

The Steelers still needed a big defensive play and a little luck to win.

Hinkle took care of the defensive play, intercepting quarterback Joe Montana's sideline pass to Bill Ring and returning it 43 yards to the San Francisco 3. Gary Anderson kicked the game-winner — a 21-yard field goal — with 1:42 left.

"Hinkle made a fantastic play," Steelers linebacker Jack Lambert said. "I thought the ball was over his head, but he made a heck of an effort to get to it. It's amazing considering his knee is bothering him as much as it is."

San Francisco kicker Ray Wersching took care of the luck. He pulled a 37-yard field goal try wide left after Montana moved the 49ers from their 26 with 1:36 and no timeouts left to the Steelers' 20 with 10 seconds remaining.

"Everything — the snap, the hold — was perfect but me," Wersching said. "When I hit the ball, it felt good and I thought the kick was good. Then, I looked up and saw that it wasn't going through. I guess my placement foot was too close to the ball."

"I knew he was going to miss," Hinkle said, "because we worked our butts off and deserved to win."

"I knew he was going to miss, too," Webster said. "That was justice."

Not so much for the Steelers. But for their offensive linemen.

Despite two fumbles inside the Steelers' 25, Mark Malone bounced back and directed his team to a 24-17 victory.

PITTSBURGH PROVES IT IS A TEAM WITH GUTS

By Ron Cook, *The Pittsburgh Press*

DENVER, DEC. 30, 1984 — CORNERBACK DWAYNE WOODRUFF spoke for the defense.

"Our attitude is simple. Teams aren't going to score on us. Period. It doesn't matter if they start at our 1-yard line or the 4 or the 20. They're not going to score. If they do, we're not doing our job."

Quarterback Mark Malone spoke for the offense.

"After they went ahead (17-10) in the third quarter, I told the guys in the huddle, 'If you want to win this game, now's the time. You've got to win it right now.'

"It was amazing to sit there and watch their reaction. It was like someone shot them up with adrenaline. They went berserk and we went up the field."

Guard Craig Wolfley spoke for the team.

"I'm not sure how I can explain the feeling we have. It's just that we feel like we can't die in the game. Somehow, someway we're going to get it done.

"You might say," Wolfey said, pausing for effect and smiling the smile of a man who just pocketed $18,000 and laughed at everyone who said it couldn't be done, "that this football team has guts."

Yes, at last, you might say the Steel-

SCORE BY PERIODS

Pittsburgh	0	10	7	7	24
Denver	7	0	10	0	17

----

ers have guts.

There are reasons:

■ They defeated the Denver Broncos — the National Football League's third-best team, thanks to a 13-3 record — in an American Football Conference first-round playoff game.

■ They outplayed the Broncos worse than the 24-17 score indicates.

■ They pulled the upset before 74,981 hostile fans at Mile High Stadium, where the Broncos had won 13 of their past 14 games.

■ They survived two Malone fumbles inside their 25, three missed Gary Anderson field goals and a blocked Craig Colquitt punt.

■ They outdefensed the NFL's second-most opportunistic defense.

■ They rushed for 169 yards against that defense — fifth-best in the league vs. the run.

■ They earned a trip to the AFC championship game at Miami Sunday.

■ And, perhaps in the biggest display of courage, they talked of beating the Dolphins — who mugged them, 31-7, at Three Rivers Stadium Oct. 7 — and advancing to the Super Bowl.

"We're one game away from The Big One," Malone said. "If that doesn't get you ready to play, nothing will.

"We're a far different team than when we played Miami before. And they're a different team. Back then, we wondered, 'Can those guys be beaten?' Now, we know they can be beaten. They've shown that. They've shown they can make mistakes, too."

"I'm glad the game's at Miami," linebacker Robin Cole said. "They already came to our place and stuffed us. It's time for us to go down there and shut their people up."

"I'm sure no one will give us much of a chance, but that's fine with us," free safety Eric Williams said. "That just pulls us together. We talk about how this paper says this about us and that paper says that and we can't understand it. We've beaten several good teams now and people still say we're sorry."

No longer.

Williams muzzled the critics and eliminated the Broncos when he stepped in front of wide receiver Ray Alexander, intercepted a John Elway pass and returned it 28 yards to the Broncos' 2 with 2:45 left. Fullback Frank Pollard scored the game-winner three plays later on a 2-yard run.

"It still seems like a dream," Williams said. "I expected someone else to do something like that. Not me."

Williams' play was typical of the Steelers' defense:

■ It allowed only seven points after Malone lost fumbles at the Steelers' 23 and 22 in the first four plays.

■ It ended a second-quarter drive at the Steelers' 6 when nose tackle Gary Dunn intercepted an Elway pass.

■ It allowed just three points early in the third quarter after Roger Jackson blocked Colquitt's punt out of bounds at the Steelers' 4.

■ It held running back Sammy Winder — 1,153-yard rusher and the Broncos' lone Pro Bowler — to 37 yards on 15 carries.

That makes six 1,000-yard rushers it has throttled this season. Eric Dickerson, Gerald Riggs, Wendell Tyler, Marcus Allen, Freeman McNeil and Winder combined for 293 yards on 99 carries — a 3.0 average.

"We have the kind of defense that, if you're an offensive player, you don't want to sit down when you come off the field," Malone said. "You stand on the sideline anticipating them making the big play. You almost expect it."

The Steelers' defense broke once, allowing the Broncos to go ahead, 17-10, when Elway threw a 20-yard touchdown pass to wide receiver Steve Watson with 7:15 left in the third quarter. Watson finished with 11 catches for 177 yards.

Enter Malone, who made his inspired speech.

"It's amazing the way the attitude on this team has changed around and grown. Earlier in the year, when we

Running primarily with Frank Pollard (30) and Walter Abercrombie (34), the Steelers rushed for 169 yards against one of the league's best defenses.

made turnovers or mistakes, we didn't respond and bounce back like we should. Now, we're a team that never says, 'It's all over. Let's go home.' We keep going 100 miles an hour until the game's over."

Rookie wide receiver Louis Lipps sparked the game-tying, seven-play, 66-yard drive.

He started it with a 34-yard kickoff return and ended it with a 10-yard touchdown catch with 3:19 left in the third quarter. In between, he caught 23- and 17-yard passes.

Running back Walter Abercrombie took over in the fourth quarter.

He carried five times for 30 yards

as the Steelers moved to the Broncos' 9 with 3:40 left. Coach Chuck Noll was encouraged, even after Anderson missed a 26-yard field goal that kept the Broncos even.

"I liked the way we ran the football. We have to run it and control it against Miami. We have to keep it away from them. They're a big-play team so we have to be a big-play team."

The Steelers were just that two plays later when Williams made his interception.

In the fourth quarter, when the Steelers needed a touchdown to win the game, they gave the ball to Frank Pollard.

Steelers owner Art Rooney with his team's first three Super Bowl trophies. He added a fourth after the Steelers' 31-19 win in Super Bowl XIV.

ART ROONEY: A LEGEND IN THE NFL AND IN LIFE

By Steve Halvonik, *Pittsburgh Post-Gazette*

PITTSBURGH, AUG. 26, 1988 — ED MCCASKEY WAS A LOVE-struck college student, singing in a smoky Philadelphia bar, the night Art Rooney Sr. paid him a visit.

Rooney, the founder and owner of the Steelers, was in the company of Bert Bell, a co-founder of the Philadelphia Eagles who had just become Rooney's right-hand man in Pittsburgh.

The two men were in Philadelphia at the request of George Halas, their good friend and owner of the Chicago Bears. Halas wanted them to get the skinny on this McCaskey, who was courting his daughter Virginia, a student at Drexel.

Virginia was talking marriage, and Halas wasn't sure he liked his daughter dating a saloon singer, even if the kid was doing it only to pay his way through the University of Pennsylvania.

The year was 1941.

"As you know, George Halas was at his height then," McCaskey said. "I was walking on campus one day and two guys in double-breasted camel's hair overcoats, one with a cigar in his face, walked up to me.

" 'You McCaskey? I'm Bert Bell and this is Art Rooney. Halas sent us here to investigate you.' "

McCaskey said the two men left and caught up with him later that night at the saloon. They had been to see Bill Lennox, the ticket manager at Penn.

" 'Bill Lennox said you're OK, and if you're OK with Bill Lennox, you're OK with me,' " McCaskey said Bell told him.

"Then Art took his cigar out of his face and said, 'If you're OK with Bert, you're OK with me. And whoever said Halas was an angel?' "

Rooney died yesterday morning at age 87, eight days after being stricken with a stroke. His many friends and admirers honored him in the way he would have liked most: with a good story.

"Cigars and stories. That's what I think of first when I think of Mr. Rooney," said Lynn Swann, the former receiver. "He was always telling stories. And the miracle of it is, he never told the same story twice."

Rooney was truly a legend in the National Football League; a larger-than-life figure who was blessed with the common touch. A man called "The Chief" who never once acted the part.

"One time he was up in Canada and he sent me a postcard right in the middle of the off-season," said Gary Dunn, the Steelers' nose tackle who was released by the team this week. "I picked up this postcard and I'm reading it and it says, 'Gary how's your off-season going? I'm up here in Canada and just been thinking about you. Hope you're doing fine and hope your mother's fine, and we're looking forward to a good year this year and I want to thank you.'

"I'm reading it and I'm looking at the bottom and it says, 'Art Rooney.' And it just set me back. I just couldn't believe that someone like him would take the time, in the middle of a trip somewhere, to send my something like that. It really meant a lot to me."

Rooney, who formed the Steelers in 1933, was the last living link to the founding fathers of the NFL. He lived long enough to see his team shake off four decades of losing and become the dominant team of the 1970's, winning four Super Bowls in six seasons.

"Art Rooney led his beloved Pittsburgh Steelers for more than half a century in the NFL, but he was a man who belonged to the entire sports world," said NFL Commissioner Pete Rozelle. "It is questionable whether any sports figure was any more universally loved and respected. His calm, selfless counsel made him a valuable contributor within the NFL. But he will be remembered by all he touched for his innate warmth, gentleness, compassion and charity."

Rooney's death follows that of Mayor Caliguiri, who died May 6.

"The passing of Art Rooney has taken from us another civic and community leader who was the essence and embodiment of the spirit of our city," said Mayor Masloff. "There are very few men and women whose names are synonymous with their particular city, but Art Rooney will always mean Pittsburgh to all of us."

Rooney wasn't just the patriarch of the Steelers; he was a friend to the other sports franchises in the city.

"The entire Pittsburgh Pirates organization is deeply saddened by the passing today of Art Rooney," said Carl F. Barger, president of the Pirates. "He was a devoted friend of the City of Pittsburgh and the Pittsburgh Pirates. Very rarely can the word 'legend' be properly attached to someone, but it is certainly appropriate in describing

The Chief in 1967.

how deeply he will be missed."

"I think he symbolized the style of the Steelers and the style of Pittsburgh," said Edward J. DeBartolo Sr. the Penquins' owner, who bought Randall Park in Ohio from Rooney and his associates. "He was respected by everyone. I know that's a trite expression, but everyone did respect him. He's going to be a big loss."

Two other members of Pirates' management, General Manager Syd Thrift and Manager Jim Leyland, both recalled that Rooney seemed to know when a kind word was needed.

"He always seemed to show up at the right time to give me encouragement and support," Thrift said. "I had a deep appreciation and love for this great human being who represented the true heart and spirit of Pittsburgh."

"I think the thing I'll remember most is that during the darkest hours for me when I took this job, Mr. Rooney would show up in my office," Leyland said. "I don't know how he figured it out, but he would always show up at those times. He knew what I was going through, and he was there to cheer me up and tell me to hang in there. I'll never forget that. In a short period of time, I think we became close friends, and I had a tremendous amount of respect for him."

"He's the kind of guy you wish would live 87 more years," said Joe L. Brown, the Pirates' former general manager. "He was one compassionate, caring guy. Particularly when things weren't going well — and there were years like that when I was there — Art would come around and sit and chat a while. Without appearing to, he would make life seem happier and everything seem rosier. He cared about his city, and I think the city cared for him."

"He certainly is one of the most respected people in Pittsburgh, and probably is the singular most powerful force in this century when it comes to sports in Pittsburgh," said Paul Martha, the president of the Civic Arena Corp., who played for the Steelers from 1960-65.

The Steelers moved from the old National Football League to the American Football Conference's Central Division in 1970, but Rooney remained close to his old friends in the other league. "I always root for the Steelers, the Chicago Bears and New York Giants," he once told McCaskey, who became the Bears' chairman of the board in 1983, after Halas' death.

Rooney's granddaughter, Kathleen, is married to Chris Mara, the son of Wellington T. Mara, the Giants' owner and president.

"Mr. Rooney leaves a legacy of decency which he has contributed to the NFL for half a century," Wellington T. Mara said yesterday.

A mark of Rooney's greatness was that he earned the friendship and respect of some of the Steelers' greatest rivals.

"He's one of the greatest guys in sports," John Madden, the former Oakland Raiders coach, told USA Today. "We had some giant battles with the Steelers, but Art Rooney was always above that. Win or lose, he would treat you the same. There's a saying, 'Shut up until you win, then talk like hell.' He was never like that."

"The Chief was a gentleman and a gentle man," said Art Modell, owner of the Cleveland Browns. "He was a true sportsman, a fierce competitor and one of my dearest friends since the first day that he welcomed me to the NFL 28 years ago. Pat (Mrs. Modell) and I will miss him dearly."

Rooney touched the lives of many people, from his neighbors on the North Side to national figures like James Michener, who wanted to do a book about him. He even left his mark on coaches he couldn't hire.

"There are few people you meet in your life that you respect any more than Mr. Rooney and his family," said Joe Paterno, the Penn State football coach, who turned down a chance to coach the Steelers in 1969.

"He was my kind of guy," Paterno said. "Loyal. Never took himself seriously. Always concerned about everybody but himself. He didn't make money just to make money. He was the easiest touch, I suppose, in the whole

Art Rooney, circa 1929, played semi-pro baseball. His college yearbook called him "a young baseball player of great promise."

The Chief visits with his star running back, Franco Harris, in the locker room prior to kickoff of Super Bowl XIV.

city for the right kind of people. He's the kind of guy you just hope you have a little of in yourself."

Mike Gottfried, the Pitt football coach, said "our thoughts and prayers are with his family."

Although he never thought of himself as a big shot, Rooney was one of the most important and influential men in the NFL. He helped hold the league together during World War II, and in 1960 was among those supporting an expansion franchise in Dallas.

"He was one of the great men of the game," said Tex Schramm, the Cowboys' president. "He was one of the builders or our sport. He went through the tough times that too few of those today who are enjoying the success of the league had to go through. He was just a great individual, a great person, and a man I loved very dearly."

After Halas' death, Rooney grew closer to the McCaskeys, calling faithfully three times a week to find out how Ed and Virginia were doing.

When the Bears returned recently from an NFL exhibition game in Sweden, Rooney called to ask about Virginia's health after such a long trip.

"If I had to be somebody else, I'd like to be Art Rooney," McCaskey said. "I've learned so many lessons from him. His religiousness, his sense of fair play, his decency. I think his greatest quality is his fairness with everyone. He's such a beloved figure to people in all walks of life. I've been with him in Pittsburgh when people just walked up to him."

Despite his decreasing involvement with the Steelers, Rooney remained a popular figure in the NFL. At the league meetings last winter in Phoenix, he was given a standing ovation by the other owners when he entered a conference room one afternoon.

STEELERS BOUNCE OILERS, 26-23, IN OVERTIME

By Ed Bouchette, *Pittsburgh Post-Gazette*

HOUSTON, DEC. 31, 1989 — GARY ANDERSON HIT A 50-YARD field goal with 11:39 left in overtime yesterday, giving the Steelers a 26-23 victory over the Houston Oilers in the NFL American Conference wild-card game.

It was the Steelers' first playoff game in five years. They play at Denver at 4 p.m. next Sunday.

The game was the first wild-card game to go to overtime since the Oilers' 23-20 victory over Seattle in January 1988.

Houston had come from behind in the fourth quarter, scoring two touchdowns to take a 23-16 lead. But with 46 seconds left in regulation, the Steelers tied it, 23-23, on Merril Hoge's 2-yard plunge.

Houston did not reach midfield on its final possession of regulation.

The Steelers got the ball deep in their own end to begin overtime and were stymied. After a 26-yard Harry Newsome punt, the Oilers took over but promptly turned the ball over.

Steelers cornerback Rod Woodson hit Lorenzo White, who coughed up the ball near the Houston sideline. Woodson recovered the ball at the Houston 46.

Hoge ran 11 yards for a first down to the Oilers' 35 and Tim Worley ran for 2 more yards to the 33.

On fourth down, Anderson booted

SCORE BY PERIODS

Pittsburgh	7	3	3	10	3	26
Houston	0	6	3	14	0	23

the 50-yarder to win the game.

Twice in the first half, the Steelers were faced with fourth down and less than a yard. Coach Chuck Noll made different decisions on them, once going for the yardage and the second time going for the field goal.

The first one came late in the first quarter with the game scoreless. The Steelers had the ball on the Oilers' 9-yard line. They went into their regular set with both receivers split wide. Bubby Brister then pitched the ball to Tim Worley, who ran right. Linebacker Robert Lyles got suckered inside on the play, Worley turned it up and was untouched until he bowled over safety Bubba McDowell at the 1 and landed into the end zone.

The touchdown gave the Steelers a

Gary Anderson's 50-yard field goal gave the Steelers a 26-23 overtime win.

Merril Hoge's 49-yard run on a draw play was the longest of his career.

7-0 lead with 2:53 left in the first quarter. Rookie Jerry Olsavsky created the opportunity for the touchdown by breaking through untouched up the middle and blocking Greg Montgomery's punt to give the Steelers the ball at the Houston 32.

After the Steelers' touchdown, Houston mounted a drive from its 1. The Oilers, converting three third-downs, reached the Steelers' 3, where they had third down for a fourth time. This time,

Merril Hoge led the Steelers in rushing in 1988, 1990 and 1991.

however, guard Mike Munchak jumped offsides for a penalty that moved it back to the eight. From there, Warren Moon bounced a pass in the end zone toward Haywood Jeffires and the Oilers settled for a 26-yard field goal from Tony Zendejas to cut the Steelers' lead to 7-3.

They made it 7-6 on Zendejas' 35-yard field goal after Worley caught an 8-yard pass from Brister, then fumbled when he was stripped by cornerback Steve Brown.

Houston took over at the Steelers' 41 after the fumble, and when Oilers coach Jerry Glanville was faced with a

fourth-and-1 at the Steelers' 17, he opted to kick the field goal to cut the score to 7-6.

The Steelers put together a long drive late in the second quarter aided by Hoge's 49-yard run on a draw play, the longest of his career.

But, with second and 2 at the Oilers' 9, the Steelers couldn't get a first down. Hoge got a yard up the middle, then got nowhere on third off tackle. On fourth down and less than a yard at the 8, Noll sent Gary Anderson into the game to kick a 25-yard field goals with 1:57 left.

GRITTY STEELERS BOUNCED BY BRONCOS, 24-23

By Steve Hubbard, *The Pittsburgh Press*

DENVER, JAN. 7, 1990 — IT WAS, DENVER COACH DAN REEVES said, "a great game." It was, Broncos defensive end Ron Holmes said, "the type of game that really give you heart problems."

But in the end yesterday, it was the Steelers whose hearts stopped, ached and finally broke. They dominated the Broncos for three quarters, led them for nearly four quarters, played magnificently and courageously and still they lost.

Lost by a point, 24-23, when Denver drove 71 yards and scored with 2:27 left and the Steelers dropped the ball, then fumbled it, on their last-gasp effort to once again prove miracles happen.

And so the Broncos (12-5) will entertain the Cleveland Browns (10-6-1) in the American Football Conference championship game and the Steelers will entertain "what if" fantasies. They came tantalizingly close. And frustratingly far away.

"We'd rather get blown out than lose like this," Tim Worley said. "We played our hearts out. We don't feel any satisfaction. We came here to win."

And they would have if they could have taken back any one of half a dozen plays.

"You'd rather lose, 40-0, and say, 'Hey, we stink,' than lose by one point after beating their tails off for three quarters and eight minutes," Mike Mularkey said.

"It hurts to come so far, get so close

SCORE BY PERIODS

Pittsburgh	3	14	3	3	23
Denver	0	10	7	7	24

and come up short," David Little said. "It was like that little train going up, up, almost over the hill, only to get pushed back. It's harder to lose this way than to get blown out."

Maybe it's harder in the short run, but not in the long run. Because even in defeat, the Steelers proved they are made of heavy mettle. They proved they have talented youth who should only get better. They doubled their victory total of a year ago, from 5-11 to 10-8. They have not arrived, they cannot end their journey now, but they are closer to their destination than they have been in a long time.

"I'm mad because we didn't win," Bubby Brister said. "It's an empty feeling because we played well enough to win.

"But I'm proud of everybody. We

Steelers quarterback Bubby Brister (6) looks for an opening in the Broncos' secondary.

don't have any reason to hang our heads. We don't have anything to be ashamed about. We've come a long way. We have something to build on for next year. The future's going to be bright."

Perhaps the future never looked more lustrous than in defeat.

An offense that lagged behind the rest of the league from start to finish scored 17 points in the first half against a defense allowing a league-leading 14.1 per game. The Steelers romped to 251 yards in the first half — more than they had averaged for a whole game — and finished with a season-high 404. Last in the league in third-down conversions, they converted nine of 15 (for 112 yards) against the AFC's best third-down defense.

Brister, knocked woozy during the game and left hobbling after it, shook off the blisters and cobwebs of nine consecutive so-so statistical days to complete 19 of 29 for 229 yards, one touchdown and no interceptions, and his numbers would have been far better if not for four drops.

Merril Hoge, breaking more tackles than Manuel Noriega breaks laws, bull-dozed the Broncos for 120 yards on 16 carries and another 60 on eight catches.

"It's my biggest day," Hoge said, "but it's just a start. It's definitely not a peak.

We're a young team and this is just the beginning.

"It's an upsetting time and a little dis-appointing time, but it's got to be an exciting time, too, because we know we can play with anybody in this league. This is just one step toward being a championship team. This is something to build on."

Defeat but not despair.

"This group has all the heart, all the good stuff you need to be a champion," Coach Chuck Noll said. "I'm just proud as heck of them. They grew in all man-ners. They weathered some tough stuff."

Such as losing their first two by the combined score of 92-10. Such as get-ting shut out three times and losing six times in their first 10 games. Such as being ridiculed even after making the playoffs. But they beat the Houston Oil-ers in their House of Pain and they near-ly did the same yesterday before 75,868 Mile High maniacs.

"We proved a lot of people wrong, we proved we belonged, we proved we can play with the best of them," Keith Willis said. "We can walk out with our heads held high."

"America woke up today," Hoge said. "We showed them we're a good club. Nobody gave us much respect coming

into this game. We were 10-point under-dogs. That's ridiculous."

It certainly looked that way most of the day. Hoge ran four times for 29 yards as the Steelers took the opening kickoff 65 yards to make it 3-0. Hoge's 45-yard cutback run, Worley's 33-yard catch and Hoge's 7-yard touchdown run keyed a five-play, 93-yard drive to make it 10-0. Brister's 9-yard pass to Louis Lipps com-pleted a 12-play, 77-yard drive to make it 17-7 with 26 seconds left in the half.

But Mark Jackson ran by Dwayne Woodruff, Little and Rod Woodson for a 26-yard catch. Then Ricky Nat-tiel was given a 16-yard gain on a pass that appeared to be dropped and David Treadwell kicked a 43-yarder to pull the Broncos within seven at the half. Reeves called that a turning point because it gave the Broncos momen-tum when they had none.

Worley gave them much more, when he fumbled for the 11th time in 17 games after being crunched by Greg Kragen and Karl Mecklenburg.

"Four or five guys hit me," Worley said. "I didn't see nothing but darkness. I was just dizzy. I didn't know where I was at first. I don't think my fumble hurt."

But it did. On the very next play

HOGE HAS HUGE RUN OF SUCCESS

By Steve Hubbard, *The Pittsburgh Press*

Dick Hoak played with Hall of Famer John Henry Johnson. He coached Hall of Famer-to-be Fran-co Harris. And Rocky Bleier, Frenchy Fuqua, Frankie Pollard, Earnest Jack-son, Tim Worley and a few dozen others. He has been in pro football since 1961.

And he could not remember a bet-ter example of classic will-not-be-denied power running than he saw from Merril Hoge yesterday.

Hoge ran for 120 yards on 16 car-ries, and it seemed like he broke tack-les or carried Denver Broncos on his back for about 119 of those. He also

caught eight passes for 60 yards. "I've seen guys run for a lot more yards," Hoak said. "I've never seen anybody run for that tough of yards. As much yardage as he got, it was all hard yards. Even when there were people in the holes, he was running over them. Breaking tackle after tackle."

He's been getting that a lot lately from Hoge. Hampered most of the season by a torn hamstring and sep-arated shoulder, Hoge is semi-healthy, and it shows. He carried 18 times for 90 yards in the regular sea-

Louis Lipps (83) celebrates his nine-yard touchdown catch.

third of the day and seventh without a miss in the playoffs. And seven seconds into the fourth quarter, the Steelers led, 23-17.

But, Little said, "We let them get away."

They escaped once when the Broncos strangely opted for a quick punt on fourth-and-3 from the Steelers' 35. But the Steelers came up a yard short, then came just short of recovering Johnson's fumbled punt return. Johnson made up for it moments later, when, on a second-and-inches flea flicker, he ran by Everett for a 36-yard catch. Everett got a leg cramp on the play. Seven plays later, Melvin Bratton's dive on third-and-1 made it 24-23.

The Steelers had time for another miracle. But Stock dropped a pass at the 37, Brister threw one away under pressure and Chuck Lanza, filling in for a fatigued Dermontt Dawson, snapped low to Brister in the shotgun and Brister bobbled it, bent over to pick it up and missed, as did Hoge. The Broncos recovered and the Steelers were done. At least until July.

"We'll be right back here (the playoffs) next year," Worley said. "I promise you."

John Elway looked left to Clarence Kay, suckering in free safety Thomas Everett, then fired right to Vance Johnson for 37 yards and a 17-all tie.

"He did look," Everett said, "but it wasn't the best of looks. It was a breakdown on my part, just not a very well-played down."

Still, Hoge's 18-yard run and Mark Stock's 30-yard catch set up a field goal and Everett's 26-yard interception return set up another, Gary Anderson's

son finale and 17 times for 100 yards in the playoff victory at Houston. But his 180 rushing-receiving yards yesterday were not enough to prevent a 24-23 loss to the Denver Broncos.

Sill, it was the first time a Steelers back had run for 100 yards in consecutive playoff games. It was the fourth-best single-game playoff game by a Steeler back; Harris had games of 158, 153 and 132. It was the first time this season a back had gained 100 yards on the Broncos — and Hoge had his 100 (on 10 carries) with

two minutes left in the first half.

"We wanted to destroy the Denver myth," Coach Chuck Noll said, "that they can stop the run. They said it couldn't be done."

The Steelers did it, and without complicated formulas.

"I'll tell you what made the running game work — Merril Hoge," Noll said. "Merril did just a great job. Great second effort. And catching the ball. He was almost like a one-man offense out there. He just did exceptionally well."

Hoge's previous best as a pro was 102 yards last year against the Philadelphia Eagles.

Most of the nation never heard of the 1987 10th-round choice and even fewer can pronounce his name.

But Hoge, as in Dodge — or is it Rolls-Royce? — won some respect on national television yesterday.

"I hope so," he said. "That's not what I came out to do today. I came out to win this game. It just happened I had a good game and earned some respect."

THE TIME IS RIGHT FOR STEELERS' WIN

By Steve Hubbard, *The Pittsburgh Press*

CINCINNATI, NOV. 10, 1991 — THE NFL DOES NOT GIVE POINTS FOR style or coming close or getting better. This isn't figure skating or horseshoe tossing. This is pro football and you are measured by victories and losses whether your name is Chuck Noll or Neil O'Donnell, Joe Walton or Bubby Brister.

Doesn't matter if you play pretty or putrid. Just win, baby. Doesn't matter if you beat the 1-9 Cincinnati Bengals, as the Steelers did, 33-27, in overtime yesterday in Riverfront Stadium, or the 10-0 Washington Redskins, as the Steelers will attempt to do next week in Three Rivers Stadium. Just win, baby.

They had had enough moral victories. O'Donnell needed a real one. The Steelers needed a real one. They needed it bad and they got it big, in a fairly well-played and exceedingly exciting game.

"It was a big win, no doubt," O'Donnell said. "I've been frustrated waiting for my first victory. I finally got one. I feel a little relieved."

He won for the first time in four starts. The Steelers won for the first time in four years against Cincinnati, the first time in five weeks against anybody. They finally won a close game after losing twice by a field goal and once by a touchdown in a game they could have, should have won. But all

SCORE BY PERIODS

Pittsburgh	0	6	7	14	6	33
Cincinnati	10	7	0	10	0	27

Neil O'Donnell completed 24 of 39 passes for 309 yards, including three TD's.

coming close did was add to their anxiety.

"We had a chance in the Giants game," O'Donnell said. "We had a chance at Cleveland and then at Denver last week. I've been frustrated just falling short. I hate to lose. I'm the first one to point the finger at myself. We finally came out on top. It gives me some confidence. I'm happy."

He should be. In his fourth start, he completed 24 of 39 passes for 309 yards. By contrast, Bubby Brister has three 300-yard games in 51 starts. More important, O'Donnell again showed poise beyond his years, rallying the Steelers from an 11-point deficit by throwing three touchdown passes in the game's final 14½ minutes. He hit Ernie Mills for 35 yards to pull the Steelers within 24-20 with 7:59 left, found Louis Lipps for 12 yards to put them ahead, 27-24, with 1:24 left, then spotted a wide-open Eric Green for 26 yards to win it with 8:28 left in overtime.

"It's the first close one we've won in a while and we're proud of that," Coach Chuck Noll said. "We haven't had a whole lot of success in this town. We're celebrating and rightly so."

It wasn't just that they won. It was the way O'Donnell won it, the way everybody won it. The Steelers made big plays all over the place. After the Steelers spotted the Bengals 17-3 and 17-6 leads, after they squandered a chance to pull within 17-9 when Gary

Eric Green won the game for the Steelers with a 26-yard touchdown catch in overtime.

ing ourselves," Noll said. "It was real touch-and-go from a mental standpoint until then."

"It was a momentum swing," Williams said. "It was the turning point of the game because everybody got excited off that."

Still, after Aaron Jones got a 15-yard penalty for a late hit for the second consecutive game to help the Bengals go on a 12-play, 78-yard drive capped by Ickey Woods' second touchdown run and second Ickey Shuffle, the Bengals led, 24-13, with 9:50 left.

That's when O'Donnell went to work. He hit Warren Williams for 21 yards, Merril Hoge for 25, and Mills for 35 and the touchdown. Mills, who has 4.3 speed, ran by Wayne Haddix, a 1991 Pro Bowler waived by the Tampa Bay Buccaneers and practicing with the Bengals for the first time Thursday, to score on his first pro catch.

"I know Ernie has great speed and once he got loose, I gave it a shot," said O'Donnell, who lofted the ball in perfectly.

Hardy Nickerson and David Little held Woods to 1 yard on third-and-2 and O'Donnell got the ball back at his 44 with 3:46 left. He hit Mills deep again, this time for 30 yards, and then after Hoge was stuffed for a 2-yard loss trying to turn the corner on third-and-5 from the 10, Lipps beat rookie Antoine Davis, a 12th-round draft choice just activated off the practice squad, and dived over rookie Fernandus Vinson at the 1 for the go-ahead score.

"My first thought was to get the first down and then after that get whatever I could. That's the name of the game: Get in the end zone," Lipps said.

But with Esiason again using his

Anderson missed his fourth field goal in three weeks (after missing one the first seven weeks), cornerback David Johnson separated Boomer Esiason from the ball on a blindside blitz and Jerrol Williams, starting because of Bryan Hinkle's bruised ribs, scooped it up and ran 38 yards for a touchdown and an emotional jumpstart.

"We kept stubbing our toes, hurt-

Greg Lloyd made the biggest play of the game when he stole the ball from Cincinnati running back Ickey Woods and returned it 19 yards.

masterful play-action fakes and throwing for 361 yards on 32-of-43 passing, the Bengals drove for the tying 37-yard field goal by Jim Breech, only to have it wiped out by Rodney Holman's holding penalty. No matter. Ten yards back, Breech drilled it down the middle with five seconds left to send the game into overtime.

The Steelers came up a yard short and punted, but six plays later, Greg Lloyd made the play of the game, poking the ball away from Woods, picking it up and returning it 19 yards. Center Bruce Kozerski's flagrant face-mask penalty gave the Steelers the ball at the Bengals' 29, already within Anderson's range, albeit not very com-

GREEN GETS WEIGHT OFF SHOULDERS

By Bob Smizik, *The Pittsburgh Press*

It was him again, just like last Sunday. Waiting for the ball again. Waiting to score a touchdown again. Waiting with a chance to decide the outcome of the game again. Waiting, waiting, waiting.

Waiting is tough when victory or defeat in a National Football League game is at the end of the wait. Waiting is tougher still when you're all alone and have time to think about catching the ball. Or not catching the ball.

Now here comes the ball. He has what seems like years to think about it as he runs and everybody in Riverfront Stadium fixes on him. Finally, the ball comes down. This time it's in his hands — not off his shoulder pads. This time it's a touchdown. This time the Steelers win.

Eric Green didn't drop this one. He nestled it. He snuggled it. And then he ran into the end zone with it. The game was over and the Steelers had a 33-27 overtime victory against the Cincinnati Bengals.

It had been a long week for Green. A week to forget what had happened in the end zone in the final minute of the Steelers' loss to the Denver Broncos. It might not have been a loss if Green had snuggled that one. But it went right through those enormous hands on fourth down and the Steelers were beaten by seven points.

"It was tough," Green said in the Steelers' locker room yesterday. "It was on my mind. That's life in football. Those who never drop a pass, never have one thrown to him.

That's how I look at it."

His teammates helped, particularly Louis Lipps.

"Louis was the first guy to come over to me. He said, 'Put it behind you and go from here. You're going to be a good one in this league.'

"Louis Lipps is one of the people I look up to in this league. If he says put it behind you, then I know that's the best thing for me to do."

Green said it was forgotten by the time he reported to practice Tuesday. Most certainly, it's forgotten today after this victory the Steelers had to have. A lost to Cincinnati — and they trailed, 17-6, at the half — and the season threatened to become very ugly. Ahead there is no sign of victory. Ahead, there are the Washington Redskins, Houston Oilers, Dallas Cowboys and Oilers again, teams whose combined records are 24-5.

This win leaves the Steelers 4-6 and, at least, hopeful. A defeat would have left them 3-7 and wondering if

fortably because of a series of bad snaps and bad kicks.

So on third-and-7 from the 26, Walton, the beleaguered offensive coordinator, didn't play it safe because a field goal wasn't. Anticipating a blitz, Walton designed a play-action pass with Hoge as a safety valve with a chance for a first down. And, anticipating the Bengals might play a zone, he changed Green's pass pattern. Instead of running short across the middle, Green ran deep toward the flag. The cornerback jumped on Hoge and Green was open by at least 5 yards. Green caught it at the 4 and scored easily.

"That was a great call by Coach Walton," O'Donnell said. "No one thought we'd play-action that late in the game. The one thing I didn't want to do is get sacked, so when I came out of my play-action, I looked upfield real quick and I just saw Eric wide open."

His first thought: "Get him the ball."

His second: "Don't screw it up."

A week before, O'Donnell had disdained short passes to his backs that would have been good for first downs and instead threw to the end zone, only to throw wide of Lipps and see Green drop what would have been the tying touchdown. This time, there were no interceptions, no big mistakes.

"No doubt about it, I learned from it," O'Donnell said.

And he, and Green, atoned for their mistakes. The more O'Donnell eliminates those mistakes, the more likely he will become the regular starter and Brister, who Friday said he wouldn't accept being the backup next year, will depart.

"He definitely has confidence in himself and that confidence is rubbing off on the coaches, and they feel confidence calling that type of play knowing Neil is going to make the play go," Lipps said. "He's getting better every game. Winning just makes it sweeter."

Winning just makes it matter.

they would win again this season.

It was a terrific victory, filled with remarkable plays and legitimate heroes. Heroes such as Green and quarterback Neil O'Donnell, who passed for 309 yards, and linebacker Greg Lloyd, who stripped Ickey Woods of the ball in overtime, picked it up and ran 19 yards to set up the winning touchdown, and yeah, such as offensive coordinator Joe Walton.

Walton gets no peace in this town, hasn't had any almost since the day he arrived. His offense is universally disrespected, his play-calling relentlessly questioned.

But no one will question what Walton called on the last play of the game.

After the fumble, Lloyd had put the ball at the Bengals' 29. It was within Gary Anderson's field-goal range, but not his most comfortable range. Another 5 yards would have been nice, 10 wonderful.

Merril Hoge ran twice and got 3 yards. Another run seemed certain. But not to Walton. He would stun the Bengals with play action.

"It was a lag, draw, trap pass to Merril," said Green.

A pass? Why not, said Walton.

"I didn't think it was much of a gamble. We have very good (pass) protection on the play. If they blitz, they leave the fullback wide open."

The Steelers were expecting a blitz, expecting Hoge to catch the pass about 5 yards downfield.

But Green could get behind the secondary because Walton changed his route on this play. Normally Green crosses shallow. But when Walton gave O'Donnell the play on the sideline during a timeout, he told him to have Green run a seven route — deep to the corner.

Green was surprised. "Neil came back and said, 'Big guy, Joe said run a seven.'

"I had to ask Neil twice, 'What are you talking about?' "

"He said, 'Just do it. Just do it.' "

He did it. The Bengals went for the play action and Green sprinted unaccompanied to the end zone.

"It was a great call by Joe Walton," O'Donnell said. "No one thought we'd have play action down there. They thought we'd kick a field goal with our great kicker, Gary Anderson. But we play-actioned. I faked and I saw Eric wide open. So I gave it to him."

Green's confidence hadn't been wounded by last week's drop. "If one pass would hurt my confidence, I'm a mentally weak football player.

"I'm glad my coaches put me in a position to make the catch. You can easily say, 'We're not going to go to this guy because he doesn't work well in pressure situations.' But they didn't do that to me."

He waited for a week to learn how the coaches would handle him. He waited for seconds in the overtime to learn how he would handle his second chance. Both were worth the wait.

CHUCK NOLL: THE COACH OF CHAMPIONS

By Ed Bouchette

THE SUMMER DROUGHT CHAR-BROILED A FIELD AT ST. Vincent College to the point that fissures in the baked ground made it difficult to walk in the sweltering afternoon. Chuck Noll strode up a hill and slowly made his way over the craggy dirt toward the Pittsburgh Steelers' dormitory on the tiny campus in Latrobe, Pa.

To Noll's right, a herd of kids thundered toward him, kicking up dust as they bolted from behind a rope, carrying pens and notebooks. They circled the Steelers' coach and he stopped to sign their pads.

"What's your name?" he asked one.

"Jim Brown," the young boy answered.

"I had a teammate named Jim Brown," Noll said. "Pretty good player."

Wherever he went in football, Chuck Noll was surrounded by greatness. Whether he was blocking for Hall of Famer Jim Brown, playing for Hall of Famer Paul Brown, coaching for Hall of Famer Sid Gilman or soon-to-be Hall member Don Shula, Noll's pro football family tree majestically rose like few others. He eventually went to work for another Hall of Famer, Art Rooney, and turned the NFL's laughing stock into one of the most successful franchises in sports history.

Along the way, Noll spawned more Hall of Famers, men like Terry Brad-shaw, Franco Harris, Mean Joe Greene, Mel Blount, Jack Lambert, Jack Ham and ultimately himself, the coach. They named the Super Bowl trophy after Vince Lombardi, but no coach won more of them than Chuck Noll.

"We had a lot of great players," Ham said. "But in no way would we have won those games or championships if it were not for one man — Chuck Noll. ... We might have been able to get along without Bradshaw, or Joe Greene or Jack Ham or some of the other guys but we would not have won without Chuck Noll.

"He was the glue that pulled this whole thing together. Without him, we wouldn't have won the championships and you wouldn't see busts of all us guys up there in Canton. All I know is that we were damn lucky we had Noll."

"He was," Greene said simply, "the best there is."

He took over a franchise that had never won a championship, never won

Chuck Noll surveys his troops at practice prior to the 1975 season.

a playoff game and turned it into the best, maybe the best ever. The Steelers won the first game he coached in 1969, then lost the remaining 13 that season. By 1972, they were division champs and by '74 they began a run like no other — four Super Bowl winners in six years.

Noll set the tone early, drafting the little-known Greene from North Texas State in '69 and dumping the team's biggest star, wide receiver Roy Jefferson, when he would not conform to his rules. The Rooneys gave him final say in the drafting of players and he used it on two of the finest drafts in NFL history. The Steelers, in 1971, drafted Frank Lewis, Ham, Dwight White, Larry Brown, Ernie Holmes and Mike Wagner. In 1974 they picked Lynn Swann, Lambert, John Stallworth, Mike Webster and signed Donnie Shell as a rookie free agent.

Art Rooney Jr. headed the Steelers' scouting department then and he acknowledged Noll's genius at both identifying talent and coaching it.

"I always said, if I ever had 15 minutes of fame, 11 came from Noll and the rest from my dad. A lot of guys may have been better scouts, but they never got the fame I did because of the way Chuck put it all together."

His teams won 209 games in his 23 years with the Steelers before he retired in 1991 just shy of his 60th birthday. Although Noll was inducted into the Pro Football Hall of Fame in his first year of eligibility in 1993, he sought none of the fame that went with the territory. Such was his anonymity at times that his name was often misspelled. It was even listed as "Knoll" in a video in the Pro Football Hall of Fame in Canton.

Noll won more Super Bowls than any other coach in NFL history.

While running back Steve Davis watches, Noll shouts instructions to his offense.

During his entire coaching career, he made just one sales pitch, and that was for a local Pittsburgh bank as a favor to a friend.

The late Paul Brown once took note of Noll's low-key approach to publicity as a sign that he was devoted to coaching, not selling himself.

"The players know there's no monkey business there," Brown said in 1990. "He's made it his life's work, which means he isn't trying to sell autos on the side and that kind of stuff. That

would be degrading to me as a coach, to be selling stuff. You got a profession, you put your mind on it all the time. It's year-round."

More than that philosophy of Brown's rubbed off on Noll, who was a linebacker and messenger guard for Brown's Cleveland teams in the 1950's. Noll learned that, besides talent, there was nothing more important than the game's fundamentals.

He became above all else one of the NFL's great teachers, a profession he

set out to pursue before he wound up in pro football. His most joyous time of the year was not playoff time or the regular season but the spring mini-camps, when he had more time to devote to the young players. Once, late in his career, Noll was spotted at training camp relaxing in the club's hospitality room late at night. His idea of relaxation, though, consisted of getting down in a three-point stance, teaching some visiting young coaches from a small college the intricacies of the Steelers' trap-blocking scheme.

"What is really attractive about coaching to me is when you're able to help somebody," Noll said. "You work on the technique and you get it done, and he turns around and he's got that sparkle in his eye like, 'Where did you get that? Boy, does that work.' ... Those are the kinds of things you remember more than the victories."

They are the things that others remember about Noll, too, including Tampa Bay coach Tony Dungy, who played for Noll and later coached on his staff in Pittsburgh.

"My memories of Chuck would be the teaching process and the fact that he made the game simple," Dungy said, "and the confidence he instilled in everyone."

Shula said Noll's style of coaching and teaching was "as good as anyone who ever walked the sidelines."

Noll retired from the Browns in 1959 to try his hand at coaching. The University of Dayton, his alma mater, rejected him as its head coach. But someone had remembered him from his playing days in Ohio and gave him a break with a new league — the American Football League. That someone was Sid Gillman, the San Diego Chargers' coach.

"We saw him at the University of Dayton when I was at Cincinnati and we played Dayton," Gillman said. "He stood out like a sore thumb. Matter of fact, we recommended him to Paul Brown. Then, when I was looking for a staff with the Chargers, he called several times. He wanted to get into coaching. I felt that anyone who played for Paul and was a messenger had to be very bright.

"Boy, you talk about having convictions. He was stubborn. All the good ones are stubborn, I guess."

Joe Greene explains: "I've never

A frustrated Mel Blount (42) and Noll walk off the field following the Steelers' 31-28 loss to San Diego in the AFC playoffs in 1983.

been in contact with anyone (like Noll) who was able to stay focused and stay committed to the proper things — not get distracted by all of the things that are involved in playing competitive sports. Distractions just were not part of his game plan."

Noll left Gillman in 1966 to join Shula's Colts in Baltimore as secondary coach. Brown, Gillman and Shula were three of the best the coaching profession had to offer and Noll studied from them first-hand.

"You learn something from everyone," Noll said. "Sid was one of the game's prime researchers and offensive specialists. In six years, I had more exposure to football than I normally would have received in 12 years. ... That was a great training ground for me in the American Football League at the start. It was a real break, one of many I've had."

He said he learned about organization and attitudes from Shula.

"When you're around a winner," Noll said, "it rubs off."

Dan Rooney noticed many of those qualities in 1969 when he hired Noll after the Colts went down to the biggest upset in Super Bowl history to the New York Jets. The Steelers had offered the job to Joe Paterno, who turned it down. Their second choice turned out all right.

"I remember how impressed I was at his stableness," Rooney said. "He was very calm and collected."

That calmness carried him through the 1-13 first season, and the draft picks that everyone tried to talk him out of. Joe Greene was Joe Who? Even Noll's own scouts wanted him to take someone else. Noll was offered small fortunes in trade for the first pick in the 1970 draft. He hung tough, though, and picked Bradshaw. His first-round draft choices from 1969 through 1974 included Greene, Bradshaw, Franco Harris and Lynn Swann. Not a bad collection.

"There's no question we ended up being fortunate getting good football players, people who were winners, and guys who could play together," Noll said. "It was very frustrating for Joe that first year. But then we added Bradshaw and others. You could begin to see the light at the end of the tunnel."

And once that freight-train got on a roll in Pittsburgh, there was no stopping it. Not only did Noll assemble the talent and then coach it to the pinnacle, he was able to hold them together — despite the egos, the big-money talent — and go 4-0 in Super Bowls over a six-year period. Many people believe that was Noll's greatest accomplishment, not letting the egos and the hype get in the way of his team's mission.

"There is no question," Lambert said, "that during the Super Bowl years he had a group of guys with tremendous talent, but he kept those gifted players focused, cohesive and on an even keel. He played a major role in the fact I have four Super Bowl rings."

Noll came off as aloof to the public, a cold man with an icy stare. He stood on the sidelines showing little emotion, rarely complimenting a player. He certainly wasn't one to run over to his quarterback and slap him on the back. One of Noll's rare displays of emotion came when Bradshaw turned away from his coach as he was talking to him and Noll angrily grabbed his quarterback's face-mask and jerked him to attention as he finished his instructions.

"He wasn't one who put his arm

Noll won only one game in his first season as Steelers coach, but persevered and eventually won four Super Bowls.

The Chief congratulates Noll, who holds the Vince Lombardi Trophy after the Steelers won Super Bowl XIV.

around you and pump you up," running back Rocky Bleier said. "His way was 'I don't have time to motivate you. My job is to take self-motivators and show them how to become better.' And it's so true. He wasn't very comfortable at having to go pat guys on the back or jack them up before the guys."

Said Ham: "He coined the phrase 'self-starters.'"

But Noll may have been among the most sensitive and wordly men among the NFL's coaches. He cultivated roses and fine wine, flew his own plane, piloted his own boat and had a deep curiosity about life.

"Contrary to popular belief of some, Chuck is a very sensitive individual," former Steelers wide receiver John Stallworth said. "I believe that he struggled throughout his time as a head coach, and maybe even before that, to hide that sensitivity, to the point of appearing insensitive sometimes."

Even a lowly sports writer occasionally got a glimpse of this. In 1988, one of them came home from a Steelers' scrimmage to find that his wife not only had left him, but wiped out their bank account and took everything in their apartment. Noll heard about it and one day walked up to the writer and handed him an envelope.

"Here," Noll said, "I want you to have this."

There was $200 inside.

"A lot of people had the idea he was really a tough guy," Dan Rooney said. "But he always had the position of trying to keep players beyond their careers. That's something some of them don't even realize."

Among them were Dwight White and Joe Greene, half of the vaunted Steel Curtain front four. Noll cut promising Dwaine Board to keep White around one more year and Board became a vital member of the 49ers' Super Bowl run. Greene could hardly play in his last few years in the league.

"To the people on the outside looking in," Ham said, "Chuck was very uncaring and stoic about his players. In reality, he cared immensely about his players."

Some players saw rare glimpses of Noll's sensitivity while he was still coaching them. He and Bradshaw wound up in Terry's dorm room singing and playing the guitar one night during training camp. During the Christmas season in 1977, Lynn Swann and other players with their wives and girlfriends came caroling outside Noll's house. Chuck invited them all in.

"He offered us a drink, showed us a number of pictures — his wall of wildlife he photographed himself," Swann said. "We got to see a little world of Chuck Noll. He even pulled out his ukelele and we were singing songs."

But it wasn't until he retired after the 1991 season that Noll finally allowed his personality to take root publicly. He was introduced before a Steelers game, threw out the first pitch for the Pirates, flipped the coin at the Super Bowl, went on more speaking engagements than he had done in his 23 years combined as a Steelers coach. He appeared on radio and television, accepted an honorary degree at his alma mater, the University of Dayton, and recruited students for the college. He became a spokesman for several charitable organizations. Noll's love of the arts also prompted him to do a radio commercial for "The Phantom of the Opera." He even served as chairman of a ball in Pittsburgh. He traveled overseas to Germany and Japan to teach clinics for the NFL.

And he was loving all of it.

"I didn't have time when I was coaching," Noll said. "If you start doing a lot of that, then you're not focusing on football. I could have been out every night when I was coaching, but then your family, which gets shortchanged anyway, gets shortchanged more."

He was slightly embarrassed about his election to the Hall of Fame. Noll considers football the ultimate team sport, so he figures the whole team should have gone into Canton.

"In football nothing is accomplished by yourself. Everything is dependent on the people around you.

"One of the fortunate things we had in the 70's was, we had some outstanding people. I'm talking about ownership, coaches, talented players, equipment, the whole organization."

And one hell of a head coach.

Noll is carried off the field by Franco Harris and Joe Greene after defeating Minnesota in the 1975 Super Bowl.

STEELERS END ON HIGH NOTE, TRIP BROWNS

By Ed Bouchette, *Pittsburgh Post-Gazette*

PITTSBURGH, DEC. 27, 1992 — BARRY FOSTER RUSHED FOR another 100 yards, the Steelers capped their best regular season since 1979 and they all get a week off for their efforts.

Happy holidays, said quarterback Bubby Brister.

"We're happy where we are, we're happy Barry got his record, we're happy to get the week off. We're just really happy with the way we're going," Brister said.

By nudging the Cleveland Browns, 23-13, the Steelers ended a two-game losing streak and finished the regular season at 11-5. They next play at home either Jan. 9 or 10 and need only two victories to make their first trip to the Super Bowl in 13 years, a goal Coach Bill Cowher set early in his regime.

"I don't know who we're going to play in two weeks, but I know when we're going to play them," Cowher said. "We're going to play them right here in this stadium."

Foster rushed for 103 yards, tying Eric Dickerson's NFL record with his 12th 100-yard game. That gave him 1,690 yards. He lost the NFL rushing title to Emmitt Smith on the last

Barry Foster (29) rushed for 103 yards, which tied Eric Dickinson's NFL record of 12 100-yard games in one season.

SCORE BY PERIODS

Cleveland	0	3	7	3	13
Pittsburgh	7	10	3	3	23

day but it was the only disappointment yesterday, Brister said.

Foster gave the Steelers a 7-0 lead on a 7-yard run in the first quarter, their first touchdown in three games. They never trailed after that, although Cleveland (7-9) would not go quietly. The Steelers pumped their lead to 17-3 by halftime on Brister's 2-yard pass to tight end Tim Jorden and Gary Anderson's 26-yard field goal.

The Browns, however, came back in the second half after quarterback Bernie Kosar left the game with a reinjury of the right ankle he broke in the second game of the season. Mike Tomczak replaced him and flipped a 38-yard pass to Michael Jackson to cut the lead to seven.

But Anderson kicked field goals of 29 and 28 yards around one by Cleveland's Matt Stover to hold off the Browns.

"This win was a must for us," half-

back Leroy Thompson said. "By not scoring in the last two games, the offense was embarrassed and Coach (Ron) Erhardt was embarrassed. He told us we need to come out and have a big day and everybody set their mind to do that."

Nobody did a better job of it than Brister, who lost the starting job to Neil O'Donnell in the preseason. With O'Donnell nursing a broken fibula, Brister started his third straight game and had the best game of either quarterback since the first third of the season.

Nevertheless, Cowher said O'Donnell will return as the starter if he's healthy in two weeks.

In his first year as Steelers coach, Bill Cowher's record of 11 wins and 6 losses was an impressive one.

After losing his job to Neil O'Donnell in preseason drills, Bubby Brister played his best game of the 1992 season against Cleveland.

STEELERS PAY BACK BILLS, END 8-GAME SKID

By Ed Bouchette, Pittsburgh Post-Gazette

PITTSBURGH, NOV. 15, 1993 — THE STEELERS LAST NIGHT emphatically staked a claim to the prime turf in the AFC — and burned it smack through the heart of their chief antagonist.

The Buffalo Bills came here with the best record in the NFL and an eight-year winning streak against the Steelers, including two last season.

It all ended with a crushing, 23-0 victory for the Steelers before 60,265, a regular-season record in Three Rivers Stadium.

The victory moved the Steelers to 6-3, atop the AFC Central Division, while the Bills slipped to 7-2.

"I think," quarterback Neil O'Donnell said, "we had to prove to ourselves we could beat them."

The Steelers accomplished it all without running back Barry Foster, who sprained his left ankle on the first drive and did not return. Coach Bill Cowher said Foster will probably miss at least two weeks. His replacement, Leroy Thompson, gained 108 yards on 30 carries and Merril Hoge added 64 yards on 10 carries.

"Between Leroy and Merril, we have a couple of guys who can run the football pretty good," Cowher said.

Buffalo lost more than a game. Bills quarterback Jim Kelly suffered a concussion late in the first half and did not return. Wide receivers Andre Reed (wrist) and Don Beebe (head) left the game in the second half.

SCORE BY PERIODS

Buffalo	0	0	0	0	0
Pittsburgh	7	3	10	3	23

The Steelers made it look easy, scoring in every period.

They took a 10-0 halftime lead on Thompson's 9-yard run and a 37-yard Gary Anderson's field goal. Tight end Eric Green, who led the Steelers with six catches, got things going to start the second half. He caught a 1-yard touchdown pass from O'Donnell and Anderson added field goals of 19 and 31 yards.

The victory may not have evened the score for the Steelers, who lost to the Bills, 24-3, in the playoffs here last January. But it could go a long way toward

Neil O'Donnell congratulates Leroy Thompson after his 9-yard touchdown run in the first quarter.

some post-season success for them this season.

"You've got to beat teams like that to go where you want to go," said fullback Merril Hoge.

"The difference was we came out and shoved it down their throat in the second half. We have not done that since I've been here. You have to do that. That said the world about our football team."

The Bills, who had beaten the Steelers five straight times, appeared to be steaming toward their fourth AFC title.

Last night, all that might have changed.

"The message is: We're coming and you better be ready," said tackle John Jackson.

Cowher tried to downplay the importance of the victory but did say, "The fact we finally beat the team that won this conference three years in a row means something."

It was the Bills' first shutout loss since they fell at Miami, 28-0, on Dec. 22, 1985.

O'Donnell completed 16 of 27 passes for 212 yards and no interceptions. He was sacked four times. Kelly was just 7-of-19 for 93 yards and no interceptions. Frank Reich, who was at the controls when the Bills ripped the Steelers last January, was 4-of-9 for 41 yards in the second half.

Thurman Thomas, the AFC's leading rusher, was held to 40 yards on 13 carries as the Bills managed only 157 yards on offense to the Steelers' 400. The Steelers inundated Buffalo by keeping the ball for 44 minutes 51 seconds, compared to just 15:09 for the visitors.

The Steelers jumped on top, 7-0, on Thompson's 9-yard run with 5:31 left

O'Donnell led the Steelers to a 23-0 shutout win over Buffalo after losing to the Bills in the 1992 playoffs.

in the first quarter. It capped a convincing first drive by the Steelers of 81 yards on 15 plays, taking 7 minutes, 17 seconds.

Thompson entered the game when Foster sprained his left ankle in the middle of the drive when linebacker Mark Maddox broke up a screen pass to him.

Thompson carried three straight times of 3, 6 and 9 yards for the TD. On the scoring run, he dashed up the middle, cut deftly to his left and ran into the end zone without a hand ever touching him.

The Steelers made it 2-for-3 when they put together another scoring drive on their third try, ending in Anderson's 37-yard field goal and a 10-0 lead with 9:14 left in the first half.

Buffalo, meanwhile, could go nowhere in the first half until a last-minute surprise. The Bills' first six drives began at their 20 or less and they did not get beyond their own 45-yard line in the first five.

They were backed up to their own 18 with a third-and-10 and 44 seconds on the clock when Kelly went deep to Andre Reed. Cornerback Rod Woodson was on Reed but he appeared to lose the ball and the receiver. Reed caught it for a 51-yard gain and the Bills set up shop on the Steelers' 31.

Two plays later, defensive end Kenny Davidson saved three points for the Steelers by sacking Kelly for an 11-yard loss back to the 40. With time running out, Kelly then threw incomplete on the final play.

The third quarter looked a whole lot like the first two.

The Steelers took the opening drive and went 70 yards for a touchdown.

Eric Green, having another monster game, caught a 14-yard pass to the 1. O'Donnell then faked a handoff to Thompson, rolled right and hit a wide-open Green in the right corner of the end zone.

STEELERS SQUEEZE INTO PLAYOFFS, 16-9

By Ed Bouchette, *Pittsburgh Post-Gazette*

PITTSBURGH, JAN. 2, 1994 — IT WAS TOO FAMILIAR — THE dropped passes, the quarterback sacks, the lack of touchdowns, the early deficit.

Everything that marked the Steelers' fade the previous six weeks clung to them yesterday in Three Rivers Stadium in their final game of the regular season.

Except for one thing. This time, the Steelers somehow overcame all that and beat the Cleveland Browns, 16-9. And, thanks to some help from their friends, they managed to make the playoffs as a wild-card team. The Steelers will play at Kansas City, the AFC West champs, on Saturday at 12:30 p.m.

The final piece of the puzzle that put the Steelers into that game fell into place last night when their bitter division rivals, the Houston Oilers, knocked the New York Jets out, 24-0.

They also needed the New England Patriots' overtime victory against Miami.

"The goal," said fullback Merril Hoge, "is to get in there and win the championship."

"We kept saying all week long — take care of business, beat Cleveland and we'll be in the playoffs," safety Darren Perry said.

"If you get in," cornerback Ron Woodson said, "you can wipe the slate clean."

SCORE BY PERIODS

Cleveland	0	9	0	0	9
Pittsburgh	0	3	3	10	16

Now that they've made the playoffs, Coach Bill Cowher won't have to shave his mustache. Yesterday, he told his team he'd shave it if they didn't make it. He said he had little doubt the Oilers would win. "I bet my mustache on it."

Cowher will go against his former mentor, Chiefs Coach Marty Schottenheimer. "It was a case of going to Denver or Kansas City. I'd rather take the shorter trip," Cowher said.

For most of the game yesterday, the Steelers seemed determined not to make it. They fell behind, 9-3, and trailed, 9-6, entering the fourth quarter. Promis-

Eric Green had three receptions on the Steelers' fourth-quarter game-winning drive, including the 14-yard TD pass.

ing drives were compromised by dropped passes — two by tight end Eric Green and one by wide receiver Jeff Graham — and by the Browns' seven sacks of quarterback Neil O'Donnell as many in the crowd of 49,208 at Three Rivers Stadium booed.

But at the end, Green came through. He led the Steelers with six receptions, including three on the winning drive. The last one was the biggest, a 14-yard touchdown pass from O'Donnell with 7:16 left that put the Steelers in front, 13-9.

It was the only touchdown of the game and it came after a blistering half-time harangue by linebacker Greg Lloyd, who criticized his offense for its non-chalant play.

"I thought it was time to step up and tell it like it is," said Lloyd, who surprised even some of his teammates by playing yesterday despite a pulled hamstring. "Some things you can't candy coat. But when you're getting your butts kicked each week, then the message has to be sent."

For whatever reason, the Steelers' offense responded in the fourth quarter.

"It's something to build on," wide receiver Dwight Stone said of the offensive awakening. "It came at the right time."

The Browns nearly sent it into overtime on a frantic drive in the final 1:11. But linebacker Kevin Greene sacked quarterback Vinny Testaverde on second down for a 4-yard loss back to the 17.

Cornerback D.J. Johnson then broke up two passes from Testaverde to Michael Jackson in the corner of the end zone.

The first pass looked as if it might have been complete, but an official ruled Jackson was bobbling the ball as Johnson shoved him out of bounds. Jackson went in the air and had his hands on the last one, but before his feet hit the ground, Johnson knocked the ball loose.

"I knew the general direction it was going," Johnson said. "He can jump high. I said 'Wait for the ball to come down,' and at some point I wanted to knock it away."

Many of the Browns (7-9) thought Jackson had a touchdown on the first one.

"Basically," Cleveland coach Bill

Lloyd Sparks Steelers

By Bob Smizik, *Pittsburgh Post-Gazette*

Leadership generally comes in two forms: words and deeds.

The Steelers' Pro Bowl linebacker, Greg Lloyd, defined both styles yesterday at Three Rivers Stadium. Defined them so superbly the Steelers advanced to the promised land of the National Football League playoffs with a 16-9 victory over the Cleveland Browns that was carved by Lloyd's halftime rhetoric and his second-half heroics.

The Steelers' season would have ended around 4 p.m. yesterday if Lloyd had not had his say at halftime, when the Steelers trailed, 9-3. He verbally attacked his teammates' lackadaisical offensive performances and then went out and physically attacked

the Browns, forcing two fumbles, both of which had a major impact on the outcome of the game.

It was clear from Lloyd's angry message the play of the offense wasn't the only thing bothering him. His comments could easily be viewed as a repudiation of Bill Cowher's coaching philosophy.

"Something should have been said a long time ago, not by me but by the coaching staff," Lloyd said.

"Coach Cowher says if you don't have anything positive to say, don't say it. I haven't said anything because of that. But this is a do or die situation. I think somebody had to do it. It was enough of saying, 'We're going to be all right, we're going to be all

right.' I got tired of people saying we're going to be all right.

"I wish I had said this at the start of the season."

Lloyd's anger was stirred in the first half as the defense played admirably and the offense was pathetic in its attempts to move the football.

Lloyd's words and actions were all the more meaningful because of his own physical condition. He had been listed as questionable with a hamstring pull after missing last week's game against the Seattle Seahawks.

"I'm playing hurt. I probably shouldn't have played. It hurt, but I had to play through it. There's a difference between being injured and being hurt. I was just hurt.

"I'm out there busting my butt trying to make plays and we got guys that are healthy who are sitting back and playing nonchalant football. That's unacceptable on this level."

"He came in and threw a tantrum,"

Belichick said, "it came down to one call from going into overtime."

The game belonged to the kickers and the defenses. Gary Anderson staked the Steelers to a 3-0 lead with a 36-yard field goal in the second quarter.

Cleveland's Matt Stover then kicked three in a row from 36, 47 and 44 yards. Anderson made it 9-6 on his second field goal, from 38 yards in the third quarter.

The Browns had a chance to extend their lead but Belichick opted to punt from the Steelers' 32 rather than try a 49-yard field goal in the third quarter. The punt went into the end zone. Later, he ordered a punt from the Steelers' 37 that went into the end zone.

"We were playing pretty good on defense," Belichick explained. "We had a chance to back them up and take them out of field position."

The Steelers' offense again produced decent statistics. Leroy Thompson had 91 yards rushing on 26 carries and Merril Hoge added 48 on just four. O'Donnell completed 22 of 39 passes for 226 yards and no interceptions.

The Steelers' defense that had tumbled from its No. 1 perch in the NFL rankings to No. 3 last week, stuffed Cleveland's running game for just 61 yards. Testaverde did complete 15 of 30 passes for 249 yards and no interceptions, but he could not get the Browns in the end zone after they routed the Rams, 42-14, the previous week.

A big difference for the Steelers yesterday was the return of Lloyd, one of their two Pro Bowl starters. Lloyd missed the game in Seattle with a pulled hamstring and the Seahawks rushed for 267 yards.

Lloyd played yesterday, although he stayed out of their dime defense. He forced two fumbles.

"He was like Superman out there today," said defensive end Donald Evans, expressing awe at how Lloyd could play at such a level on an injured leg. "A lot of times, if you get a wounded lion, you have hell on your hands. Greg's a low-key guy, but on game day, he turns into an animal."

Yesterday, the Steelers themselves turned into something they seemed determine to avoid becoming over the past six weeks — a playoff team.

running back Leroy Thompson said. "He's not afraid to speak out. As soon as we got in here, he started. He yelled for a couple of minutes. He took a break for some Gatorade and came back and went at it for several more minutes.

"I take it with a grain of salt. I can motivate myself. But other guys need a kick in the butt to get motivated."

Lloyd was angry as soon as he entered the locker room.

"You walk in here and you can see guys are worried about their flights (home). I didn't actually see that, but that's what it felt like. They were messing with my money. I wasn't ready to go home.

"Basically, I tried to motivate them and tell them not to make excuses. We have to forget about going home, forget about who's up in the stands watching. I told them they were messing with my money. It's just a matter of getting it done. This whole place

was quiet. I don't know if they were angry or didn't like it. Who cares?

"Cleveland came in here and wasn't ready to play and we weren't taking advantage of it. I was tired of the defense having to do everything. Just once I'd like to see the offense spark the defense."

The Steelers went three-and-out on their first two second-half possessions but on a Browns' first down from their 23, Lloyd broke through to sack Vinny Testaverde and force a fumble. Joel Steed recovered for the Steelers.

"I had a one-on-one with the back," said Lloyd. "That was a mismatch. I saw Testaverde set. I reached around him, and chopped him in the wrist."

The offense had the spark it needed and, four plays later, Gary Anderson kicked a 38-yard field goal to move the Steelers to within three points.

Properly inspired, the offense scored early in the fourth quarter on an 80-yard drive to take the lead. But the Browns came right back, moving 43 yards in two plays to the Steelers' 38. That's when Lloyd stepped up again.

Leroy Hoard took a handoff from Testaverde, and Lloyd liked what he saw.

"From studying film, I knew right where the ball was going. There was good support that allowed me to get to the ball. We've been taught to strip the ball in those situations. I noted he didn't have two hands on the ball and I popped his wrist."

The Steelers' Kevin Greene recovered, and although there were some uncomfortable moments later, the Browns had been defused.

And Lloyd had inspired a victory. Was he afraid of any repercussions from his outburst? Not at all. He is a man who can say what he wants.

STEELERS KICKED OUT OF POSTSEASON

By Ed Bouchette, *Pittsburgh Post-Gazette*

KANSAS CITY, MO., JAN. 8, 1994 — THE STEELERS YESTER-day distributed the Cliff's Notes version to their whole season.

Their 27-24 overtime loss to the Kansas City Chiefs in a wild-card playoff game carried the fingerprints of '93 all over it.

They bolted boldly ahead and looked unbeatable before fading with help from another botched special teams play.

"We had them on the ropes and they got off," moaned defensive end Donald Evans.

Nick Lowrey's 32-yard field goal at 11:03 into overtime sent the Chiefs on to Houston next Sunday and ended a frustrating campaign for the Steelers.

But it was a blocked punt with 2½ minutes left in regulation — one that allowed the Chiefs to tie it on Joe Montana's 7-yard touchdown pass to Tim Barnett on fourth down with 1:43 left — that the Steelers will remember most of all.

"This is seven months of discouragement coming up," linebacker Kevin Greene said.

"This," said cornerback Rod Woodson, "is the most disappointed I've ever been by a loss."

The Steelers, eight-point underdogs, built a 17-7 lead on the strength

Eric Green is examined on the sidelines by the trainer during a break in the action.

SCORE BY PERIODS

Pittsburgh	7	10	0	7	0	24
Kansas City	7	0	3	14	3	27

of a 30-yard Gary Anderson field goal and Neil O'Donnell touchdown passes of 10 yards to tight end Adrian Cooper and 26 to wide receiver Ernie Mills.

They were giving Montana a tough time, blitzing him and knocking him to the turf. Evan smacked into him in the first quarter, bruising Montana's ribs. Montana moved to the sidelines for four plays. During that span, back-up QB Dave Krieg threw a 23-yard TD pass to J.J. Birden for the Chiefs' only score of the half.

Lowrey booted a 23-yard field goal late in the third quarter to cut the lead to 17-10 and then Marcus Allen tied it for the Chiefs on a 2-yard run with 8:58 left.

The Steelers lurched back in front, 24-17, on Eric Green's 22-yard TD pass from O'Donnell with 4:11 left.

When the Steelers then stopped

Montana and the Chiefs on three downs, they seemed headed for another week of play.

All the Steelers needed to sew things up was get a first down or two.

They didn't come close. Two runs went nowhere. On third down, Jeff Graham dropped a pass and the Steelers were forced to punt.

"We got the ball with three minutes left on the clock," Green said. "We've got to make first downs and kill it."

Instead, the punt team put the gun to the Steelers' head one more time. Tight end Keith Cash, a former Steeler, roared past blocker Tim Jorden virtually untouched and blocked Mark Royals' punt. The Chiefs' Fred Jones picked it up and ran to the 9, where he was caught from behind by Gary Jones.

"You can't get a kick blocked. That's totally uncalled for," said Coach Bill Cowher, who saw the Steelers give up four TD's on punt or kick returns this season. "Maybe it typifies the way this year has gone."

Cowher went after Royals when he came off the field. Cowher later said of the blocked punt, "I just know in that situation you've got to get the ball off and we didn't do it."

Royals said Cowher told him he did not get the punt off quickly enough.

"I never see what happens in that situation," Royals said. "I just try to grab it and kick it. If I'm looking up at the rush, I'm in trouble to start with. I just try to catch it and kick it, and they made the play on it and we didn't make the play."

Jorden took the blame for not blocking Cash. Normally as guard on the punt team, he moved to tackle to replace injured Reggie Barnes. Jorden was supposed to quickly check Albert Lewis rushing from the inside and then block Cash on the outside. He never got to Cash.

"It wasn't anything different," Jorden said.

But the Chiefs still hadn't scored, thanks to Jones' saving tackle.

Two 1-yard runs by Allen around an incomplete pass left the Chiefs with a fourth down and goal at the 7. With no timeouts left, if Kansas City did not score on the next play, the Steelers could have run out the clock.

But Montana, who had a rough start when he missed his first seven passes of the game, hit a wide-open Barnett in the back of the end zone. Lowery kicked the extra point to tie it, 24-24.

"There's no doubt that Joe Montana is a good quarterback," safety Darren Perry said, "but we gave them way too many plays. We made some mistakes and he did an excellent job of finding the open man."

The Steelers almost lost it in regulation. They got the ball on their 22 with 1:39 left and O'Donnell threw three passes, completing one for 5 yards.

Kansas City did not block Royals' punt this time, but Montana directed them from the Chiefs' 28 to the Steelers' 25 in one minute. Lowery, however, kicked his 43-yard field goal attempt wide right with seven seconds left as the Steelers jumped up and down in jubilation.

Kansas City went nowhere after winning the coin toss. The Steelers managed a drive to the 50 that died. Montana and the Chiefs then mounted the game-winning drive beginning at their 20.

The big play came on second-and-9 at the 50. Montana connected with Cash for 18 yards to the 32, putting the Chiefs barely within Lowery's range. Birden assured him of an easier kick when he made a diving catch along the sidelines for a 10-yard pickup to the 18.

Chiefs coach Marty Schottenheimer sent Lowery in to boot it on third down to make sure he had another chance if a bad snap occurred.

The snap was good and so was the redeeming kick for Lowery.

"I owed it to my teammates, that's my job," he said.

A playoff game and a season had slipped through the Steelers' fingers.

"It hurts," Perry said, "but it's typical of the whole year — up and down."

Over and out.

Gary Anderson's second-quarter field goal gave the Steelers a 17-7 lead.

STEELERS APPLY MIAMI VISE, DROP DOLPHINS IN OT

By Ed Bouchette, *Pittsburgh Post-Gazette*

PITTSBURGH, NOV. 20, 1994 — DAN MARINO LIVES FOR games like these. Twenty-eight times during his career he had brought the Miami Dolphins from behind in the fourth quarter to win.

Yesterday, he brought them back to tie with no time left, then had the Dolphins perched on the Steelers' 38 with a first down in overtime.

Dan Marino, back in his hometown, moved in for the kill.

Instead, the Steelers blew up in his face, stopped his charge and put on one of their own to beat the Dolphins, 16-13, on Gary Anderson's 39-yard field goal with 3:52 left in overtime.

"What a thrill!" exclaimed linebacker Kevin Greene.

The pulsating victory behind a new quarterback and the same old stifling defense raised the Steelers' record to 8-3, tied for the best in the American Conference, tied with Cleveland in the Central Division, and moved Coach Bill Cowher to tears.

"I've been here for 2½ years and I can honestly say it may be one of the best victories that I've been associated with," said an emotional Cowher, his eyes moist. "I couldn't be more proud of a bunch of guys, to show the resiliency they showed today."

Miami fell to 7-4, just one game ahead of second-place Buffalo in the

SCORE BY PERIODS

Miami	0	7	3	3	0	13
Pittsburgh	3	3	0	7	3	16

AFC East.

"I'm so frustrated at this point," said Miami linebacker Bryan Cox. "When the game was on the line, they came up with the plays and we didn't."

The Steelers had contained Marino much of the day, only to see him take the Dolphins 62 yards on nine plays in the 1:53 to tie the game on Pete Stoyanovich's 48-yard field goal that sailed through with no time left.

The Steelers had taken a 13-10 lead midway through the fourth quarter on Barry Foster's 10-yard run, their first offensive touchdown in 14 quarters and

Dolphins halfback Bernie Parmalee is gang-tackled by a trio of Steelers, led by Levon Kirkland (99).

two overtime periods, or 217 minutes and one second.

The overtime turned unexpectedly back and forth like a hurricane.

Quarterback Mike Tomczak, who started and played well for the injured Neil O'Donnell, completed a 32-yard pass to Ernie Mills as the Steelers whisked downfield with the first possession of overtime.

However, Foster was stopped for no gain on fourth-and-1 at the Miami 39 and the Dolphins came right back.

They moved to a first down at the 38 and were just 5 yards shy of Stoyanovich's range. But Greene spilled Bernie Parmalee for a 4-yard loss and Joel Steed sacked Marino for a 5¡-yard loss. Ray Seals stripped Marino of the ball on that play, linebacker Levon Kirkland scooped it up and ran it in for what seemed like the game-winning TD, but

the officials had ruled the play dead.

"I thought it was a fumble," said Steed. "Ray stripped it, Levon picked it up and ran with it. I thought it was six points, game's over. But they said he was in the grasp."

Marino had one more chance, but threw incomplete to O.J. McDuffie and the Dolphins punted.

The Steelers began on their 13 and Tomczak went to work again. He threw a screen pass that Foster turned into a 27-yard gain to the 40 that looked to Tomczak like "a bowling ball going downfield."

On third down from there, Tomczak was flushed left under pressure, stopped and tossed a pass to fullback John L. Williams for 23 yards and a first down at the Miami 37.

"Mike's an elusive guy. He was trying to make a play," Williams said.

He made one more, hitting tight end Eric Green for 13 yards over the middle to the Dolphins' 21. Cowher did not hesitate, waving Anderson into the game to win it right there.

"Let's kick it," Cowher said. "We've been in too many overtimes already this year."

That's three overtimes in the past four games, two of them won on Anderson field goals. Yesterday was his ninth game-wining field goal and made him 20 of 21 this season.

"I was just glad that the offense finally came through and got us down there," Anderson said.

The Steelers' offense has struggled mightily this season, but came alive under Tomczak. Miami did a good job to limit Foster to 88 yards on 31 carries, but Tomczak made them pay.

He completed 26 of 42 passes for a

LLOYD'S EMOTIONS RUN WILD

By Gene Collier, *Pittsburgh Post-Gazette*

What might have resulted from the thick chaos that was yesterday's Steelers-Dolphins game had it not been officiated by the visually challenged is certainly anyone's guess. As Greg Lloyd said in a postgame locker room cooking in equal parts pride and relief, "We could have easily been on the other side of this."

Across nearly five periods of football, two of the better teams in the AFC exchanged enough monstrous athleticism and enough total brain cramps that, combined with the league's ever-worsening officiating, this game turned itself inside out at

least a half-dozen times before Gary Anderson won it for Pittsburgh with a 39-yard field goal more than 10 minutes into overtime.

But what would have happened had a Mike Tomczak-led offense done anything other than get off the floor and win the football game after Lloyd, the All-Pro linebacker with the All-World public machismo, berated it with an idiotic display of his mounting disgust near the start of the fourth quarter? And right in the middle of the field, fuel-injecting the hostility of more than 59,000 witnesses fed up with 45 consecutive touchdown-free possessions stretch-

ing back to before Halloween.

What would have happened had, the offense remained impotent, its lasting memory that of being targeted for public ridicule by its own teammate and leadership model, good old No. 95?

Bill Cowher could easily be concerning himself with that today, but he isn't, and he was having none of it yesterday either.

"I don't think it had any impact," Cowher said as his own emotions were just re-entering the Earth's atmosphere 10 minutes after his club went to 8-3. "I think Greg is just a very emotional player. If you watch during a football game. You see him exuding emotion a lot. That's just Greg being Greg and I hope he doesn't change."

Lloyd is the hot emotional engine of a hot emotional defense, a defense

career-high interceptions. He nimbly escaped a good rush and was sacked just once.

He outplayed Marino, who completed 31 of 45 with one TD, a 2-yarder to Keith Jackson in the second quarter, and one interception by Kirkland.

Marino, sacked just 10 times entering the game, was dropped four times by the Steelers, who blitzed him on 29 plays by one press box count. Linebacker Chad Brown had two sacks.

"We blitzed a lot," said Dom Capers, the Steelers' defensive coordinator. "It's our game and you go with the flow. We felt that was the best way to attack him."

The Steelers, who lead the league in sacks, now have 40.

"When's the last time you've seen Marino like that?" asked defensive end Ray Seals. "He was jittery out there.

Cowher receives post-game congratulations by Dolphins coach Don Shula.

We were bringing it as a team."

The Steelers also smothered Miami's running game, limiting the Dolphins to just 37 yards rushing, with Parmalee getting 29.

In the locker room afterwards, line-

backer Greg Lloyd talked about how he got no sleep Saturday night just thinking about the game, and Rod Woodson said the adrenaline was still pumping through him.

"The attitude and confidence we have in ourselves ... is contagious," said Woodson.

It was the third straight victory for the Steelers and, if the playoffs were held today, they would be the top-seeded team in the AFC. Cleveland and San Diego, both losers yesterday, also are 8-3, but the Steelers have the best record within the conference (8-1).

Said Cowher: "I told them afterwards, 'I don't care what Cleveland did; I don't care what Kansas City did; I don't care about anybody else. We've just got to go out and take care of business.'"

Business hasn't been much better.

---

that registered four more sacks yesterday on no less difficult a target than Dan Marino, who hadn't been sacked more than twice all season.

As Lloyd's offensive teammates came onto the field trailing 10-6 with 12 minutes left, Greg let 'em hear some of his displeasure, and then let everybody in the building know what he'd just done. He threw down his helmet, put his hands on his hips, walked slowly toward the sideline, and then kicked his helmet into the shin of a member of the chain crew, crumpling him.

"You get worked up," Lloyd said. "I just said, 'We're stopping 'em, and stopping 'em, you gotta wake up on that side,' " Lloyd said. "I said, 'Get across the 50. Kick a field goal. Do something. Wake up!' "

In a totally unrelated event, the offense woke up. Scored a touch-

down six plays later to take a 13-10 lead. Lloyd and the hot emotional defense went out there to protect that lead and watched Marino shred that defense for 62 yards in nine plays to a tying field goal as the clock expired.

In what I suppose was a phenomenal display of restraint — or was it just standard professionalism? — no one from the Steelers' office went out there and spiked his helmet at Lloyd's feet in reciprocal disgust.

"We all know Greg; he just shows his emotions," veteran guard Duval Love. "When he does that, it's not a criticism of the offense. It's just that he knows we're capable of playing better. But we know what we have to do. We're professionals. You can't go out there and get 400 yards every game. The other guys are getting

paid, too."

What makes Lloyd's point, much less his display, all the more invalid is the very nature of the different tasks. You can't play offense like Lloyd plays defense. You can play defense on nearly unbridled emotion. It's a positive. Offense has to be played with patience and calculated precision. Emotion is an impediment. You can't score touchdowns merely by getting as mad as Greg Lloyd.

A lot of people are emotional during these games, but it seems only one berates his teammates. When it all cooled down yesterday Cowher spoke sincerely about yesterday being "a step toward growing together" for this team.

Had Anderson's kick not flown between the uprights, it could have a step toward tearing apart.

STEELERS STAY HOME FOR PLAYOFFS, 17-7

By Ed Bouchette, *Pittsburgh Post-Gazette*

PITTSBURGH, DEC. 18, 1994 — BILL COWHER JOGGED OFF the field, shook hands with Santa Claus, then doffed his cap many times to the screaming fans in the end zone.

The Steelers will spend Christmas Eve in San Diego. They will spend the playoffs at home, on their own field, where a record crowd roared its approval of the Steelers' 17-7 thumping of Cleveland yesterday.

That gave them the AFC Central Division title with a 12-3 record, a bye in the first round and home-field advantage throughout the playoffs. The AFC team with home-field advantage has made it to the Super Bowl six of the past seven years.

"We showed we could win this game with all the smack this team has been talking," Steelers linebacker Kevin Greene said of the Browns, 10-5 and a wild-card playoff team. "Maybe we shut up some people today; maybe we didn't. All I know is we won the AFC Central Division and we got home-field advantage."

The Steelers had home-field advantage two years ago and lost to Buffalo in their first game. But Cowher said he'll take his chances again.

"Were you at the game today?"

Neil O'Donnell completed 10 of 18 passes for 176 yards and one touchdown.

SCORE BY PERIODS

Cleveland	0	7	0	0	7
Pittsburgh	14	0	0	3	17

Cowher asked about the largest crowd in Three Rivers Stadium history, most of them twirling gold Terrible Towels on a raw evening. "That should speak for itself. There's an energy you can draw from crowds ... The best thing about it is we get to do it again."

They might even get to do it against the Browns.

"We know we'll meet this team again," said tight end Eric Green.

If so, they will want to repeat whatever they did in the first quarter.

For the first time this season, the Steelers scored touchdowns on their first two drives. Neil O'Donnell, who had another good day in the pocket, threw a 40-yard touchdown pass to Yancey Thigpen with 11:30 to go in the first quarter. He came back with a 42-yard pass to Ernie Mills and a 17-yarder to Eric Green. Those two passes set up a 1-yard TD run by Barry Foster, who rushed for 106 yards on 32 carries with two broken bones in his back.

The Steelers, barely 11 minutes into the game, were poised to send the Browns packing back up the turnpike by halftime.

But an 84-yard Cleveland drive ended 10 seconds before halftime on Vinny Testaverde's 14-yard pass to Mark Carrier, and the tone suddenly turned.

"We didn't panic and get away from what we wanted to do," Cleveland coach Bill Belichick said.

They didn't panic, and they also did not score again. The Browns, thwarted by penalties, turnovers and an inability to come up with big plays, could not score in the second half. The only score in the second half was Gary Anderson's 49-yard field goal in the fourth quarter.

"We moved the ball," Belichick said, "but we had some mistakes all the way around. A couple of our skilled players dropped the ball."

Cleveland lost three turnovers yesterday and the Steelers none, making it 8-0 in two games between the teams. Testaverde threw two costly interceptions. Safety Gary Jones made a diving pickoff at the Steelers' 3 to thwart one drive. Testaverde threw into quadruple coverage on another, and linebacker Chad Brown intercepted it in the fourth quarter at the Browns' 36. That set up Anderson's 49-yard field goal that put the Steelers ahead by 10 with 9:50 left.

"I got a wet ball," Testaverde said. "They were slipping throughout the game. It slips out, and I made a low throw and it seemed like it went right to him."

Funny, O'Donnell, using the same ball, threw no interceptions and completed 10 of 18 for 175 yards.

Cleveland's Leroy Hoard, who managed just 25 yards rushing, had a critical fumble — his fifth of the season — when he was stripped of the ball early by Joel Steed at the Steelers' 41. Ray Seals recovered to kill another promising Browns' drive.

At that point, Belichick pulled out Hoard, a Pro Bowler, and stuck Earnest Byner at running back.

"I hurt the team," Hoard said. "We didn't need it at that time. I would have taken myself out of the game, too."

If not for those turnovers, things might have been different yesterday. The Browns outgained their hosts, 331 yards to 276. Also, Testaverde avoided the Steelers' crushing pass rush that has been the NFL's best. They sacked him just once.

"They did a nice job of picking up what we were doing," said Steelers defensive coordinator Dom Capers.

For Lloyd, Even a Win is Painful

By Bruce Keidan, *Pittsburgh Post-Gazette*

At the end of the day, Greg Lloyd stood in front of his locker and tried to decide in response to a question if it would be faster to recount the injuries he had suffered or to list those few body parts he had not hurt.

Someone had taken a mile-long Ace bandage and wrapped it around his upper torso and both his shoulders. Bags of ice peeked out here and there. A large cigar with an evil bouquet dangled delicately from his left hand. A football game is only a football game, but a good cigar is an oxymoron.

This particular panatela was a victory cigar. By defeating the Hated Cleveland Browns, 17-7, the Steelers had in one fell swoop won the AFC Central Division championship and all the perks that accrue to the conference's highest-seeded team. Such as a bye to the second round of the playoffs and homefield advantage thereafter until they are beaten or advance to the Mother of All Football Games, which is played at a neutral site.

Much as he wanted to grip the cigar in his teeth and blow smoke rings, Lloyd could not. A dozen microphones formed a blockade in front of his mouth.

"Where doesn't it hurt?" someone asked.

If the NFL had a three-knockdown rule, Lloyd would have lost by TKO in the second half. The whistle would sound, and he would be prone on the hard plastic turf of Three Rivers Stadium, still as deep waters. Three times the trainers and team physician rushed to his side. Three times the crowd of 60,808 sucked in its breath. Three times he got up and made his way to the sideline under his own power — wobbling a little, but finding his way. Three times he returned to the game.

"You throw your body around out there, and you pay a price for it," he said.

He was hit in one shoulder by a

"We didn't hold back. The key was the turnovers."

That and stopping the Browns' bruising running game, Cleveland managed just 86 yards rushing. Testaverde did provide 250 through the air, but his two interceptions and Eric Metcalf's dropped pass in the end zone with 31 seconds left in the game added up.

"It seems like every time we play the Browns it's they coulda done this and they coulda done that," said Cowher, agitated when questioned about the Browns' missed opportunities. "If you want to give them credit, go ahead. Just look at the final score."

Cleveland, though, gave the Steelers a nudge toward their first score. The Steelers were all set to punt on fourth-and-1 at the Cleveland 45, but safety Bennie Thompson bolted over the line of scrimmage before the snap. The 5-

yard penalty gave the Steelers a first down at the 40.

On the next play, O'Donnell threw deep down the right side. Thigpen was double-covered by cornerback Don Griffin in front and safety Stevon Moore behind. No matter. He leaped in the air at the 3, caught it and ran into the end zone for the touchdown.

"It was a cover-two zone, and Neil made a great throw," Thigpen said.

The Browns were in a zone again on the next series when Mills went right down the middle to catch O'Donnell's 42-yard pass that led to the next TD.

"That's the stuff we've been working on," O'Donnell said.

Ron Erhardt, the Steelers' offensive coordinator, said the Browns ganged up to stop the run and the plan was to go deep to loosen them up.

"Those are things we really worked

on," he said.

Despite their early success, the Steelers could not shake Cleveland. They seemed to have things safely in hand with 2:04 left on fourth-and-1 on the Browns' 14, but Anderson's 32-yard field goal hit the left upright and bounced away.

Testaverde then guided the Browns from their 23 to the Steelers' 2. Four passes from there fell incomplete, including a drop by Metcalf and a fade to Michael Jackson that was knocked away by Rod Woodson on fourth down with 26 seconds left.

"They moved the ball down there well," Woodson said.

But they could not cross the goal line as the Steelers swept the Browns for the first time since 1981.

"It was a major hurdle to cross," Cowher said. "But at the same time, our goals and our dreams are higher."

Cleveland helmet while making a tackle. The shoulder went numb.

He was hit in the other shoulder by friendly fire. A Cleveland receiver caught between Lloyd and a cornerback dived like a submarine fleeing a depth-charge attack. He lost feeling in that shoulder, too.

He stuck his head someplace it didn't belong. Under a shoe, perhaps. His brain said, "This is how Michael Moorer felt when George Foreman flattened him." His eyes wouldn't focus for a few minutes. Someone said, "How many fingers am I holding up?" He said, "I don't know, but I do know how many fingers I'm going to hold up if you try to keep me from going back in this game."

Between knockdowns, he made five unassisted tackles, forced a fumble and knocked down a pass. The

Browns had the good sense to stay away from him whenever possible, but the Steelers' defense is like the Hydra, and avoiding one of the monster's head doesn't do you much good.

None of Lloyd's dents and dings are severe enough to prevent him from playing in San Diego next week, in a game the Steelers do not need to win but do not want to lose.

They have come a long way for a team that was chewed up and spat out by Dallas here on the opening day of the season. But for all their accomplishments, they have a long way to go.

They didn't prove anything yesterday that they were not convinced of already. They are the best and the most consistent team in the AFC. That and their won-loss record will

get them a week off and the right to sleep in their own beds for as long as they stay in the AFC's postseason tournament. That and the energy they draw from their partisans could come in handy if, as is not unlikely, they find themselves facing these same Browns again in three weeks.

But the Steelers have been down this road before. They had an opening-round bye and the home-field advantage against Buffalo in the conference semifinals two years ago. If memory serves, it did them no good.

"We are a more mature team this time," Bill Cowher, their coach, noted as night fell on Three Rivers Stadium. "I think we'll be able to handle it better this time."

In the words of the prophet Muhammad Ali, if you can do it, it ain't braggin'.

STEELERS GET TOUGH WITH BROWNS, 29-9

By Ed Bouchette, *Pittsburgh Post-Gazette*

PITTSBURGH, JAN. 7, 1995 — CLEVELAND'S EARNEST BYNER taunted the Steelers during introductions, then saw a Terrible Towel flutter to the ground.

Byner jumped on it. It was rookie defensive end Brentson Buckner's towel.

"I'm supposed to be scared because he's doing this?" Buckner asked.

The rest of yesterday afternoon the Steelers spent wiping their feet on the Browns in Three Rivers Stadium.

This time, the blitz belonged to the Steelers' offense, which scored its first three times down the field and blew things open on the way to a dominating 29-9 playoff victory at Three Rivers Stadium.

It was over at halftime yesterday, when the score was 24-3.

"I think after awhile," linebacker Greg Lloyd said, "they just didn't want to play."

The surprisingly easy victory was the Steelers' third over the Browns this season and moved them onto the doorstep of their fifth Super Bowl appearance. They will play the winner of today's Miami-San Diego game for the AFC championship here next Sunday a game they haven't won in 15 years.

"This is a new time," Steelers President Dan Rooney said, "a wonderful

SCORE BY PERIODS

Cleveland	0	3	0	6	9
Pittsburgh	3	21	3	2	29

time."

And yesterday, it was like old times.

The Steelers broke the Browns' backs with the second-best running game in their playoff history. Barry Foster rushed for 133 yards to lead a ground game that carved out 238 yards, second only to their 249 against Minnesota in Super Bowl IX in January 1975.

"Our offensive line was coming on the sidelines and saying 'They can't

Yancey Thigpen dances into the end zone after a 9-yard TD pass from Neil O'Donnell 16 seconds before intermission.

Steelers running back John L. Williams is congratulated by Coach Bill Cowher and Neil O'Donnell after his 26-yard second-quarter TD run.

stop us,' " said fullback John L. Williams, who had 43 yards.

"They blocked the world," said rookie Bam Morris, who had 60 yards.

Three times down the field and it was 17-0 — on Gary Anderson's 39-yard field goal, Eric Green's 2-yard touchdown pass from Neil O'Donnell and Williams' snappy 26-yard burst up the middle.

Matt Stover kicked a 22-yard field goal to give the Browns three points, and the Steelers came back with seven more points 16 seconds before half-time. Cornerback Tim McKyer created the opportunity by intercepting another one of those misplaced Vinny Testaverde passes, and O'Donnell converted it by throwing a 9-yard TD pass to Yancey Thigpen.

"It's the best half of football that I've witnessed since I've been here," said Steelers coach Bill Cowher. The second half turned into one big party as 58,185 celebrated the Steelers' first playoff victory in Three Rivers Stadium in 15 years.

"It's a great feeling," Williams said, "when we can go to the sidelines and just laugh and joke and talk about what's going on. That's exactly what we did. We went out there and had fun."

The inconsequential second-half scoring included Anderson's 40-yard field goal, Testaverde's 20-yard TD pass to Keenan McCardell, and safety Carnell Lake's sack of Testaverde in the end zone for a safety.

It was one of just two sacks of Testaverde yesterday, but the Steelers proved once again they did not have to sack the Cleveland quarterback to beat him.

Testaverde suffered through four drops in the first 18 minutes — two by

rookie Derrick Alexander — and two interceptions in the first half. He completed just 13 of 31 for 144 yards.

"I was aggressive, but the dropped passes hurt," said Testaverde. "I only thought I threw one bad pass in the first half, and it cost us."

That would have been the one to McKyer. The Steelers held a 17-3 lead at the time, and Ernie Mills had just fumbled the ball to Cleveland after catching a 50-yard pass from O'Donnell.

Cleveland had the ball on its 26 with just under a minute left and Testaverde was trying to make something happen.

He did, for the Steelers. Testaverde aimed a pass toward Alexander along the right sideline. McKyer muscled in front of him, picked it off and ran it back to the 6 to set up Thigpen's TD catch 16 seconds before intermission.

"I couldn't believe he threw that ball," McKyer said. "That's the one he'll look at the films and wish he had back."

In the meantime, O'Donnell was having a nearly perfect afternoon running the Steeler offense. He completed 16 of 23 passes for 186 yards, two TD's, no interceptions and no sacks.

Green made a diving catch over the middle of a perfectly thrown pass in the end zone for the first TD, a 2-yarder.

"Neil said, 'Just get open' and that's what I did," Green said. "Neil was getting the ball to all his options, all his receivers and spreading it around."

O'Donnell's best move all day wasn't even a pass. Leading, 10-0, the Steelers had a third-and-2 on the Browns' 26. They lined up in an I-formation with Williams in front of Foster. O'Donnell took the snap, whirled

completely around from his right and smoothly handed off to Williams up the middle.

The Browns, most notably defensive tackle Bill Johnson, never saw it coming. Williams blew through a huge hole, shook off safety Louis Riddick and ran 26 yards for a TD.

Linebacker Carl Banks tore his helmet off and threw it into the end zone so hard it almost caught Williams from behind.

"When he scored up the middle, you saw them finger pointing and guys slamming their helmets," offensive tackle Leon Searcy said. "We had them on their heels and we just wanted to put them away."

They did, for the third time, and they got pleasure out of burying a team that had taunted them all week, during introductions and right up to the end.

"They're all about acting tough, and we're all about being tough," linebacker Chad Brown said. "They want to push you after the play. We want to push you during the play."

Buckner, who got the Steelers' first sack of Testaverde, never did get his Terrible Towel back. But he said there's more where that came from and gladly offered it up for the cause. It was, he said, the most aggressive step Byner took all day as the Steelers stuffed the Browns' running game, allowing just 55 yards.

"He showed me a lot of courage by coming out there," Buckner said of the taunting by Byner. "But he showed it at the wrong time. He should have showed me courage when Testaverde said 'Hike.' "

Instead, the Steelers told the Browns to take one.

STEELERS RALLY PAST BEARS, 37-34

By Ed Bouchette, *Pittsburgh Post-Gazette*

CHICAGO, NOV. 5, 1995 — AND ON THE NINTH GAME, THEY rose again from the dead.

"All I can say is, we're baaaack," crowed Steelers tackle Leon Searcy.

Norm Johnson booted a 24-yard field goal in overtime to give the Steelers a 37-34 win over Chicago.

Acting like vampires when the sun goes down, the Steelers crawled out of their Soldier Field coffin yesterday and burst out of the graveyard that was becoming their season. They came back after trailing the Chicago Bears three times, then won on Norm Johnson's 24-yard field goal in overtime, 37-34, and in the process slipped a stake through the Bears' lifetime winning streak against them in Chicago.

"This," said quarterback Neil O'Donnell in a rip-roaring Steelers locker room, "is just the start of a lot of big things to come."

The victory moved the Steelers into first place in the AFC Central Division by themselves with a 5-4 record after Cleveland was upset at home by Houston. The Steelers play the Browns next Monday night at Three Rivers Stadium.

The Steelers snapped the four-game winning streak of the Bears, who slipped to 6-3 this season and 12-1 forever in Chicago against the Steelers.

"We finally put the Chicago thing to

SCORE BY PERIODS

Pittsburgh	0	17	3	14	3	37
Chicago	3	7	14	10	0	34

bed and now we can use it as a slingshot to more momentum," said cornerback Carnell Lake. O'Donnell pitched a 10-yard touchdown pass to Ernie Mills on fourth down with 1:06 left in regulation to bring the Steelers within one point of tying the Bears.

After Coach Bill Cowher sent his offense onto the field for a two-point conversion try to win it all, Chicago called a timeout. That gave Cowher a chance to think harder about his decision and he sent Johnson out to tie it by kicking for one point.

"My better senses made me decide not to," Cowher said of the aborted two-point try. "I wanted the outcome of the game to be decided by the players, not by my decision."

The Bears won the coin flip in overtime, went three-and-out and the Steelers took over on their 31. O'Donnell threw a 12-yard pass to Mills on third-and-11, hit halfback Erric Pegram for a

Steelers coach Bill Cowher enjoys his postgame walk to the locker room.

14-yard screen pass and found Charles Johnson for a 12-yarder in a crowd to give them a first down at the Chicago 32.

Pegram made a first down by inches at the 22 on third down, and on another third down, John L. Williams ripped up the middle for 8 yards to the 8. Williams carried again for 2 yards before Cowher whistled to the bullpen for Johnson and the win.

"It was a decent spot," Johnson said of the somewhat muddy middle of the field, "so I was not concerned."

The winning field goal ended an exciting game but one filled with mistakes that included nine turnovers.

Chicago quarterback Erik Kramer, who had thrown just four interceptions all season, tossed three yesterday to Greg Lloyd, Darren Perry and Willie Williams to go with two lost Bears fum-

bles. Pegram also lost two fumbles for the Steelers and O'Donnell threw two interceptions.

But O'Donnell and Pegram more than made up for those errors. Pegram tied his career high with three touchdowns on runs of 1 and 6 yards and a 7-yard pass. O'Donnell had the fourth-highest passing game of his career, completing 34 of 52 for 341 yards and two TD's. Never has he brought a team from behind the way

he did yesterday to win it.

"Everyone talks about Elway and Marino, Elway and Marino," Steelers offensive coordinator Ron Erhardt said. "Tonight you saw another great — O'Donnell. He brought them back."

Time and time again the Steelers came back.

Chicago took a 3-0 lead on Kevin Butler's 40-yard field goal on the first drive of the game.

The Steelers drove 72 yards on 14 plays — the last Pegram's 1-yard dive into the end zone, to jump in front 7-3 after nose tackle Brentson Buckner stripped Chicago's Robert Green of the ball for a fumble.

In what would become a pulsating theme of success for the rest of the game, O'Donnell hit a third-and-15 pass for 27 yards to wide receiver/quarterback Kordell Stewart on the drive.

"We got this quarterback-to-quarterback thing going," O'Donnell said.

But a 52-yard kickoff return by Nate Lewis gave Chicago the ball on the Steelers' 26, and three plays later, Kramer found Curtis Conway for a 6-yard TD pass that put the Bears back in front, 10-7.

Back came the Steelers to tie it 10-10 on Johnson's 40-yard field goal on the next series.

They then went ahead, 17-10, just before halftime on the biggest interception return of Greg Lloyd's career. From the 50, Kramer dropped back to pass and Lake blitzed from the slot on the dime defense. He leaped in front of Kramer, who threw for Conway. Lloyd intercepted it and ran 52 yards to the 4 with 1:56 left.

The Steelers, who have had few problems in the red zone the past two games after ranking 28th in the league from inside the 20 previously, jammed it into the end zone on O'Donnell's 7-yard pass to Pegram on third down.

Chicago tied it 17-17 on the opening drive of the second half when Kramer passed 12 yards to fullback Tony Carter. The Bears came right back after a poor, 22-yard punt by Rohn Stark gave them the ball on the Steelers' 39. Kramer hit tight end Ryan Wetnight with a 14-yard TD to give Chicago a 24-17 lead, and it appeared as though the Bears were ready to put it away.

But the Steelers' offense, criticized heavily this season, put Johnson in position to kick a 46-yard field goal to make it 24-20.

Safety Anthony Marshall's diving interception set up a 27-yard Butler field goal early in the fourth quarter to extend the Bears' lead to 27-20. The Steelers evened the score again after Mills returned the kickoff 49 yards and Pegram ran untouched for a 6-yard TD behind blocks by Justin Strzelczyk and John L. Williams.

Chicago then stunned the Steelers with 8:46 left in the game. Pinned back on their 3, O'Donnell threw on second down toward the right. Defensive end Alonzo Spellman stretched and batted the pass straight up into the air. Bears linebacker Barry Minter caught it at the 2 and ran into the end zone for a 34-27 lead.

It stayed that way until Mills snatched O'Donnell's TD pass near the end and the Steelers pulled it out in overtime, their first since they went 2-1 in overtime games last season.

"This game went exactly as we expected," defensive end Ray Seals said. "We expected a tough game with two physical teams. We went into overtime and we beat them. Oh, this is big, man."

Big because after losing so many games they were supposed to win — Jacksonville, Cincinnati, Minnesota — they finally won a game few thought they could.

"No one gave us a chance and we had our backs to the wall," Searcy said. "We saw an opportunity to take over our division, and Cleveland lost and we control our destiny now."

O'Donnell, bruised from five sacks but as happy as he's been, saw it more than a victory.

"This is one of those games that brings a team a lot closer together," he said.

STEELERS RETURN TO AFC TITLE GAME

By Ed Bouchette, *Pittsburgh Post-Gazette*

PITTSBURGH, JAN. 6, 1996 — AND SO THE STEELERS HEAD to their second straight AFC championship, but not before they provided one, final, nervous reminder about last year's title game — the blown lead.

"It was just like San Diego," wide receiver Yancy Thigpen said.

Only this time, Thigpen made sure it did not end like San Diego. As the Steelers' lead over Buffalo dwindled from 19 points to five in the fourth quarter, Thigpen made a brilliant catch that stopped the oozing and turned the Steelers back on course to beat the Bills, 40-21, in their playoff game at Three River Stadium yesterday.

"We didn't want to squander another opportunity," explained linebacker Kevin Greene. "We did that last year."

Thigpen beat safety Greg Evans, stretched backward, yanked Neil O'Donnell's pass out of the air and fell flat on his back for a 21-yard gain at the Buffalo 38. Four plays later, a revived Bam Morris ripped 13 yards through two Buffalo tacklers for a touchdown that gave the Steelers a 33-21 lead and breathing room with 6:16 left.

"We jumped on them early, but against a team like that you can't relax," said Thigpen, who erased the memory of his dropped pass in the Green Bay end zone two weeks

SCORE BY PERIODS

Buffalo	0	7	7	7	21
Pittsburgh	7	16	3	14	40

ago. "We have to deliver that knockout punch. We finally did."

It was the first time anyone has been able to deliver it against Buffalo in the playoffs. The Bills had won 10 straight playoff games in the 1990's (not counting Super Bowls, of course) including

Steelers linebacker Kevin Greene celebrates after the 40-21 win over Buffalo.

the greatest comeback victory in NFL history when they beat Houston in 1993.

"You guys have seen Buffalo in the playoffs," Steelers coach Bill Cowher said. "No lead is too safe."

The victory pits the Steelers next Sunday against the winner of today's game between Indianapolis and Kansas City. If the Colts win, the AFC championship will be played at Three Rivers Stadium again. A Chiefs victory puts the game in K.C.

"You have to enjoy the ride," Greene said. "But we're not going to be popping bottles and exploding balloons yet."

They did burst out of the gate yesterday against a Bills team that was without its best defensive player in history, end Bruce Smith. He stayed home with the flu and the NFL's leading pass rush did not sack Neil O'Donnell once.

Morris ran for 106 yards and two fourth-quarter touchdowns for the Steelers, but it was their passing game and four Norm Johnson field goals that provided the 26-7 lead.

The Steelers scored the first two times they had the ball. Thigpen ran a post to catch a 43-yard pass from O'Donnell, halfback Erric Pegram swept 17 yards to the 1 and John L. Williams crashed in behind Morris for TD and a 7-0 Steelers lead.

Ernie Mills and O'Donnell then hooked up on the kind of big play

Ernie Mills' theatrical end-zone catch put the Steelers ahead, 14-0, in the second quarter.

they've produced all season. O'Donnell, from his 10, threw high into the back of the end zone over three Buffalo defenders. Mills leaped beneath the goal posts, caught the pass, was hit by safety Kurt Schultz and landed with just one foot inbounds.

The officials ruled that Schultz forced him out and thus called it a TD, over a vigorous protest by the Bills.

"If I have any complaints about the officials," Buffalo coach Marv Levy said, I'll deliver them to the NFL office."

Mills smiled sheepishly and said he

did not know if it was a touchdown.

"I feel like we would have gotten in there anyway if it wasn't," he said.

The Steelers eventually made it 20-0 in the second quarter on Johnson field goals of 45 and 38 yards and, with actor Kevin Costner watching from the Steelers' owners box, the game for Buffalo was turning into the biggest fiasco since "WaterWorld."

Then, a crack in the Steelers' momentum developed.

Rohn Stark, who finished with the lowest punting average in the AFC, managed his longest of the day for only 33 yards and Buffalo got the ball at the Steelers' 49 with 1:40 left in the first half.

Kelly hit Steve Tasker with a 26-yard pass to the Steelers' 1 and Thurman Thomas ran it in for a TD that made it 20-3. The Steelers raced downfield to get a 34-yard Johnson field goal 11 seconds before the half, but the Bills' score seemed to perk them up.

"We got a little complacent there, our offense got cold and we made a few turnovers," Greene said.

The first turnover came as the Steelers seemed prepared to put it away on their first drive of the third quarter. O'Donnell, from the Bills' 9, put a pass on the outstretched hands of Kordell Stewart at the 3.

The ball slipped through, however, and Evans intercepted it.

Carnell Lake changed things around when he stepped in front of Andre Reed and intercepted a Kelly pass that set up Johnson's 39-yard field goal and a 26-7 Steelers lead with 6:36 left in the quarter. It seemed to be over.

"Hey," Pegram reminded everyone, "it was Jim Kelly and the Buffalo Bills. It was no screw-up team."

It was soon to be Alex Van Pelt and the Buffalo Bills. Kelly did not have a good day. He completed only 14 of 29 passes for 135 yards, one TD and was intercepted three times. He also took a beating. He was hit early by linebacker Chad Brown and end Ray Seals. But it wasn't until Greg Lloyd and Bill Johnson slammed him to the ground after he threw a pass that he separated

O'DONNELL COMES THROUGH

By Bob Smizik, *Pittsburgh Post-Gazette*

It was best of times and worst of times for O'Donnell, who was sharp in clutch

This was Neil O'Donnell at his finest, the quarterback who had come of age to take control of an offense in desperate need of leadership. And this was Neil O'Donnell at his worst, hesitant, inaccurate and unwilling to take charge.

First he was this, then he was that against the Buffalo Bills yesterday at Three Rivers Stadium. It was a scatter-gun performance of consummate artistry and blatant ineptitude.

But with the game in the balance, with momentum swinging wildly toward the Bills, with minds throughout the stadium recalling the one that slipped away against San Diego last season, O'Donnell became the quarterback he had been most of this season. He took the game away from Buffalo and led a Steelers resurgence that produced a 40-21 victory and a berth in the American Football Conference championship game for the second consecutive season.

Buffalo linebacker Bryce Paup, the NFL Defensive Player of the Year, said of the Steelers' offense, "It's head and shoulders above where it used to be. They're a complete team now. They can easily go the distance if they play the way they did."

O'Donnell came out in stunning near-perfection as the Steelers threatened a blowout by scoring touchdowns on their first two possessions. They were classic drives, highlighted by O'Donnell's ability not only to hit his receivers, but hit them perfectly so they were able to pick up yardage after making the catch.

He completed 3 of 3 passes for 54 yards on the first drive as the Steelers moved 76 yards in nine plays. He came back with a 3-for-4 performance for 26 yards as the Steelers moved 58 yards in 10 plays.

And then it came apart.

The offense that produced nine first downs in the first two possessions produced only two in the next four. The offense that had averaged 7 yards a play on the first two possessions averaged 1.7 on the next four.

It wasn't so noticeable because the ineptitude hadn't spread to the scoreboard. Excellent field position enabled the Steelers to turn two of

Bam Morris' fourth-quarter TD gave the Steelers a 33-21 lead.

his shoulder.

Van Pelt, who played for Pitt and the Steelers, came on, gave Tasker the ball for a 40-yard pickup on an end-around and fired a 2-yard TD pass to tight end Tony Cline.

It was 26-14 but the worry did not cascade from the 59,072 at Three Rivers until another poor Stark punt, this one of 31 yards, gave the Bills the ball at the Steelers' 36. Van Pelt began the drive but Kelly came on to finish it by pitching a 9-yard TD pass to Thomas that made it 26-21 with 11:23 left.

The momentum was shifting faster than anxious Steelers fans in their seats, and they weren't the only ones worried.

"I was pretty tight," linebacker Jerry Olsavsky conceded.

But Thigpen's catch served as Advil to a growing Steelers' headache, Olsavsky and linebacker Levon Kirkland came up with interceptions and Morris ran through Buffalo as if he were auditioning for "Dancing With Wolves."

"Greg Lloyd kept saying to everyone, 'There's no tomorrow, there's no tomorrow,'" Pegram said.

But there is and by 7 o'clock tonight they should know their opponent next Sunday.

"It boils down to a three-game season and we're 1-0," tackle Leon Searcy said. "Two and one, 1-1 doesn't get it. We have to go undefeated."

those futile possessions into field goals to take a 20-0 lead.

But, clearly, O'Donnell's game was not the same.

That didn't seem to matter to Coach Bill Cowher, who disdained a conservative approach when the Steelers got the ball back late in the first half following a Buffalo touchdown.

"When there's 45 seconds left in the half, I used to say, 'Just take it, let's kneel on it,'" Cowher said.

O'Donnell said, "I think Bill has a lot of confidence in our two-minute offense now. I always did. Sometimes it doesn't work, but I think if you look at us the past 20 weeks, we're doing a pretty good job scoring points right before the half and at the end of the game."

Cowher told O'Donnell to go for it, which he did, throwing four times and completing passes of 14, 22, 8 and 9 yards to set up a 34-yard field goal by Norm Johnson.

It should have set up a return to form in the third quarter. It didn't.

In one stretch, O'Donnell missed on seven consecutive passes as the Steelers went three and out on three consecutive possessions.

When Buffalo scored early in the fourth quarter to make the score 26-21, the Steelers appeared to be in trouble.

"The momentum was going their way," tackle Leon Searcy said. "They were stopping us and their offense was putting points on the board. It was very frustrating. It seemed like we were being overly protective of the lead and not going out there and playing football. We just gathered together and said, 'We are going to go out there and play football and ignore the scoreboard.'"

O'Donnell passed 13 yards to Ernie Mills for a first down on the Steelers' 39, but two plays later it was third-and-8 and a play of monstrous implications loomed.

From the shotgun, O'Donnell found Yancey Thigpen about 20 yards downfield and near the Steelers' sideline. The pass wasn't perfect. Thigpen had to dive. But it was a first down that gave the Steelers the momentum to go on for a score, then another to take the drama out of the game.

Next week, it's either Kansas City or Indianapolis. More will be required to produce victory.

"In the third quarter our offense fell into a little lull," said O'Donnell, who completed 19 of 35 passes for 262 yards.

"I don't know the reasons why. But it's something we'll look closely at, because down the road they get better and better. So we'll have to play all four quarters."

Yes, he will.

BOUNCE IN THE END ZONE GOES THE STEELERS' WAY

By Ed Bouchette, *Pittsburgh Post-Gazette*

PITTSBURGH, JAN. 14, 1996 — FRANCO HARRIS WAS THERE, on the Steelers' sideline, as was Kordell Stewart. They know a little about creating miracle football endings, but this time they could only watch and wait as Jim Harbaugh's prayer on the last play of the AFC championship was launched from the 29 toward the goal line.

Indianapolis receivers and Steelers defensive backs packed into the end zone like bachelors waiting for the garter toss. The stakes: a trip to the Super Bowl.

"It seemed like it took forever," Steelers safety Darren Perry said. "You could just see this big ball. It looked huge and it looked like it was coming in slow motion."

And after Perry tipped it and others swiped at it, the ball came right down into the lap of Colts wide receiver Aaron Bailey on the ground. He seemed to have it, but the ball rolled off his chest, onto the turf, the officials ruled it incomplete and the Steelers were going to the Super Bowl.

"It was," Bailey moaned, "almost another Immaculate Reception."

But close didn't count for the Horseshoes, as Bailey's non-catch on the final play and Ernie Mills' game-deciding 37-yard reception with 1:51 left propelled the Steelers to a 20-16 victory over the Colts in the AFC championship.

The game had everything that last year's title game had but with two big dif-

SCORE BY PERIODS

Indianapolis	3	3	3	7	16
Pittsburgh	3	7	3	7	20

ferences. The favored Steelers won this time and they came from behind to do it.

"Maybe it was poetic justice," said Steelers coach Bill Cowher, who had tears in his eyes after the biggest win of his career. "Having been there again with the ball in the air and an opportunity to win a championship. Now I'm 1-1. It was a great feeling."

It finally erased the memories of last year's upset loss to San Diego in the title game and puts the Steelers in the Super Bowl for the first time in 16 years. They will play Dallas, a team they beat in Super Bowls X and XIII. An early line has the Steelers as 11-point underdogs.

Bam Morris (33) scores the game-winning touchdown with less than two minutes left in the game.

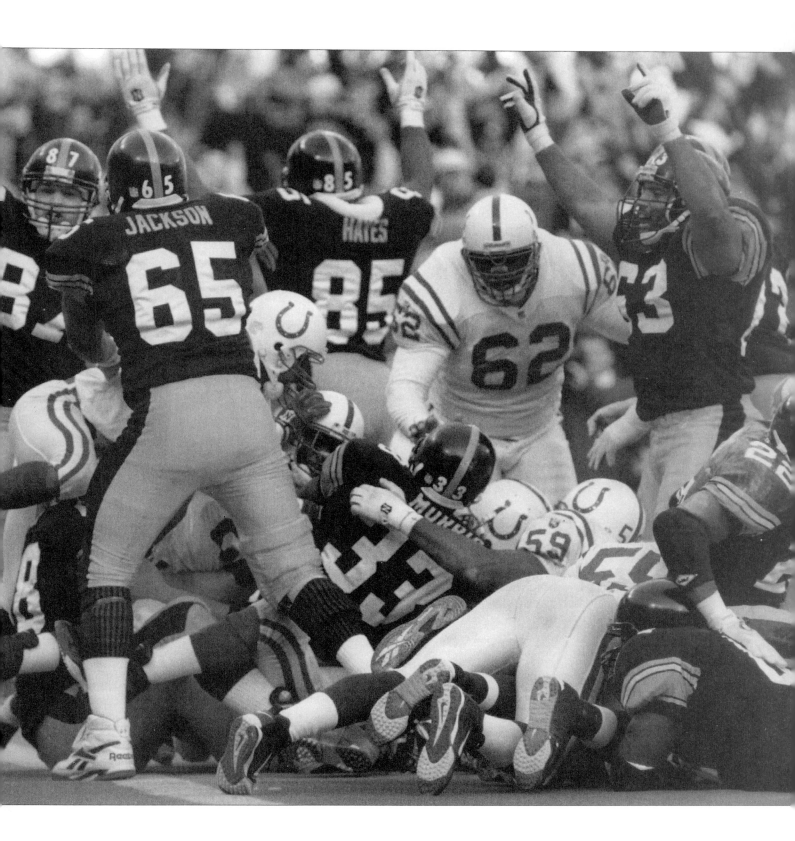

"When I saw the ref go like this," said Steelers defensive end Ray Seals, waving his hands, "it was over, baby. Cinderella's gone. We're in."

Indianapolis, though, played more like Godzilla than the 11-point underdogs that the Colts were. They scored on three Cary Blanchard field goals, one in each quarter, and trailed, 13-9, in the fourth only because of a disputed touchdown reception by the Steelers' Kordell Stewart to go with two Norm Johnson field goals.

Then Harbaugh silenced the 61,062 at Three Rivers Stadium like no one since Stan Humphries and Tony Martin of San Diego. He beat a Steelers blitz and lofted a 47-yard touchdown pass to Floyd Turner to put Indy on top, 16-13, with 8:46 left, and the Steelers were being haunted again.

"Yeah," Seals admitted, "it was in the back of your mind, 'Damn, is this going to happen to us again?' But last year we didn't finish. This year, we pulled it out and that's the difference in this team."

They put together some magic of their own before and during their winning touchdown drive.

The Steelers reached the 50 but could not convert a third-and-5 on their next series and punted to Indy with 6:29 left. The Colts' Lamont Warren fumbled on the first play from the 9 but guard Joe Staysniak recovered and the break the Steelers needed had just eluded them.

On third-and-1, however, with 3:57 left, the Steelers created their own break — with a broken play on defense. Warren took a handoff and headed left. Safety Myron Bell was supposed to blitz on the play but did not. Seeing this, cornerback Willie Williams dashed in from the opposite side, sliced through the Colts backfield and brought Warren down by the ankles for no gain.

"I saw Harbaugh give the ball off to Lamont and I just had to make the tackle," Williams said. "If I didn't make the tackle he probably would have made first down and it would have been a different ballgame."

Instead of keeping a clock killing drive going, the Colts had to punt and Hastings returned it 12 yards to the 33.

With 3:03 left, quarterback Neil O'Donnell began a drive that had the looks of last year's that ended 3 yards short against San Diego. He threw to Stewart for 13 and to John L. Williams for 7. He then nearly threw the game away when his pass for Mills went straight into the hands of linebacker Quentin Coryatt. But Coryatt dropped it after Mills swiped his left arm.

"I thought he had the ball and I just swung my arm and tried to hit it and knock it out," Mills said.

The Drive Was Drama at Its Best

By Bob Smizik, *Pittsburgh Post-Gazette*

It is often the thinnest of lines that separate victory from defeat in an athletic contest and that line was squeezed to an infinitesimal width yesterday at Three Rivers Stadium as two teams that clearly possessed the hearts of champions competed for the American Football Conference title.

The Steelers came away the victor, 20-16, over the Indianapolis Colts. But at no time in this game — not even until seconds after the final play — could they feel sure of the outcome, certain of their destiny. It was football drama at its finest, a game to do both teams and the sport proud.

With the victory the Steelers move on to the promised land of the Super Bowl for the first time in 16 years.

They'll not think about how close they came to losing this game but how they won it.

What will be remembered is the 37-yard pass from quarterback Neil O'Donnell to wide receiver Ernie Mills to the Indianapolis 1 and the bull rush into the Colts' line by Bam Morris that produced the touchdown.

What will be forgotten — in Pittsburgh, at least — is how linebacker Quentin Coryatt could have ended this final drive when it was three plays old if he had hung on to an almost certain interception.

But given this second chance — and this was the fine difference between these teams — the Steelers did not falter.

With the tension suffocating, with the label of the great choke team on the 90's awaiting them, they grabbed at this unexpected opportunity and put together the kind of drive that had brought them to this game.

And although there was time to construct this drive any way he pleased, it was only appropriate Coach Bill Cowher would place his Super Bowl hopes with O'Donnell, the man who brought the team to this game.

After the Colts had taken a 16-13 lead with 8:46 remaining, the Steelers, even with the help of a 21-yard pass interference play, could muster nothing on their next drive. When they got

"If he catches it, it's over."

They faced sudden death two plays later, on fourth-and-3 with barely two minutes to go. O'Donnell not having one of his best days, came up big at the end. He slipped a 9-yard pass to Andre Hastings for a first down.

"They lost me in the shuffle and Neil made a great throw," Hastings said.

"I think he threw it between three guys and hit me in the numbers."

That was the throw that saved the game; the very next one won it.

Mills, on first down, ran a semimove and go — and out and up from the right side. He beat cornerback Ashley Ambrose by a step and O'Donnell put the ball right on his outstretched hands inside the 5. Hugging the sideline, Mills got his right foot down and dragged his left one inbounds before he hit the sideline for a 37-yard catch to the Colts' 1.

"I took a quick peek left (at Yancey Thigpen) and then went back over to Ernie's side," said O'Donnell, who completed 25 of 41 passes for 205 yards.

"Ernie made a great move on the guy, and I gave him a chance to go get it. I told him that in the huddle, that I was going to give one of those guys a chance to get it. Now you have to go get it."

The ball was at the 1 and Bam Morris, who had carried only five times before that, came in to run behind fullback John L. Williams. On first down, he dived, flipped over for no gain and tore a hole in his pants.

"When it was second-and-1," Morris said, "John L. Williams looked at me and said, 'Whatever it takes, get it in.' "

Morris got the handoff again and followed Williams off right guard. The Colts stopped him for an instant, before

he plunged into the end zone to put the Steelers ahead by four.

"I just kept pumping my feet like I was running in water," Morris said.

There was 1:34 left, and the Colts were out of miracles. But Indianapolis believed it was a miracle that allowed Kordell Stewart's 5-yard TD catch to stand up 13 seconds before halftime.

TV replays showed that Stewart stepped out of the back of the end zone and then returned to catch the pass that put the Steelers ahead, 10-6. It should have nullified the play, but the officials did not see him when he stepped out of bounds.

"It appears as if it happened so close to one of our officials that he probably didn't look down at his feet," said referee Bernie Kukar.

"He (field judge John Robison) was looking to see if there was any contact. And unfortunately, he only has two eyes.

the ball back, three minutes three seconds remained.

It was clear to them this would be their final chance. And it was just as clear a repeat of the AFC title game last year, when their final drive failed, was heavy in their thoughts.

"Everything pointed to what happened to us last year," tackle Leon Searcy said. "That was in the minds of a lot of guys. But we weren't going to let it happen. We had to come out with the win. We had confidence in Neil."

O'Donnell found Kordell Stewart for 13 yards and on a screen-pass John L. Williams fought for 7. It was second-and-3 on the Indianapolis 47 and O'Donnell hit Coryatt in the chest. But the intended receiver, Mills, was able to help dislodge the ball. The Steelers were alive.

An O'Donnell pass to Andre Hast-

ings near the sideline sailed high.

"It was the wind," Hastings said, when it was suggested the fault for the pass was O'Donnell. "The ball didn't end up where it started to go. That wind was more difficult than people thought."

Now it was fourth-and-3. Was Cowher thinking punt?

"No, that was the game. We only had one or two timeouts. That was it."

Searcy was unwavering, but this was hard to handle. "It was too much pressure," he said.

"We called crossing patterns and hoped they would go into man coverage," O'Donnell said. "But they stayed in zone."

O'Donnell had time — the Colts rushed only three players almost all game — and took it. Suddenly, Hastings was open. O'Donnell took his shot.

"That play was unbelievable. I fired it as hard as I could."

"Neil made a great throw," Hastings said. "He threaded it between three defenders and it hit me in the numbers."

On the next play, O'Donnell threw almost perfectly to Mills. After the Steelers scored, the Colts made a final, valiant effort that came within inches of success.

"We might not be the champions," said Colts defensive tackle Tony Siragusa, "but in my heart everyone in this locker room is a champion."

The same for the other room. But these are the real champions, the team going to the Super Bowl. The team that was 3-4 after seven games had won of its past 11.

They're going to the Super Bowl. They've earned it.

STEELERS SUFFER FIRST SUPER BOWL LOSS

By Ed Bouchette, *Pittsburgh Post-Gazette*

TEMPE, ARIZ., JAN. 28, 1996 — THE DALLAS COWBOYS HAD to sweat for it, but they emerged yesterday as a dynasty in midstream and the Steelers helped with their coronation.

SCORE BY PERIODS

Dallas	10	3	7	7	27
Pittsburgh	0	7	0	10	17

Dallas won an unprecedented third Super Bowl in four years by holding off the Steelers for a 27-17 victory, joining San Francisco as the only teams to win five Lombardi trophies.

The Steelers trailed by just three points with four minutes left before cornerback Larry Brown intercepted his second Neil O'Donnell pass of the second half and returned it 33 yards to the Steelers' 6. Emmitt Smith then ran it in for a 4-yard touchdown with 3:43 left that ended the Steelers' comeback from 13 points down in the first half.

While they made an exciting game of it, the underdog Steelers became the 12th straight AFC team to fall victim in the Super Bowl and it was their first loss in the championship in five tries.

"It's been one great run," Steelers coach Bill Cowher said. "We didn't get to the top of the mountain, but it was a great run along the way."

The Steelers' comeback brought a gracious response from Cowboys owner Jerry Jones at the trophy presentation.

"I want to tell all you Steeler fans ... what a great team you have and what a ballgame."

Both of Brown's interceptions led to Dallas touchdowns, their only scores of the second half. He picked one off midway through the third quarter and returned it 44 yards that led to a 1-yard TD run by Smith.

Brown's two big plays earned him the game's MVP award, the first by a cornerback ever in the Super Bowl and the first defensive back so honored since safety Jake Scott of Miami in Super Bowl VII.

O'Donnell also threw a third interception on a Hail Mary pass on the last play of the game. Those were the only turnovers in the Super Bowl. Cowher said the first interception resulted because the ball sailed on O'Donnell — no receiver was anywhere near it — but that the second occurred because of a miscommunication between O'Donnell and his receiver, Andre Hastings.

"The bottom line is two big plays,"

Yancey Thigpen scored Pittsburgh's first touchdown over Dallas' Deion Sanders in the final minute before halftime.

Kevin Greene watches the seconds tick down on the Steelers' hopes in Super Bowl XXX.

quarter, they dominated more than half the game on offense and defense, and used a successful onside kick in the fourth quarter to create an opportunity to win.

"I'd like to commend Pittsburgh for the way they played," Dallas coach Barry Switzer said. "They dominated the second half."

Dallas took that 13-0 lead on Chris Boniol field goals of 42 and 35 yards, and a 3-yard TD pass from Troy Aikman to tight end Jay Novacek.

Neil O'Donnell threw a 6-yard scoring pass to Yancey Thigpen 15 seconds before halftime for the Steelers, who got scores in the second half when Norm Johnson kicked a 46-yard field goal and Bam Morris ran over from the 1 with 6:36 left in the game to put them within three points.

That last touchdown came after the Steelers converted an onside kick with 11:20 left and trailing by 10. Johnson kicked off short to the right sideline and Deon Figures scooped it up at the Steelers' 48.

Kordell Stewart moved behind center to convert a fourth-and-1 at the Steelers' 49 in the first quarter but they weren't so lucky on two third-quarter calls.

The Steelers had third-and-2 on their 47 and trailed by 20-7 when they tried Morris up the middle for no gain on two straight plays.

"We came here to win the game, not to play to lose," Cowher said. "Those fourth-down calls, any one of them, I would do again."

Morris outgained Smith, 73 yards to 49. Aikman, though, outperformed O'Donnell by completing 15 of 23 passes for 209 yards and the biggest stat of the Super Bowl — no interceptions. Levon Kirkland and Ray Seals

Yancey Thigpen celebrates his second-quarter touchdown in the end zone.

Cowher said. "We couldn't get a turnover and they had the turnovers and that's the difference sometimes.

"Neil got us here. Without Neil O'Donnell, we wouldn't be playing the last of January."

O'Donnell threw just seven interceptions all season. Yesterday, he completed 28 of 49 passes for 239 yards and

was sacked four times.

"It was not characteristic of Neil O'Donnell," the quarterback said. "It's just too bad we fell a little short because we had an opportunity to win it."

Without Brown's interceptions, the Steelers probably would have won the game. After a shaky start and a 13-0 deficit midway through the second

COWHER DARES TO COME UP A SUPER CHAMPION

By Gene Collier, *Pittsburgh Post-Gazette*

When he arose out of his crouch at the intersection of the sideline and the Pittsburgh 48 to a blinding crackle of flashbulbs in the desert night, Bill Cowher seemed to walk in a semi-daze.

Jerry Jones met the first Steelers coach to lose a Super Bowl a couple of steps later, then Cowher wandered toward the center of the field, brushed the right paw of Leon Lett, then found Barry Switzer as the mob thickened. Their exchange was brief, and he was channeled toward the Steelers' tunnel, paused to hug his wife and chat briefly with one of his daughters, and he left the floor of the Super Bowl.

Maybe Cowher never will return to this stage, but the Super Bowl would be worse for it, because in his first try, he coached the kind of game critics of this event have begged for most of its glorious-despite-itself 30-year history.

Cowher gambled at almost every opportunity across the green felt of Sun Devil Stadium, and the fact that his Steelers lost Super Bowl XXX to a superior Dallas Cowboys team should never tarnish his daring and his accomplishments.

In a forum best known for the numbingly conservative tactics of fearful coaches, Cowher was little short of a revelation. Let the Super Bowl records show that Cowher was little short of a revelation. Let the Super Bowl records also show that Cowher:

■ Went for it on fourth-and-1 from his 49 on Pittsburgh's second possession of the game.

■ Went for it on fourth-and-2 from his 47 with more than a quarter to play and his team down less than two touchdowns.

■ Ordered an onside kick with 11:20 to play and his team trailing by only 10 points, the earliest onside kick in the history of the Super Bowl.

"We thought about doing it to open the game," Cowher said. "I guess if we didn't get it there where we got it, we'd have been in a kind of touchy situation, but just like with the fourth down plays, I'd do every one of those plays again.

"We came in here trying to win the game. We didn't come to try not to lose it."

As gambles go, Cowher won two and lost one, and I'm not sure any of those three were the right thing to do, but, as a matter of style, every game would be a superior spectacle if it were directed by Cowher's jut-jawed philosophy.

Cowher's offense just made too many mistakes to let the coach's swashbuckling win the game. The difference between those teams is essentially this: with Rod Woodson physically less than his gifted self, Pittsburgh's top players are very good, whereas Dallas' top players are great. That's generally all you need for a 10-point Super Bowl, and that's what makes Troy Aikman throw no interceptions in the Super Bowl and only one in three postseason games while Neil O'Donnell is throwing three in the Super Bowl and six in three postseason games.

Two O'Donnell throws that wound up in the hands of Super Bowl MVP Larry Brown, who returned them a combined 77 yards and sparked two touchdowns, were the ballgame.

Pittsburgh's defense saw to it that the Cowboys mounted only one scoring drive of their own making and Pittsburgh's offense overcame a balky start. Pittsburgh's special teams, especially Norm Johnson, played a whale of a game.

Cowher had this team relaxed and ready to play, and it gave a talented team all it could take. So when you end up matching talent for talent, always the bottom line, teams will have to start recognizing the one slice of great talent on the Steelers' sideline belongs to the head coach.

Bill Cowher instructs his players on the sideline.

After a memorable season, Steelers quarterback Neil O'Donnell experienced many frustrating moments in Super Bowl XXX.

Steelers Defense All Heart, Stops Smith

By Bob Smizik, *Pittsburgh Post-Gazette*

There's no glory in defeat, nor should there be. The object of any game played by professional athletes is to win, and that is doubly so in what has become the ultimate American game — the Super Bowl.

Still, what a gallant performance by the Steelers' defense. What a show of heart, guts, will and talent. What a effort against significant adversity. What an accomplishment by men most everyone expected to be dominated.

The Steelers lost in Super Bowl XXX to the Dallas Cowboys, 27-17, last night at Sun Devil Stadium. But the Steelers' defense played like winners — like champions.

The game plan was grand in design but totally unnecessary. It called for the defense to stop Emmitt Smith, who was nothing more than the best running back in the National Football League and who was playing behind nothing more than the best line in the NFL. But, really, who stops Emmitt?

The Steelers did.

It was a performance carved out of sheer determination and an unyielding belief that no one plays this phase of the game better.

Smith, who had rumbled for more than 100 yards in both of his previous Super Bowls, gained 49 yards on 18 carries. But that was only a small part of the story.

The first time Smith touched the ball — the third play of the game — he bolted off left tackle, through an enormous hole and past a prone Greg Lloyd, who had been placed on his back by Cowboys guard Larry Allen. It was a 23-yard gain.

It looked like a portent of what was to come. Lloyd, the leader of the defense, had been trampled and with him went the rest of the defense. The Cowboys, the overwhelming favorites, had flexed their muscles and the Steelers had collapsed. Not exactly.

That was it for Smith. Oh, he scored two touchdowns to set a Super Bowl record of five for a career. But they came on runs of 1 and 4 yards.

On his final 17 carries, Smith gained 26 yards. The supposedly unstoppable Smith had averaged 2.7 yards for the game and 1.5 yards in his final 17 carries. Smith had been held to his lowest output of the season. The game plan had worked but still the Steelers lost.

The defense was slow starting, allowing the Cowboys two field goals and a touchdown on their first three possessions.

"Early on we were a little sluggish," Coach Bill Cowher said. "After that we did a very good job. After the first quarter, we went toe-to-toe with them."

Cowher was being too modest. His defense dominated what many believe to be the most electrifying offense in football. Dallas scored two second-half touchdowns, but both came after interceptions of Neil O'Donnell passes had given the Cowboys field position inside the Steelers' 20.

Although the final score doesn't indicate it, the Steelers seemed in position to tie or win the game midway through the fourth quarter. They had rallied from a 13-0 first-half

each had a sack of Aikman and Chad Hennings had two of the Cowboys' four sacks of O'Donnell.

The Steelers' Hastings also led all receivers with 10 catches for 98 yards and Ernie Mills had eight for 78. Michael Irvin led the Cowboys with five catches for 76 yards.

The Steelers outgained Dallas, 310 yards to 254.

"Pittsburgh played a great ball game the whole day," Smith said. "I have a lot of respect for them. They just started coming at us and kept coming. They never quit. They never let down. And fortunately we made enough plays to win."

The Steelers salvaged an otherwise horrible first half by scoring that touchdown with 13 seconds left on O'Donnell's pass to Thigpen.

The 54-yard drive began with 3:52 left and took 13 plays, including three big third-down plays. One came on third-and-20 when O'Donnell hit Hastings with a pass inches short of the first down. Stewart came in and ran a quarterback sneak off right guard to pick up 3 yards to the Dallas 42.

Next, O'Donnell found Mills with a 7-yard pass on third-and-7. Then, on third-and-13 at the Dallas 23 and only 23 seconds left, O'Donnell threw high and hard to Mills, who leaped and

deficit to trail, 20-17, with momentum decidedly on their side. It was the defense that put them in that position.

After the Cowboys had rumbled for 193 yards in the first half, they got only 61 in the second.

"I think the main thing was that we just settled down," Steelers safety Darren Perry said. "We were on edge a little bit until we got comfortable and said, 'Hey, we can play with this ball team.'"

Which is what they did. It was a stunning performance, perhaps the best of the season against Dallas.

"Their offense drove down the field one time on our defense," said cornerback Rod Woodson, "and other than that I don't think they did much of anything against our defense. I felt going in at halftime we were just getting warmed up. We had just gotten the kinks out."

No one was more aware of the Steelers' defensive excellence than Smith.

"Pittsburgh played a great ball game the whole day," he said. "I have a lot of respect for them. They just started coming at us and kept coming. They never quit. They never laid down."

And they did everything a defense could do — except win.

Steelers All-Pro cornerback Rod Woodson had knee surgery after the first game of the season, but worked overtime to come back and play against Dallas in Super Bowl XXX.

brought it down at the 6.

It was first down, but only 17 seconds remained. Thigpen lined up wide right, opposite cornerback Deion Sanders. Thigpen slanted inside and Sanders pushed him just as O'Donnell's pass arrived for a TD that gave the Steelers life at the half, trailing by just 13-7.

Before that score, it appeared Dallas would blow them out before the half. Midway through the second quarter, they had almost wiped out the point spread, leading 13-0.

The Cowboys scored on their first three possessions.

Bonoil got things going when he kicked a 42-yard field goal on the game's first drive, a series that included a 20-yard pass to Michael Irvin and a 23-yard run by Smith in which Larry Allen bowled over Greg Lloyd.

The Steelers' offense went three and out and Dallas quickly made it 10-0. Sanders, playing both ways, beat Willie Williams on a post pattern for a 47-yard catch on a perfectly-thrown ball from Aikman to the Steelers' 14.

Novacek, who worried Cowher all week, then came up big. He caught a 10-yard pass to the 3 on third-and-13, then followed with his touchdown catch of 3 yards.

BILL COWHER: TOUGH AS STEEL

By Ron Cook

THE LATE, GREAT PITTSBURGH STEELERS OWNER, ART ROONEY Sr., would have given Bill Cowher his highest praise. You almost can see The Chief biting down on his big cigar, hear him saying through the smoke, "I like him. He's a Pittsburgher."

Cowher is the quintessential Pittsburgh guy in many ways. He likes nothing more than going through the fast-food drive-through with his three young daughters or having a cold Iron City on his father's front porch. Yet, he lives in the toney Pittsburgh suburb of Fox Chapel and drives a black Saab convertible.

Cowher is the perfect coach for the 90's. His Steelers players call him the perfect players' coach. He has been there and done that as an NFL player. He knows the pressures and demands that go with the job. And, my gawd, he's emotional, enthusiastic, energetic. "He's droolin'. He's slobberin'. He's head-buttin'. He's screamin'," linebacker Kevin Greene once said. "You gotta love a coach like that." Yet, Cowher has absolutely no use for a free spirit such as the NBA's freaky Dennis Rodman. "He wouldn't have to worry about putting on his shoes with me," Cowher said. "He'd be gone."

Cowher is the ultimate control freak, as most successful football coaches are. Yet, he gave in to the fans — the fans, for goodness sake — when he tried to move the Steelers' bench from one sideline to the other at Three Rivers Stadium. "There was an overwhelming response," Cowher said, shrugging. Yes, the people spoke.

William Laird Cowher is many things, but he also is this: The second-winningest NFL coach from 1992-95. His regular-season record, 43-21, was exceeded only by San Francisco's George Seifert (48-16). His team was one of four to go to the playoffs each season. It went to the AFC Championship game after the '94 season and to the Super Bowl after the '95 season.

Cowher, 39, did what few thought he could when the Steelers made him their 15th head coach on Jan. 21, 1992. He escaped the mighty legacy of Chuck Noll, who built a 209-156-1 record and won four Super Bowls in his 23 seasons as coach. He is constructing a mighty legacy of his own.

"This team is its own team," Steelers President Dan Rooney said a few days before the Dallas Cowboys beat Pittsburgh, 27-17, in Super Bowl XXX, the Steelers' first Super Bowl appearance in 16 years.

That loss shouldn't detract from Cowher's marvelous coaching job in 1995. The regular season began against the Detroit Lions on a hot, steamy September Sunday when All-Pro cornerback Rod Woodson tore up his right knee on the ninth defensive play and quarterback Neil O'Donnell went down in the second quarter with a broken bone in his right hand. It didn't end until O'Donnell threw the second of two crushing interceptions to Cowboys cornerback Larry Brown on Super Bowl Sunday.

The season wasn't supposed to be that good. The Steelers traded leading rusher Barry Foster during the off-season. They lost Pro Bowl guard Duval Love and their immense and immensely talented tight end, Eric Green, to free agency. They failed to sign kicker Gary Anderson, whom the fans adored and knew as Mr. Reliable. The architect of their Blitzburgh defense, Dom Capers, left to became head coach of the Carolina Panthers.

Then, Woodson and O'Donnell were injured. The Steelers beat the Lions, 23-20, on that horrible afternoon but still sputtered to a 3-4 start. No one who watched them get blown out at home by Cincinnati, 27-9, in a Thursday night nationally televised

In four seasons at the helm of the Steelers, Bill Cowher has taken his team to the playoffs each year.

game on Oct. 19 would have wagered a nickel they would make it to the Super Bowl.

"I've been on teams that were in trouble early and you start dwelling and worrying about the past games instead of preparing for the one ahead of you," guard Tom Newberry said. "The positive thing is we were never out of the race for the division. Every week, Cowher talked about, 'Hey, we're still in position to win this division.' He said if we play well from here on out, no one will remember that you didn't have a great start. Nobody panicked."

Certainly Cowher didn't. He merely stuck out his big jaw, the one that earned him the nickname, "Goon," as a kid and, "Face," as an NFL player, the same jaw that prompted backup quarterback Mike Tomczak to once say of his boss, "If he'd sign over licensing rights, he'd make a pretty good cartoon character." That jaw has come to symbolize Cowher's resoluteness.

"The minute Woodson and O'Donnell went down, I looked at it as a challenge," Cowher said. "That, to me, is what coaching is all about. It's easy when you're winning and everything is going well. But what happens when it's not?

"I've always said it's not adversity that determines the outcome. It's how you deal with adversity that's so important.

"I told the team the same thing I told the fans and the media. 'This is a team game. The guys who have to fill in have a responsibility, but it's not just up to them. The other 20 starters have to pick up their game and we go on together. The expectations don't change one bit. Our goal still is a championship.'

"I really believe that. The players know that. You can't fool them. If you're just talking to talk and really dwelling in self-pity, they perceive that. Then, you're in trouble."

Tomczak knows about Cowher's sincerity. He experienced it after he played poorly in a 23-10 loss at Miami Sept. 18. He threw two interceptions that night and lost a fumble.

"He was positive, encouraging, upbeat," Tomczak said. "It was like, 'This is a terrible game, but it's not all your fault. Let's regroup and get after it.'

"I've had other coaches" — read:

Cowher addresses the media at a press conference announcing his selection as the Steelers' new head coach in 1992.

Mike Ditka — "who were vulgar and detrimental in that situation. They didn't do anything to help you. But with Bill, you always feel like he's on your side."

Cowher never lost his team. It helped that O'Donnell returned for the sixth game and played well the rest of the season. It helped that the Steelers finally got their running game going with Foster's replacement, Bam Morris. And it certainly helped that Cowher moved Pro Bowl safety Carnell Lake to cornerback to ease the loss of Woodson and turned rookie Kordell Stewart into "Slash," a Hydra-headed quarterback-receiver-running back who threw for one touchdown, ran for another and caught a third, bringing a much-needed spark not just to the Steelers, but to the staid NFL.

The Steelers won eight consecutive games before losing at Green Bay to end the regular season. They won their third AFC Central Division title in Cowher's four seasons. They blew out Buffalo, 40-21, in the playoffs, then hung on to beat Indianapolis, 20-16, in the AFC championship game in Pittsburgh.

It was after that game against the Colts that Pittsburgh saw a side of Cowher it had never seen. The city is used to seeing Pirates manager Jim Leyland cry. It's one reason Leyland probably is more popular than any athlete in town, with the exception of Mario Lemieux and Jaromir Jagr of the Penguins.

But on this day, tears rolled down Cowher's face. They started when the Colts' final, desperation pass rolled through the hands of wide receiver Aaron Bailey in the Steelers' end zone and continued when Dan Rooney accepted the AFC trophy at midfield. Somehow, it seemed appropriate that a likeness of Rooney Sr., the Steelers' patriarch, was on the scoreboard during the presentation. It almost was if The Chief was nodding his approval at Cowher.

"I'm just happy that the city can go through this," Cowher said. "That's why it's great. It unites everybody. It's like one big, happy family."

There also were tears in the private box where Cowher's family watches the home games. His equally emotional

Although outnumbered, Cowher makes a passionate plea with the referees.

home in time to catch the Steelers the next day.

Now his son was taking the team — his team — to the Super Bowl?

Laird Cowher's reaction that day was much the same as it was when his son was picked to be the Steelers' coach. "I just sat down because if I didn't I would have fell down."

The Bill Cowher story really be-gins in that home on Hawthorne Avenue. It begins with a life lesson Laird Cowher taught all his sons. "The only place you find success ahead of work is in the dictionary."

Bill Cowher wasn't the most gifted athlete in the games they played at nearby Crafton Park or in organized sports later. But he did work the hardest. And he had the greatest passion for winning. It's why he was a four-sport star in football, baseball, tennis and track at Carlynton High School.

Friends in Crafton describe him as a polite, mild-mannered boy. But put him on a football field? "We laughed when we said it, but we thought he was borderline insane," a former college teammate, Brad Holt, told The Pittsburgh Press in 1992. "There was something about his eyes. They were on fire. You could see the fire in them. If you looked into his eyes as he walked onto the football field, it was like he was leaving the planet. He was the most intense player I'd ever seen."

Tom Donahoe knows. As the Steelers' director of football operations, he helped hire Cowher and is his boss. But he was coaching South Park High School on Nov. 1, 1974. That night, South Park played Carlynton in Cowher's final game. Carlynton won, 47-7, but that's not what Donahoe remembers.

"Cowher intimidated everybody on my football team, including half of my coaching staff. He was scary."

wife, Kaye, received almost as much television time as he did. She played college basketball at North Carolina State, where they met, and also with the New York Stars of the Women's Professional Basketball League. She knew what this moment meant to her husband.

So did Cowher's parents, Laird and Dorothy. They raised their sons Dale, Bill and Doug on Hawthorne Avenue in Crafton, about a 10-minute drive from Three Rivers Stadium. (See, Cowher really is a Pittsburgher.) Laird Cowher, a retired insurance man and a former Steelers' season-ticket holder, was such a big fan that he routinely would drive 9 1/2 hours to see Bill play at North Carolina State, then drive

Even then, Cowher, a linebacker-tight end, had a terrific feel for the game, a feel that later would serve him well as a coach. He often would visit Carlynton defensive coordinator Bill Yost during study halls to watch film. "He was always asking questions," Yost said. "He always wanted to know more about what we were doing and why we were doing it."

"He never said much when the coaches were around, but when we got on the field he did all the talking — and everybody listened to him," said Jim James, a boyhood friend and former high school teammate.

"I remember we didn't have a goal-line defense. We never practiced it so Bill made one up in the huddle at Peters Township. He just said, 'You get down. You get down. You get down.' He positioned all of us. And it worked."

Laird Cowher, another Pittsburgher to the bone, wanted Bill to go to the University of Pittsburgh, but Pitt wasn't interested. Bill Cowher wanted to play at Penn State, but Joe Paterno didn't offer a scholarship. "After that, Bill said he wanted to go to a school that played against Penn State," said neighbor Paul Propcheck.

You might guess Cowher got at least a bit of revenge. He helped North Carolina State defeat Penn State, 15-14, in his freshman year. That was a highlight of his superb college career, although Penn State did whip the Wolfpack in each of the next three years.

Cowher was elected captain and Most Valuable Player during his senior season, but it wasn't enough to get him drafted. He signed with the Philadelphia Eagles as a free agent in 1979 but was the last linebacker waived during training camp. He tried the next year with Cleveland, won a roster spot as a special-teams standout and was the Browns' special-teams captain in 1982.

"Bill was probably as well-respected by his peers as any player I've been around," said then Browns coach Marty Schottenheimer. After being traded back to Philadelphia, Cowher was the Eagles' special-teams MVP in 1983. A knee injury in '84 ended his career.

That's when Schottenheimer re-emerged in Cowher's life. No one, with the exception of his father, would have a greater impact on Cowher. Schottenheimer was looking for a special-teams coach.

"I called Bill with a great opportunity: Making 20 percent of what he made as a player to work, oh, 80 percent harder," Schottenheimer said.

Cowher always will be grateful. He was 28 when he went to work for Cleveland, the NFL's second-youngest assistant coach. "Marty Schottenheimer gave me an opportunity. He gave it to an unknown. He's very special to me. He was the first man to believe in me."

Cowher earned rave reviews as the Browns' special-teams coach in '85 and '86 and their secondary coach in '87 and '88, although his enthusiasm got the better of him on occasions. During kick-offs, he would run up the sideline, as if he were covering the kick. Once, legend has it, he ran over Schottenheimer.

It's a good thing Schottenheimer doesn't hold grudges. He took Cowher to Kansas City with him as his defensive coordinator in '89. He pushed him hard in January of '91 for the Cleveland head coaching job, which went to Bill Belichick. Then, after Chuck Noll retired on the day after Christmas in '91, he called Dan Rooney and Donahoe to push him again.

"He's an extremely bright, hardworking individual," Schottenheimer told the Steelers. "He's a good teacher, very demanding."

What wasn't there to like about Cowher? The teams in Cleveland and

As a coach and a teacher, Cowher has few equals.

Kansas City during his time as an assistant coach went 69-41-1. The Steelers, by comparison, had been 39-42 in the previous five years and 78-80 in the previous 10.

"He never let the Mickey Mouse stuff get in the way," Chiefs defensive tackle Bill Maas said. "When you walked into his room, it was all business. You didn't say, 'Hey, Bill, how's the wife and kids?' "

The only concern about Cowher was his age. It's true, he was a successful defensive coordinator by the time he was 31. But now? To be a head coach? At 34? "I'm a young guy, but I've gone the stepladder," Cowher said. "I don't think I would be any more ready three years from now than I am now."

Dan Rooney had been pretty lucky when he hired Noll, who was 37 when he coached his first Steelers' game. He didn't mind Cowher's age as much as a lot of people. "I have to say that every time I would talk with Bill, every time I would sit down with him, you never thought of his age. His enthusiasm, his ability to coach just came through. He's a guy who can do the job."

It was a close call, but the Steelers hired Cowher over Dave Wannstedt, a native of nearby Baldwin, a Pitt graduate and Jimmy Johnson's defensive coordinator with the Cowboys. (Wannstedt would get the Chicago Bears' head job the next year.) It took Rooney and Cowher only 10 minutes to work out a four-year contract, which since has been extended through the '97 season.

Little did anyone know then how Cowher Power would energize Pittsburgh.

Cowher got off to a rough start. At his first press conference, he was so nervous he introduced his parents, brothers and a sister-in-law but forgot to introduce his wife. Oops! That night, after diving into the job, he called Kaye

and, according to the book "Dawn of a New Steel Age" by Pittsburgh Post-Gazette sportswriter Ed Bouchette, told her, "I don't know if I can take this. I don't know what I've gotten into. Honey, I may have gotten myself in too deep over my head."

That was the last time anyone saw any doubts in Cowher.

He quickly won his players' respect. More than anything, they love his enthusiasm. They see it every day. We get to see it on Sundays in the fall.

A master strategist, Cowher observes the game with keen interest from the sideline.

Cowher's most infamous outburst happened during a game against Minnesota in the '95 season. Referee Gordon McCarter penalized the Steelers late in the first half for having 12 men on the field even though television replays showed only 11. Armed with a Polaroid as proof, Cowher sprinted across the field to McCarter when the half ended and jammed the picture into his shirt pocket.

That's typical of Cowher's intensity.

He didn't care that the NFL fined him $7,500 for the incident. Nor did he care that the league docked McCarter and line judge Ben Montgomery a game's pay for the mistake. He just felt, at the time, he had to stand up for his team.

"I've got to be probably more in control on the sidelines at times," Cowher said. "But it's hard for me. That's how I am. I'm just an emotional guy. I don't do a good job of hiding it. I think that's why some people don't last too long in this job. They try to hide their emotions."

The players also love Cowher's honesty. They know where they stand with him. Ask Tomczak. Filling in for O'Donnell, he played well in games against Miami and the Los Angeles Raiders during the '94 season and was the toast of the town. But before he even could leave the field after the Raiders' game, Cowher told him he was going back with O'Donnell the next week. Tomczak appreciated his candidness. A quarterback controversy was avoided. O'Donnell led the Steelers to the AFC championship game.

Often, Cowher caters to his players. For instance, he quickly initiated a shuttle-van system at training camp to take them to lunch and dinner, better to save their legs on those hot, humid August days.

But at the same time, Cowher leaves no doubt about who is in charge of the team. His tantrums when he thinks a player isn't doing the job adequately are legendary. The guy who is such a gentle father with his daughters Meagan (10), Lauren (8) and Lindsay (5) — "If he wins a big game or loses a big game, our girls would never know it from him," Kaye Cowher said — can turn into a monster.

"If I need to get your attention, I'm sure you'll be able to hear me," Cowher said, grinning.

Cowher greets Rod Woodson as he returns to the sideline after a big play.

"Fortunately, I've never been on the end of one his butt-chewings," Greene said.

Punter Mark Royals wasn't so lucky. National television cameras caught Cowher in his face after the Steelers had a late punt blocked in their '94 playoff loss to Kansas City. It was fairly terrifying. "He just happened to be the first one I saw coming off the field," Cowher said later after apologizing to Royals. "I told him, 'If those things happen in the future, find a quicker means to the sideline away from me.' "

Cornerback Deon Figures also wasn't so lucky. He missed a team meeting before a game in '94, then had to explain why to Cowher. "He opened the door and I could feel the heat coming out of the room," Figures told The Pittsburgh Post-Gazette. "I think I lost about five pounds talking to him. It was something else." It's safe to say Figures didn't miss another meeting.

"My belief is that things have to be thoroughly done," Cowher said. "I believe the best chance you have for suc-

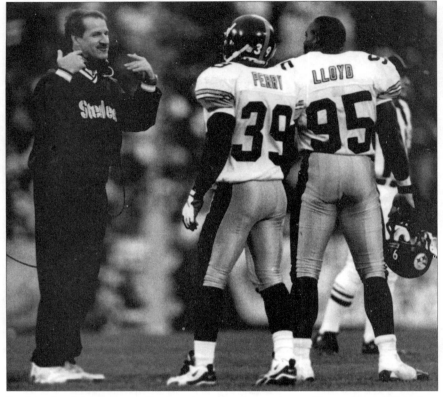

During a break in the game, Cowher gives a few instructions to Darren Perry (39) and Greg Lloyd (95).

cess is that everyone has a true understanding of what's expected of them ...

"It's not just talent that can get you someplace. If you make a commitment and you believe in it, you can obtain anything."

Cowher encourages individuality. He has tolerated numerous heated debates from his players on the sideline during games — notably, All-Pro linebacker Greg Lloyd — saying he welcomes the input. But don't try to challenge him in the locker room. Foster did late in the '94 season — the two had a screaming match in front of the team — and soon was an ex-Steeler.

"He'll never let anyone get bigger than the team," defensive end Brentson Buckner said.

That's why Cowher wouldn't ever tolerate a Rodman. "I think you lose your credibility when you turn your back on the things this guy does — not just with your team, but with the public. We're in the entertainment business. We have a responsibility to young people, to try to teach them values and ethics. Sports are positive in my mind. But if you allow this guy to get away with what he's doing, it destroys that."

That doesn't mean Cowher hasn't had his share of problems. He lost Green and guard Carlton Haselrig — two Pro Bowlers — and running back Tim Worley to substance-abuse suspensions. Nose tackle Joel Steed was suspended for steroids. Morris pleaded guilty to felony marijuana possession less than three weeks before the '96 training camp opened, putting his career

in jeopardy.

Cowher badly mishandled Foster's controversial ankle injury in the '93 season. Steelers doctors didn't think Foster needed surgery during the season. His personal doctor performed it, anyway. Much of Pittsburgh turned on Foster and considered him a malingerer because Cowher wasn't honest about the severity of the injury.

Cowher also has been criticized for his handling of his assistant coaches. He fired popular offensive coordinator Ron Erhardt, 65, three days after the '96 Super Bowl, saying he was afraid Erhardt was going to retire soon and he didn't want to lose his heir apparent, Chan Gailey, 44, to another team. But there was no explanation when special-teams coach Bobby April took the same job with a lesser team, the New Orleans Saints, that same week. Cowher and April would say only that April was returning to his hometown.

Through it all, Cowher has won. He won his first game in his first season at Houston against the heavily favored Oilers thanks, in large part, to his daring fake-punt call. (That '92 team, which was picked to finish last in the division after a 7-9 season the year before, went 11-5 and had the best record in the AFC.) He continued to win right up until the '96 Super Bowl.

Cowher has been widely honored. One highlight was his NFL Coach of the Year award in '92. Two others were his selection as the Dapper Dan Club's Man of the Year as Pittsburgh's greatest sportsman in '93 and '95. But maybe Cowher's greatest honor came when the Crafton Little Cougars retired his uniform jersey, No. 69. He played for the Mitey Mites in '68 and the Midget team in '69 and '70.

"I feel I owe a lot to the individuals in that organization," Cowher said. "I have never forgotten my roots. When you sur-

Kevin Greene (91) and Cowher enjoy a postgame celebration in the locker room during the 1995 season.

round yourself with good people, it sets you on the right direction in life."

Rooney Sr. would have loved it. That's a Pittsburgher talking.

The only better award for Cowher would be a Super Bowl trophy. It looked as if he might get it against the Cowboys, 13 1/2-point favorites. He was brilliant that day. It didn't matter that he was the youngest coach in Super Bowl history. He went for it on not one, but two fourth-down plays and also ordered a successful onside kick in the fourth quarter, swinging the momentum toward the Steelers.

"We came in here trying to win the game," Cowher said. "We didn't come to try not to lose it."

The Steelers probably would have won if not for O'Donnell's two interceptions. Cowher said he could live with those mistakes.

"I don't want people to let the falling short tarnish what has been a very special season. It's the most fun I've had coaching ... If you want to look at one game and us falling short and that's all you can remember, then I think you missed it. You missed the ride."

Cowher stuck out that big jaw. His message was clear.

This ride won't be over any time soon.

ABOUT THE EDITOR

FRANCIS J. FITZGERALD is a noted sports researcher and editor. He has recently edited the book and video box set, *Hail to the Victors: Greatest Moments in Michigan Football History* (1995); *The Nebraska Football Legacy* (1995), *That Championship Season: The 1995 Northwestern Wildcats' Road to the Rose Bowl* and *Greatest Moments in Penn State Football History* (1996).